EDUCATION, AUTONOMY AND DEMOCRATIC CITIZENSHIP

Across the globe educators are being required to respond to a changing political environment. New nations emerge out of the collapse of old empires; new democracies struggle out of old structures of oppression. Driven on by the fierce competitiveness of the 'tiger economies' of the east, old social welfare-based democracies are transformed into new market led enterprise societies.

The essays in this international collection are a response from twenty-two educators to these changes and to the reassessment that they provoke of some of the fundamental principles which shape educational thought and practice. They focus in particular on four key clusters of issues to do with the role of education in cultivating:

- **national identity** Authors from political settings as culturally distant as Lithuania and Taiwan consider what role, if any, nationalistic education might play in the context of a democratic liberal education.
- **market principles** Contributors offer different perspectives on the internationally pervasive application of the principles of the market economy to education and the consequent 'commodification' of learning.
- **personal autonomy** Different dimensions of the contested notion of autonomy are examined along with the related discourses of 'edification' and 'empowerment'.
- **democratic citizenship** From post-Soviet Russia to the new South Africa, in schools and in the context of professional training, educators examine what education for democratic citizenship might mean in practice and tease out some of the conflicts of principle which are raised in its implementation.

The contributors are distinguished scholars drawn from every continent. They write consciously for an international readership and there is constant cross reference to developments in different parts of the world. All are practitioners in education sharing an interest in the philosophical issues underlying social change. The philosophical discussion is clearly rooted in and referred back to the world of educational practice and its political context.

David Bridges is Professor of Education in the School of Education and Professional Development at the University of East Anglia, Norwich, England. His recent publications have included *Education and the Market Place* (edited with T.H. McLaughlin) and *Consorting and Collaborating in the Education Market Place* (edited with C. Husbands), both published by Falmer, and *Developing Teachers Professionally* (edited with T. Kerry) for Routledge.

ROUTLEDGE INTERNATIONAL STUDIES IN THE PHILOSOPHY OF EDUCATION

EDUCATION, AUTONOMY AND DEMOCRATIC CITIZENSHIP

Philosophy in a changing world

Edited by David Bridges

London and New York

First published 1997
by Routledge
11 New Fetter Lane, London EC4P 4EE

Simultaneously published in the USA and Canada
by Routledge
29 West 35th Street, New York, NY 10001

Typeset in Garamond by
BC Typesetting, Bristol
Printed and bound in Great Britain by
Mackays of Chatham PLC, Chatham, Kent

British Library Cataloguing in Publication Data
A catalogue record for this book is available from the British Library

Library of Congress Cataloguing in Publication Data
Education, autonomy, and democratic citizenship: philosophy in a
changing world/edited by David Bridges.
    p.   cm.
Includes bibliographical references.
    1. Education–Philosophy–Cross-cultural studies.   2. Education–
Aims and objectives–Cross-cultural studies.   3. Autonomy
(Psychology)–Cross-cultural studies.   4. Political participation–
Cross-cultural studies.   5. Education–Economic aspects–Cross-
cultural studies.   6. Nationalism and education–Cross-cultural
studies.   7. Educational change–Cross-cultural studies.
I. Bridges, David, 1941–   .
LB14.7.E39   1997
370.11′5–dc21   97-1287
                                                                        CIP

ISBN 0–415–15334–4

To my father,
Frederick William Bridges.
For conversations about politics,
and for his humane example.

CONTENTS

CONTENTS

CONTENTS

NOTES ON CONTRIBUTORS

David Aspin was formerly Professor of Philosophy of Education at King's College London. In 1988 he went to Australia where he was first Professor of Education and Head of Division at Macquarie University, Sydney, and then Dean of the Faculty of Education and Head of the School of Graduate Studies in Education at Monash University, Melbourne. After the expiry of his five-year term as Dean, he has returned to teaching and supervising students, to research and writing, and to professional and academic consultancy both in Australia and overseas, working with such agencies as IDP, UNESCPO and the OECD. His most recent publications are *Logical Empiricism and Post-Empiricism in Educational Discourse* (Heinemann 1996) and *The School, the Community and Lifelong Learning* with Professor J. D. Chapman (Cassells, forthcoming 1997).

David Bridges is Professor of Education in the School of Education and Professional Development at the University of East Anglia, Norwich, England where he is currently Pro Vice Chancellor. He works in both philosophy of education and qualitative research and evaluation and has recently directed or co-directed a number of projects in the field of professional higher education and competence based education and training. Outside the UK he has been involved in development work in teacher education in Guyana, Ghana, Ethiopia and Belize. His recent publications have included *Education and the Market Place* (ed. with T. H. McLaughlin) and *Consorting and Collaborating in the Education Market Place* (ed. with C. Husbands), both published by Falmer, and *Developing Teachers Professionally* (ed. with T. Kerry) for Routledge.

Robert Cowen is a Senior Lecturer in Comparative Education in the University of London Institute of Education. His major current research interest is re-examining and re-writing the theoretical foundations of comparative education, as counterpoint to its current overpopularisation and incorporation into advocacy politics. Formerly a Vice-President of the Comparative Education Society in Europe, and a Professor or Visiting Professor in the University of Brasilia, the Catholic University of Leuven in Belgium, the University of La Trobe in Melbourne, and SUNY, Buffalo, he is currently a member of the Editorial Board and Deputy Editor of *Comparative Education*. His last (edited) book was the 1996 *World Yearbook of Education: The Evaluation of Higher Education Systems* (Kogan Page).

Penny Enslin is Professor of Education at the University of the Witwatersrand, Johannesburg, where she headed the Department of Education between 1986 and 1995. She teaches philosophy of education and her research interests are in the areas of political philosophy and feminist theory. She has published on nation building, the public–private distinction in education, liberalism, and ideologies of teacher education in South Africa. She is currently involved in a collaborative research project on democracy and human rights education in South Africa.

Michael Fielding works at the University of Cambridge Institute of Education where much of his current work is with the *IQEA* (Improving the Quality of Education for All) international school improvement project. His current interests include the exploration of new understandings of school cultures and the importance of the public realm in schools and communities; problematising the notion of the learning organisation; the articulation of a person-centred, oppositional discourse in education; and the development of an emancipatory approach to school improvement, tentatively called 'transformative education'.

Ken Fogelman has been Professor of Education at Leicester University since 1988. After co-ordinating a programme of research for the Speaker's Commission on Citizenship, he founded the Centre for Citizenship Studies in Education in 1991. The Centre carries out research and development to promote and support the development of citizenship education in schools. He has acted as *Rapporteur General* for four Council of Europe conferences, and has published widely, including three edited books, on citizenship education.

Gaye Heathcote is Professor of Health Studies and Head of the Department of Humanities and Applied Social Studies at the Manchester Metropolitan University. She has written extensively on the theme of 'empowerment for life-skills' and is directing a number of European-funded research and development projects concerned with the autonomy of elderly people, terminally ill cancer patients and those with special educational needs. She acts as consultant to several Departments of Public Health in Eastern European Medical Universities.

Terry Hyland qualified as a teacher in 1971 and went on to complete BEd, MA and PhD degrees in educational studies at Lancaster University. He has taught in schools, further, adult and higher education, and worked in post-school teacher education at the Mid-Kent College, University of West of England and, since 1991, as Lecturer in Continuing Education at the University of Warwick. His main research interests are in vocational education and training, the post-school curriculum and higher professional learning, and his book *Competence, Education and NVQs: Dissenting Perspectives* was published by Cassell in 1994.

Akilu Sani Indabawa is a Senior Lecturer in Philosophy of Education at the Department of Education, Bayero University, Kano, Nigeria. His areas of research interest include ideology, cultural relativism and education in Sub-Saharan Africa and the political economy of education in Nigeria. He has published a number of articles in reference journals, and also contributed some chapters in books on his two main areas of research interests.

Palmira Juceviciene is Professor and Head of the Department of Management in Social Systems in Kaunas University of Technology, Lithuania. She is a member of the Science Council of Lithuania and has recently been a Visiting Scholar at the University of Cambridge in the Department of Education and in St Edmund's College.

James S. Kaminsky is Professor and Head of the Department of Educational Foundations Leadership and Technology in the College of Education at Auburn University, Auburn, Alabama. Auburn University is a Land Grant University of approximately 22,000 students. He teaches courses in the philosophy of educational research, the history of educational philosophy, and American pragmatism. Dr Kaminsky has been a member of the department since 1989. Prior to his tenure at Auburn University, he was Senior Lecturer, Department of Social and Cultural Studies in Education, University of New England, NSW. He worked at the University of New England from 1974–89. He is author of *A New History of Educational Philosophy* (1993) and has published scholarly work in *Educational Theory*, *The Journal of Educational Administration*, *The Journal of Educational Thought*, *The Australian Journal of Education*, and other journals. He has presented scholarly papers in Australia, Great Britain, New Zealand, Taiwan, and the United States. In addition, he was executive editor of *Educational Philosophy and Theory* from 1987–9.

Terry McLaughlin is Lecturer in Education at the University of Cambridge and Fellow of St Edmund's College, Cambridge. He specialises in philosophy of education and has recently been Visiting Professor in the Department of Management in Social Systems in Kaunas University of Technology, Lithuania.

Nikolai D. Nikandrov graduated from Leningrad University in 1959 and received his PhD in education there in 1973. He is now full member and vice-president of the Russian Academy of Education responsible for the overall planning and directing of research in several institutes of the academy as well as for a number of administrative functions. His main interests are in the fields of comparative education, methodology of educational research, and methods of teaching and learning. He is author of about 200 publications on these subjects, among them several books (*Programmed Learning and the Ideas of Cybernetics,* 1970; *Pedagogics of Higher Education,* 1974; *Higher Education Abroad,* 1978; *Creativity in Teaching,* 1990; *Values Education: The Case of Russia,* 1996 and others).

John Arul Phillips is associate Professor and Head of the Department of Social Science Education in the Faculty of Education of the University of Malaya, Kuala Lumpur. He specialises in curriculum and instruction at master's level and in initial training programmes for teachers and has a particular interest in the teaching of critical thinking.

Terry Phillips has researched and published in the complementary fields of language and learning in schools, education and dialogue in institutions, and communication for understanding in education for the professions. In his school-focused research he has analysed the nature and quality of talk and learning in small groups of children between 5 and 12 years old. In his studies of communication in hospitals, colleges and universities, he has examined the relationship between 'local' interactions and institutional communication structures. In the field of education for the professions, he has co-directed an evaluation of the assessment of competence in diploma-level nursing and midwifery education, and an evaluation of degree-level nursing and midwifery education. His special concern in these projects has been to identify and critically examine the discourses being 'worked out' in educational and workplace practices, to discover how these shape professionals' perceptions and understanding, and to explore the educational implications. His focus is deliberately inter-institutional and cross-professional.

Richard Smith is Senior Lecturer in Education at the University of Durham, UK, and currently Director of Combined Studies in Social Sciences there. He is editor of the *Journal of Philosophy of Education.* His publications in the area of this book include *Freedom and Discipline* (Allen & Unwin, 1985) and 'Remembering democracy', *Studies in Philosophy and Education* 1993, 12: 44–55.

Felisa Tibbitts is the Co-Director of Human Rights Education Associates, an a-political, non-profit organisation whose main mission is to support efforts aimed at introducing human rights concepts and values into educational curricula and teaching practice. Ms Tibbitts has developed large-scale political education reform projects in Romania, Albania, Estonia and Armenia and has worked as an adviser, speaker and teacher trainer throughout the region. She has written extensively on this topic, and serves as a consultative expert in human rights education with the Council of Europe and the United Nations Centre for Human Rights. Ms Tibbitts was educated at Harvard University, from which she holds a bachelor's and two master's degrees in public policy and international education.

James Tooley is University Research Fellow at the School of Education, University of Manchester, and also Director of the Education and Training Unit, at the Institute for Economic Affairs, London. He has held research positions at the University of Oxford's Department of Educational Studies and the National Foundation for Educational Research, and is an executive officer of the Philosophy of Education Society of Great Britain. Before entering educational research, he was a mathematics teacher in Zimbabwe and London. He is the author of *Disestablishing the School* (Avebury, 1995), and *Education without the State* (IEA, 1996).

Ching-tien Tsai graduated from Tainan Teachers College in Taiwan and had been a primary school teacher before he gained an MEd at National Taiwan Normal University under the supervision of Professor Huang Kuang-hsiung. He worked for the Preparatory Committee for the Establishment National Chi Nan University and lectured on curriculum. He studied for his PhD (awarded in 1996) at the Centre for Applied Research in Education at the University of East Anglia under supervision of Professor David Bridges, researching approaches to curriculum innovation in social studies in the UK and Taiwan. He is now an assistant Professor in the Institute of Education at the National Chung Cheng University, Taiwan R.O.C.

John White is Professor of Philosophy of Education at the Institute of Education, University of London. His interests are in interrelationships among educational aims and applications to school curricula, especially in the areas of the arts, history and personal and social education. His books include *Towards a Compulsory Curriculum* (1973), *Philosophers as Educational Reformers* (1979) (with Peter Gordon), *The Aims of Education Restated* (1982) and *Education and the Good Life: Beyond the National Curriculum* (1990), *A National Curriculum for All: Laying the Foundations of Success* (1991) (with Philip O'Hear), *The Arts 5–16: Changing the Agenda* (1992). In addition he has written about 100 academic papers and chapters in books.

Geoff Whitty is the Karl Mannheim Professor of Sociology of Education at the Institute of Education, University of London. He was previously Dean of Education at Bristol Polytechnic and the Goldsmiths' Professor of Policy and

Management in Education at Goldsmiths' College, University of London. He has written extensively on education policy and school reform in Britain and elsewhere. He is co-author of *The State and Private Education* (Falmer Press, 1989) and *Specialisation and Choice in Urban Education* (Routledge, 1993).

Colin Wringe has taught in secondary schools and further education and studied philosophy of education at the Institute of Education, University of London. He is currently a Reader in Education at Keele University and has written about children's rights, educational aims, political education and education for citizenship. He is a foundation member of the Philosophy of Education Society of Great Britain.

ACKNOWLEDGEMENTS

I gratefully acknowledge the support of Professor Oscar Jiaw Ouyang of National Taiwan Normal University who has encouraged us to publish (in revised form) papers by Tsai, Bridges, Cowen, Whitty, Hyland, Wringe, Smith, Kaminsky, Terry Phillips and John Phillips, Heathcote, Fielding, Indabawa and Aspin originally presented at a 1995 *International Conference on Education Reform* held at National Taiwan Normal University.

I would also like to record my enormous appreciation of the meticulous work of Miriam McGregor, secretary in the Centre for Applied Research in Education at the University of East Anglia, in preparing this material for publication and to Christine Cook for helping me to bring it to completion.

David Bridges

INTRODUCTION

David Bridges

The contributors of this book all write in consciousness of and against a background of political change in their own countries and across the world. For some, these changes – for example, the collapse of apartheid in South Africa or of Soviet imperialism in Lithuania and Russia and the progress towards democratic institutions in Taiwan (Republic of China) and Malaysia – have been welcome and much celebrated though, when the immediate celebration has quietened, the political aftermath demands a more sober and complex response. For others, the 'new medievalism' in religious zealotry and the internationalisation of the market ideology, for example, are disturbing to in the one case their liberal, in the other their communitarian instincts. For all, however, their philosophical thinking is prompted by political and related educational developments in the world and is intended to inform the future course of those developments.

The chapters represent in this sense essays in applied philosophy, and I make no apology for including elements of history, narrative, politics and sociology among the more strictly philosophical ingredients. Indeed a number of the contributors (Whitty, Terry Phillips, John Phillips, Heathcote and Fogelman, for example) would certainly not identify themselves primarily as philosophers or philosophers of education, even if, as surely any serious academic should, they get drawn, as they do here, into philosophical ideas and reflection. I am pleased to represent in a *New International Library of Philosophy of Education* a collection of papers that move thus freely across boundaries which are routinely crossed in the intellectual life of continental Europe and many other communities but which are frequently over-nervously or over-zealously defended in the Anglo-American tradition.

Though the volume draws substantially from English contributors and exclusively from those fluent in the English language, it has some real basis for the international perspective which is a feature of the series in which it is published. Its contributors are drawn from every continent, though it makes no claims to reflect the full cultural or political diversity of the international community. Significant among the contributors are writers from the newly emerging democracies in South Africa, the Asian Pacific and the former

Soviet Union, in all of which issues to do with nationhood and national identity tangle with the drive for market economics and democratic politics.

But whatever the home location of the author, nearly every chapter cross references discussion to developments across the world. It is not just big business, but also educational policy and practice which have become internationalised, as they struggle to address economic, political, social and cultural issues which feature globally in the preoccupations of politicians and educators. These include notably: the role of the school in contributing to the development of national identity and nationhood, democratic citizenship and economic prosperity; and the balance between the claims of individualism, family, community, nation and state.

The origins of this book reflect directly part of this story of political change. It had its roots in a visit I made to Taiwan in the spring of 1994. Here I encountered, to my delight, a considerable enthusiasm for philosophy and philosophy of education (statues of philosophers feature prominently in public places!), a recent determination to extend democratic institutions, and the beginnings of moves to reform educational practice in the interests of developing a citizenry better equipped to play an active part in a democratic society. Out of discussions held during this visit emerged a proposal from the National Taiwan Normal University (NTNU), supported by the Taiwanese Ministry of Education, for an *International Conference on Educational Reform*. The conference in 1995 was chaired by Professor Oscar Jiaw Ouyang, Head of the Department of Education at NTNU, jointly convened by his colleague Dr Sophia Wen and myself, supported by Professor Juang-hsiung Huang, now Director of the Institute of Education at National Chung Cheng University. It brought together philosophers (primarily) from the Republic of China and from across the world. A core of the papers in this collection – those by Tsai and Bridges, Cowen, Whitty, Hyland, Wringe, Smith, Kaminsky, Terry Phillips and John Phillips, Heathcote, Fielding, Indabawa and Aspin – had their origin in the English language contributions to this conference, though most have been substantially revised for the purposes of this publication. In this sense, ingredients of the book have been themselves part of the history of change on which its authors reflect.

The authors probably share a broad allegiance to liberal and democratic values but none of them suppose these values to be unproblematic, uncontestable or unique in their demands. A recurring preoccupation in the book is consideration of ways in which these can or cannot be reconciled with other values and allegiances which the authors also recognise.

The unifying theme is of course that of educational policy and practice, with which all contributors are engaged at a very practical level, and the social and political principles and priorities which ought to underpin that policy and practice. More specifically, the central and recurring references are to four broad collections of principles: nationalism, the market, autonomy and democracy, around which the four main sections are organised, and a fifth cluster of values to do with collectivism and communitarianism, whose compatibility with some of those first four is a frequent focus for discussion. The interconnections between these five principles are however so extensive as to make any structural division somewhat arbitrary.

PART I: NATIONALISM, DEMOCRACY AND EDUCATION

The first part of the volume focuses on the role which nationalistic education might play in the context of a democratic liberal education and the compatibility or otherwise of these principles. The chapters make specific reference to the way in which these educational aims are being articulated in Taiwan, in Lithuania and elsewhere in Central and Eastern Europe. This last context also raises issues to do with tensions between individualist and collectivist principles which are further explored in Part III below.

John White opens the section with a defence of the place of national myths in a liberal and rational democratic education. Preparation for democratic citizenship, he notes, is a key liberal aim of education but it has often been held to be at odds with the cultivation of national sentiment. This is not surprising, given the bitter history of nationalism during the twentieth century, though David Miller, Yael Tamir and others have recently been arguing that liberal and national ideas are not necessarily incompatible. However, in a recent article Penny Enslin (who contributes later in this volume) rejects the view that nation-building should be an aim of education. She writes with South African affairs particularly in mind, urging that the prime educational task facing that new country is civic rather than national education. The present chapter offers a critique of Enslin's position, concentrating especially on her claim that the mythical element found in appeals to national sentiment is logically at odds with the demand for rationality embedded in the core democratic value of personal autonomy. The chapter argues that historical myths about a nation's past are not necessarily irrational, but that school history classes need to treat them with caution, ensuring at the very least that they are presented as contestable interpretations.

The chapter by *Terence McLaughlin* and *Palmira Juceviciene* begins by asking, similarly, to what extent education in a liberal democratic context should seek to form a national identity, but they approach the question rather differently. The first part of their discussion considers the question at the level of general principle. They argue that though education and schooling may seek to transcend particularities, they cannot take place in a cultural or political vacuum. Language, literature and custom are significant ingredients of personal as well as local identity and such identities of nationhood need not be opposed to autonomy and freedom. The second part of the discussion considers more specifically some of the issues about national identity and its reassertion which are the focus of debate in contemporary Lithuania and examines some of the educational policies which are expected to serve the purpose of re-establishing national identity.

From Eastern Europe to East Asia – *Ching-tien Tsai* and *David Bridges* consider the way in which changing political values in Taiwan are reflected in developments in, in particular, the social studies curriculum. The chapter shows how traditional moral piety, 'national spirit education', and more recent demands for an education which will provide the foundations of democratic citizenship have been reflected in curriculum change and it considers to what extent traditional values and the political imperatives to retain an identity which is at once Chinese and Taiwanese can be reflected in a curriculum aimed also at the education of a democratic citizenry.

Felisa Tibbitts' chapter offers curriculum developers' teachers' and students' views about individualism/collectivism as they emerge in the reformation process of political education in the new nation-states of Central and Eastern Europe, with particular reference to Romania and Albania. It points to a number of concrete problems which arise in this context, such as designing content and instructional methods that incorporate the new individualism, as well as issues related to the perceived individualistic/collectivist dichotomy and the relationship between reformed philosophical outlooks and social realities in the emerging democracies.

PART II: EDUCATION, DEMOCRACY AND THE MARKET

The promotion of the principles of the market economy both within the more strictly economic field of the management of production, labour and prices and, by extension, as a way of arranging public service institutions in the fields of education and health, has been an almost universal feature of world politics in the last decade. This has been one of the most obvious consequences of the collapse of the Soviet empire and the discrediting of centralised planning and socialist aspirations which were assumed and declared (perhaps over readily) to be necessary implications of this collapse. For some these dramatic developments offered a new certainty and confidence in the capitalist ethic – the triumph of capitalism and of liberal democracy seemed to be one; for others they reinforced an acute sense of the end of all certainties, indeed of modernity itself. The chapters in this part reflect different perspectives on the policies and practices which have been associated with these changes.

Robert Cowen initially identifies the ways in which the Third World 'modernity' project was construed in economic terms by the development literatures of western social science. It notes the late insertion into this literature of themes of identity and social cohesion. In contrast he points out that the themes of national identity, individual autonomy and social cohesion were, in practice, central to the educational modernisation of many countries struggling for economic development in the late nineteenth and twentieth centuries. The cases of Japan and the USSR are sketched.

These models are then contrasted with the late modernity education crisis, and its emerging solutions in a number of countries where market driven educational systems have emerged. Cowen suggests in this contrast that problems of the construction of social identity and social cohesion have been undervalued in these late modernity projects.

The final argument rejects both the highly differentiated economic and moral message systems of the 'industrial' education systems of the 'western countries' in the 1950s and 1960s, and the messianic visions of social cohesion on offer in contemporary Asian systems of education. Neither set of models seems to Cowen to offer a way to rescue future oriented conceptions of multiple citizenship and social cohesion which permit a place for 'otherness'.

James Tooley observes that it is commonly argued that markets in education are opposed to 'democratic education', and that those who support markets in education must be in favour of an 'individualist' rational autonomy, an amoral democracy, and a capitalist-oriented education. By contrast, those who 'struggle' against markets uphold a 'deliberative' conception of autonomy which places individuals within the context of the 'public sphere', enjoying a rich education in the 'learning society'. Carr and Hartnett (1996) explicitly argue this; others rally around similar claims.

Tooley, however, argues in this chapter that this mis-characterises the potential of markets in education. Markets in education are not incompatible with democratic education within a deliberative democracy at all. For markets can be regulated – hence educational opportunities delivered can be within democratic safeguards – and supplemented with a funding and regulatory safety-net for the sake of equity.

More strongly, however, Tooley argues that within the democratic deliberations about the role of the state in education, a three-pronged argument can be made which could lead to an endorsement of markets in education, *in preference to* state schooling, and he outlines the ways in which this can be developed.

Geoff Whitty too focuses on the ways in which market principles are applied to educational practice, as increasing numbers of quasi-autonomous schools with devolved budgets compete for individual clients in the marketplace, and education is treated as a private good rather than a public responsibility, though his stance is less enthusiastic. Whitty's chapter considers the reasons for these changes and suggests that they involve a repositioning of education in relation to the state and civil society. He explores the implications of such changes for social justice and concludes that the reforms are tending to exacerbate social divisions between schools and between the pupils who attend different schools. He argues that there is an urgent need to strike a better balance between the rights of parents to choose schools for their children and the duties of public authorities to promote the education of all children. However, in calling for a reassertion of citizen rights alongside consumer rights in education, he also suggests that changes in the nature of contemporary societies require the development of new conceptions of citizenship and new forms of representation through which citizen rights can be expressed.

One dimension of the imposition of a market ideology on educational practice (though other ideologies could readily have produced the same effect) has been the increasing commodification of the curriculum, the notion of knowledge, education and training as something to be bought and sold on the market. With this has come too an increasing emphasis on the part that education and training play in economic success and a higher prioritisation of the vocational function of education at all levels and new kinds of accountability for that education and training.

This is the territory which *Terry Hyland* observes in his chapter. Hyland notes that the marginalisation and neglect of values and personal development objectives at school level in the UK as a result of a centrally imposed National Curriculum has been paralleled in post-school education through the vocationalisation of programmes by means of the competence-based education and training (CBET) strategy which underpins the increasingly influential work of the National Council for Vocational Qualifications (NCVQ). Such an approach to vocational education and training (VET), he argues, allows little scope for the development of personal, social and moral values and results in an excessively technical-instrumental approach, which runs counter to the ideal of fostering autonomy in education. As an alternative to this approach he outlines an 'education for work' programme – based on a Deweyan conception of vocationalism – and draws attention to the values and personal development aspects of work and employment. He recommends that such a core component should form part of the 14–19 curriculum for all students.

PART III: AUTONOMY RECONSIDERED

The notion of personal autonomy features centrally in the discourse of liberal education, of democratic values and indeed of market principles. Bridges recalls in his chapter Dworkin's observation that the concept is, however, made to do a lot of work:

> It is used sometimes as an equivalent of liberty ... sometimes as equivalent to self-rule or sovereignty, sometimes identical with the freedom of the will. It is equated with dignity, integrity, individuality, independence, responsibility and self knowledge. It is identified with qualities of self-assertion, with critical reflection, with freedom from obligation, with absence of external causation, with knowledge of one's own interests. ... It relates to actions, to beliefs, to reasons for action, to rules, to the will of other persons, to thoughts and to principles. About the only

features held constant from one author to another are that autonomy is a feature of persons and that it is a desirable quality to have.

(Dworkin 1988: 6)

The chapters in this section explore different dimensions of the notion of autonomy itself and related discourses of edification (see Kaminsky) and empowerment (see Fielding), as well as some of the communitarian principles which stand in tension with the more individualistic notions of personal autonomy (see Smith, Wringe and Kaminsky). Though most of the contributions in this section are from the UK, Indabawa's chapter serves as a useful reminder of the need to interpret and reinterpret this principle, as any others, in terms of the values and traditions of the society in which it is being applied.

Colin Wringe begins by observing that a commonly accepted account of rational autonomy as an educational goal can be set out in terms of the capacity to choose and sustain the most desirable way of life for oneself, subject to the requirement to respect the right of others to do likewise.

Communitarian and postmodernist views, however, seem to challenge the appropriateness and possibility of an individual's exercising freedom of choice in the selection of a favoured way of life. Wringe considers the educational implications of these views in some detail, and examines their tenability. He argues that the communitarian objections have educational consequences which many would find unacceptable in the modern world, and which are invalid in principle. He concludes that certain more extreme postmodernist views are patently untenable, but that others are less grave in their educational consequences than might be supposed.

Richard Smith's chapter expresses scepticism about the continuing usefulness of the notion of autonomy, which is increasingly associated with a tendency to think of persons atomistically and works alongside notions of choice and 'the market' to separate individuals from their world and their fellow human beings. If we abandon ideas of autonomy, however, we risk abandoning the marginalised and the dispossessed in our societies. Accordingly the chapter attempts to develop a view of autonomy which emphasises that our freedom is to be found in what we do with and for each other in the public realm: in reasoning, arguing, challenging and supporting each other as particular occasions require. This in turn requires an account of citizenship, of how we learn to engage politically with one another in the public world and demystify the sources of the powers to which we are subjected. Certain writings on counselling and psychotherapy, which have become our characteristic modern way of coping with the loss of autonomy, prove helpful in developing this account.

James Kaminsky argues that post-totalitarian liberalism as suggested by the work of Milan Kundera and Václav Havel, contains important suggestions for the cultural role of edification in maintaining the bourgeois order that this chapter assumes is the prerequisite of a stable, modern and pluralist democracy. The task of 'edification' is to assist the public in achieving both community and autonomy within a cultural order in which all individuals are free and equal citizens of a just community, a community which is, quite probably, democratic. Edification within a bourgeois cultural order must be connected to a theory of cultural action (democracy) and a potent means (technics). Its curriculum and organisation must therefore strongly support both democracy and technology.

David Bridges begins by reviewing some of what have been put forward as the ingredients of personal autonomy and hence ingredients for liberal education programmes dedicated to the development of personal autonomy. These have included: a grasp of the knowledge, understanding, central concepts, tests for truth and critico-creative processes constitutive of the fundamental 'forms of knowledge' or ways of knowing which have evolved historically; knowledge and understanding of the kinds of activities which we might choose to engage in for their own sake; knowledge and understanding of ways of life which we might choose for ourselves; reflective knowledge of ourselves and of the sources of our understanding and motivation.

He suggests, however, that such accounts support the idea of a superbly reflective, analytic, critical individual who might nevertheless be totally incapable of performing the minimal acts necessary for basic survival let alone acting in or upon a bustling economic, political and social world. Hence he argues for a richer, expanded notion of autonomy which includes these additional capacities.

In the educational context he uses the contrasting examples of the World Studies Project and its proposals for preparation for forms of political action acceptable in a democratic state and the Royal Society for Arts Manufacture and Industry Education for Capability initiative to illustrate the kinds of practical competence with which educational programmes might be concerned and which might constitute elements of education for personal autonomy in a social world.

Gaye Heathcote explores the notion of autonomy in the practical context of continuing professional education. Her chapter is in two parts. The first is a theoretical exploration of the nature and interrelationships of the key concepts associated with autonomy and in particular that of 'empowerment'; the second part describes, evaluates and comments on an extended illustration drawn from education for health, of personal autonomy in practice. The potential of a process-led, skills-based approach to education for personal autonomy is evaluated as a model for working in societies experiencing periods of rapid structural change and seeking to strengthen democratic citizenship.

Michael Fielding argues that empowerment is a notion that is centrally important in the debates about identity, autonomy and citizenship which lie at the heart of the social and political dilemmas many countries and regions are facing. The intention of his chapter is to render problematic the notion of empowerment in educational discourse, examine with appropriate care and attentiveness the assumptions that inform its use, map the conceptual frameworks which support and enrich these assumptions, and, finally, make a number of suggestions with regard to its future development.

Having set the contemporary scene, Fielding goes on to look at the 'neutral', process account of empowerment which claims to be context and value-free. He then builds on some of the emerging issues and sketches what he calls an emancipatory account. He considers some postmodern critiques of emancipatory perspectives before moving in a final section to take issue with aspects of postmodern accounts. The chapter closes by arguing the importance of exploratory conceptual work in this area.

The final chapter in this part, by *Akilu Sani Indabawa*, examines the place of autonomy as an educational ideal within the dominant political ideologies of West Africa, and more specifically Nigeria. Indabawa suggests that contemporary Africa rests ideologically on three pillars: traditional, pre-capitalist values, religious commitments (to traditional, Christian and Islamic religions), and to modernity expressed in liberal politics and economy. He explores the extent to which the ideal of personal autonomy can be accommodated into these competing ideologies. The analysis itself shows the cultural locatedness of autonomy as an educational ideal.

PART IV: EDUCATION FOR AUTONOMY AND DEMOCRATIC CITIZENSHIP

The theme of democracy and its educational requirements flows through every part of this book but becomes a more particular focus in this final part. In the first chapter *Ken Fogelman* considers some of the reasons behind recently increasing attention to citizenship education, and reviews developments in a range of different countries. He suggests that although information on what happens in schools has largely to be based on official or partial accounts, there is evidence that citizenship education in many countries is moving from a mechanistic 'civics' approach to approaches which address skills and values and which emphasise active learning participation and a democratic school climate. The second half of the chapter describes recent developments in England, summarising publications from the National Curriculum Council and other influential bodies, but emphasising that these were non-statutory and in a context of other pressures on schools which made their implementation problematic. A series of research studies are reviewed which indicate that teachers are largely positive about citizenship education, but practice has been highly variable because of lack of time, resources and guidance. The chapter concludes with a brief summary of the current context in England, where citizenship education is once again prominent on the educational agenda.

Nikolai Nikandrov treats education primarily in terms of the education of values among which autonomy and citizenship are prominent. He describes how the seventy years of Soviet power have produced the Soviet man, 'homo sovieticus' – very much criticised in the present-day Russia but whose characteristics are not all bad. He suggests that the value changes that took place in Russia required a reassessment of all education philosophy and practice but observes that the school of life still stands in many ways in contrast with the school of education.

Penny Enslin writes similarly from a country in which established political principles and practice have recently been overturned and which provides a complex but highly visible forum for debate about what is to replace them. She observes that in South Africa's post-apartheid democracy a key role is planned for parents in the governance of schools. Her chapter begins by exploring the vision of democracy which has emerged from the liberation struggle and the contrasting effects of apartheid on black and white families. She then builds on a feminist analysis of the family to argue that its influence is in some respects antithetical to the development of democratic citizenship. She challenges the assumption that the family is the equivalent of the private sphere, showing that the valuable features of the family may have to be sought outside the family or domestic context. Contrary to the claims of mainstream liberalism, she argues that there are oppressive family practices that undermine the development of the autonomy appropriate to full development of democracy and that they require public scrutiny and educational intervention.

Terry Phillips proposes that there is an inextricable link between the development of autonomous citizens in general and the development of autonomous professionals in particular. He argues that the curriculum for democratic citizenship is constructed in practice. It is what is done in social interactions rather than what is written down in syllabuses or policy documents. In particular, it is what is constructed in interactions with the professionals who have been invested with the power to set the intellectual, ethical and practical agendas for specialised fields of activity.

Phillips claims that professionals, who have a great deal of autonomy themselves, are major role models for others and that because of this, the preparation of students for democratic citizenship is more likely to be successful if the model of autonomy offered by professionals is itself a democratic one. Two things follow. First, that the success or otherwise of school and college programmes for democratic citizenship is closely related to whether or not teacher/lecturer preparation promotes autonomous behaviour. Second, that curricula for the education and training of professionals must be founded on dialogic principles.

Placing his argument in the context of the debate about the relationship between knowledge, social practice and culture, and providing some examples of how this works at the 'local' level in specific school or college classrooms, he suggests that attempts to change students' practice must begin with changes in the preparation of professionals, which must involve the institutionalisation of enquiry, challenge, analysis and critique. To support the claim he draws on data from research into the education and training of nurses in the UK. He concludes that possibilities for democratic autonomy occur where processes of analysis, critique and dialogue are at the heart of professional preparation.

David Aspin considers the crucial educational question of how different conceptions of knowledge and values impact on educational institutions aiming to increase autonomy in their students and to prepare them for life as citizens in a participative democracy. He examines some recent proposals for the construction of curricula and the ways in which different conceptions of knowledge influence the structuring of the curriculum and the selection of curriculum content. Chief among these are the conceptions of curriculum relating to the promotion of national economic goals, to introducing students to their cultural entitlements, and to initiating students into the various forms of cognition constituting the rational mind. All are criticised and their deficiencies contrasted with the curriculum approach resulting from the adoption of a post-empiricist pragmatic perspective on education which involves a preference for increasing students' autonomy by helping them acquire knowledge and understanding through a process of problem-based learning. An argument is developed for an integrative approach to knowledge and to teaching and learning, which encourages students to adopt a coherent and holist view of reality and their situation in the world. The educational values to be derived from the epistemological concerns of educating institutions are predicated upon personal autonomy and these lead in their turn to the notion of education for democracy which, on this argument, provides the principal criterion for the selection of curriculum content and methods of teaching and learning in the democratic school.

John Phillips' chapter starts from observations about the changing character of society around the Pacific Rim and in particular in South and East Asia. It observes the shift from an essentially agrarian to a manufacturing and information-oriented society in which the workplace, the marketplace and the home have become increasingly complex organisations and the parallel shift from essentially autocratic to increasingly democratic governments requires a higher level of participation of their citizens.

Schools have, however, failed to keep up with the implications which these changes have for teaching and learning. They continue to be preoccupied with teaching curriculum content rather than the critical processes which enable children to think for themselves in a society which is less predictable, rapidly changing and increasingly complex. The chapter, therefore, discusses the importance of teaching the process of learning and its goal in creating autonomous learners and critical thinkers and proposes strategies which incorporate those skills associated with critical, creative and content thinking, while taking into consideration the examination-oriented system of education in the Pacific Rim.

Few chapters offer simple solutions to the complex social and political issues which underpin educational discourse in the contemporary world, though several give some pretty clear illustrations of ways in which particular principles might be expressed in educational practice. In any case, facing complexity is more honest than its denial; understanding complexity more satisfying than the crude simplicities that are sometimes offered in its place; and both together a necessary condition for any kind of political or educational progress, however that progress is defined.

REFERENCES

Carr, W. and Hartnett, A. (1996) *Education and the Struggle for Democracy: The Politics of Educational Ideas*, Buckingham and Philadelphia: Open University Press.
Dworkin, G. (1988) *The Theory and Practice of Autonomy*, Cambridge: Cambridge University Press.

Part I

NATIONALISM, DEMOCRACY AND EDUCATION

2

NATIONAL MYTHS, DEMOCRACY AND EDUCATION

John White

DEMOCRACY AND NATIONAL SENTIMENT: THE COMPATIBILITY THESIS

Among the political aims of education, many liberals give a key place to pre-paration for democratic citizenship. Not all of them, by any means, also favour the cultivation of national sentiment. It is not surprising, given the bel-licose history of the twentieth century, that supporters of liberal democracy have so often lined up against enthusiasts for the nation. Liberal democrats have stood for such values as personal self-determination, limited government and a politics based on the use of reason rather than force. Twentieth-century nationalists have subordinated individuals' interests to those of the nation, loyalty to which has been presented as one's highest duty; and have too often been quick to resort to war and to internal repression to promote their chauvinist goals.

In the last few years, the often taken-for-granted inconsistency between democratic and national ideals has been questioned. A vital distinction made here is between 'national sentiment' and 'nationalism'. What we recoil against in our recent history is the latter, that is, the notion that one's own nation is in some way superior to other nations and in the light of that demands our supreme loyalty. We have seen countless examples of this, from Hitler's Germany through to Bosnia. But attachment to one's nation need not bring with it the idea that it is better than others – any more than attachment to one's family or workplace need be associated with such competitiveness. Patriotism is not necessarily nationalism.

Other features associated with national sentiment in our times also seem to be contingent. An ethnic basis, for instance. The violence which ethnic nation-alism can unleash is all too familiar. But some nations, the Swiss for instance, have heterogeneous cultural origins. What binds a nation together is not neces-sarily ethnic pedigree or a common language (Switzerland again), but the shared beliefs of its members that they belong together, have a common history and look forward to a common future. All this is perfectly compatible with liberal-democratic values. National communities can be run (more or less) democratically, as most of the countries in Western Europe, for instance, demonstrate.

Ethical attachments to fellow-nationals can in some contexts weigh more heavily with one than attachments to those outside, just as concern for one's own family members can on occasion trump other obligations. There is nothing morally amiss either when British people grieve more for the killing of the schoolchildren in Dunblane than for a similar tragedy in California, or when a person cancels her professional appointments to visit her father taken suddenly to hospital. In neither case is the local attachment a focus of overriding, enduring loyalty. Values have to be weighed against each other. National values, like family values, come out now higher in priority, now lower.

There is more one could say about misconceptions in this area. About the view, for instance, that the nation is some kind of metaphysical entity, irreducible to individuals. It is quite understandable why democrats, attached as they are to rational ways of proceeding, should bridle at conferring value on a fictive phenomenon. But once we see nations on the pattern of families, as composed of individuals related together in some way, this objection evaporates.

David Miller (1988, 1993) has been a leading defender of this compatibility thesis in recent years. Not only does he argue that democratic and national notions are not inconsistent, he holds, further, as a democratic socialist, that the political arrangements that social democracy favours presuppose that citizens be bonded together not only by ethical and political principles, but also as members of a community in which the fate of each matters to each (Miller 1989). Only by fellow-feeling for the poor, for instance, will the rich have a motive for accepting redistributive policies within their own country. Attachment to one's national community thus underpins one's civic responsibilities.

Philosophers of education attracted by the compatibility thesis have recently been exploring its applications to educational policy. Some examples are Callan (1991), Tamir (1992, see also 1993) and White (1996a, 1996b).

THE COMPATIBILITY THESIS CHALLENGED

A philosopher of education who has been more sceptical of the compatibility thesis and the educational uses to which it has been put is Penny Enslin in her paper 'Should nation-building be an aim of education?' (Enslin 1994).

Her answer is a definite 'no'. The essay is written with South African affairs particularly in mind and against the background of calls since the ending of the apartheid regime for the creation of a new South African nation. Her 'no' is certainly meant to apply in the first instance in that context. But some of the arguments which she uses to support it also seem to favour the more general conclusion that a policy of nation-building is *never* to be pursued.

A more local argument on which she relies is that South African society is linguistically and culturally diverse, and that while it is probably true that a majority share a common loyalty to the political community, the relationship of this disposition to the history of the country is deeply problematic. . . . As a result members of the society have very different sets of memories and myths, in which other members are often depicted as enemies rather than compatriots. It is difficult to locate a common nationhood here.

(Enslin 1994: 28)

One response to this might be that, while the argument points to the non-existence of a South African nation at the moment, it does not by itself rule out the possibility of creating one in the future. If it is indeed nation *building* which is at issue, why could one not try to *create* the shared beliefs about belonging together and other common bonds which nationhood demands?

A likely answer from an opponent of nation-building is that the gulfs between opposing cultural communities are just too wide to make this a realistic policy. South Africa is no Switzerland. The Swiss nation (as I was surprised to learn), came into being largely in the late nineteenth century. *Its* builders, too, had to cope with several languages and several cultures; but the cultural differences were slight as compared with those in South Africa and, more importantly, there was no history of implacable antagonism between groups.

As far as I can tell, Penny Enslin does not make this move, although she might well believe that what it says is true. It is, note, not a philosophical claim, but a pragmatic-political one. For the next few years the world will be holding its breath waiting to see if the Mandela regime and its successors will be able to bridge the chasms which surround them. It may look as if history, rather than logical deduction, will be the best guide as to whether the nation-building project is impossible. Or will it? If Enslin's central argument in her paper is valid, a philosophical route may be more reliable, after all. If it is, it would seem to be applicable not only to South African nation-building, but to any.

Enslin's argument has been constructed in the light of the case recently made for compatibility and is presented as an objection to it. What she does is to focus on one part of the compatibilists' position and to show that this contradicts the requirements of an education for democracy. Among the points, echoed by other writers, that Miller has made about the definition of 'nation' is that 'nationality is to a greater or lesser degree a manufactured item . . . a work of invention, in particular the invention of a communal national past' (Miller quoted by Enslin 1994: 29). In other words, creating what Benedict Anderson (1991) has called the 'imagined community' that constitutes a nation involves a mythical element: the nation's history is a work of invention, of fiction. This necessary presence of myths is at odds with the cultivation of autonomy required by education for democratic citizenship. In two ways: 'both in terms of what I call the logic of nation-building and because of the values which nation-building would encourage' (Enslin 1994: 30).

17

I shall not dwell on the second of these arguments. It revolves around the militarism which Enslin views as a common accompaniment of nationhood. Norway, Finland, Denmark and – yes – Switzerland furnish perhaps enough in the way of counter-examples to allow us to move on to more solid territory. The first, and more central, point is this. Part of the autonomy ideal is that one's beliefs be held in a rational way, with due regard to the evidence in their support and a willingness to change them if grounds for them prove insufficient. This is not compatible with children coming to believe myths about their nation's past. 'Education for a democratic way of life must include directing pupils' attention to the exposing of false beliefs, especially the myths which political and commercial entrepreneurs would have them embrace' (Enslin 1994: 32).

If Enslin's thesis stands, there is a logical contradiction between cultivating national sentiment and educating for democracy. This jeopardises not only the South African project, but indeed any project of nation-building. It also threatens the education of national sentiment in nations which are long-established, like France or Britain.

NATIONAL MYTHS AND NATIONAL HISTORIES

But can it stand? It rests on the assumption that the myths which form a necessary part of national sentiment are either false or at least irrationally based. That they often are is indisputable. There are no grounds for believing that the German nation is based on pure Aryan blood, making it congenitally superior in intelligence and virtue to other races. Afrikaner nationalism, as Enslin points out, has held the unfounded belief that 'every nation is rooted in its own soil which is allotted to it by the creator' (Enslin 1994: 30).

But are national myths always like this? Take the belief, associated with Britishness, that the nation's attachment to liberty has deep historical roots, stretching back at least to Magna Carta, the thirteenth-century charter wherein the barons wrested major liberties from the king. Is this belief well-founded? Sceptics may say that it is all too easy, with hindsight, to provide ancient historical pedigrees for contemporary ideologies; when one looks at these in context, however, the appearance of a link between past and present melts away. Contemporary liberalism has to do with a universal ideal of personal self-determination. It is the product of a culture which has broken with tradition-directedness, putting all the weight on the autonomous individual's fashioning of his or her own life. The barons of King John's reign, living in a pre-modern culture, had no conception of all this. They were simply caught up in a power struggle with the monarchy, taking advantage of their collective strength to consolidate their wealth and territory. Encouraging British school-children to see a feudal warlord as a proto-liberal democrat is dangerously to mislead them.

And yet ... liberal democracy is composed of many strands. One has to do with the autonomous individual, another with limitations on state power. Magna Carta *did* check the power of the English king in an enduring way. Its advocates did not have modern democratic government in prospect, but there is something of a case for saying that their work, while motivated perhaps by selfishness, in fact helped to lay one of the planks on which modern limited government, and later democratic government, were built.

As Miller says in his recent book *On Nationality* (1995), national myths are rarely based on outright falsehoods. There is no one true historical account of past events. Historians differ in their interpretations. The 'liberal' version of the Magna Carta story is not false, only one interpretation in competition with others. If one accepts this, it blunts the edge of Penny Enslin's logic-based argument. If a myth is not false or irrationally based, only a contested version of events, then the charge that the idea of the nation contradicts the rationality requirements of democracy fails to stick.

On the other hand, would it do if British schoolchildren, say, were brought up, for reasons of national identity, on a mythical history of liberalism, stretching back from Magna Carta to the pre-conquest legal system and forwards to the Cromwellian and Glorious Revolutions, the Great Reform Act and the stand against Hitler? Even though specific elements in this story were not obviously false, would it still not be an offence to their status as rational beings to foist on them such a biased account?

If this were the *only* history of their country to which they were introduced, one would have good cause to be alarmed. This is because, although other interpretations existed, children would not be encouraged to have access to them. If 'indoctrination' is definable as preventing people from critical reflection on beliefs they hold, then this would come pretty close to indoctrination. The affront to personal autonomy in this is obvious.

To avoid Enslin's contradiction, we would at least have to say that one-sided national histories celebrating the nation's alleged virtues must be supplemented by other interpretations so as to encourage pupils to make up their own minds. But this would seem to make the contradiction easily bypassable. The desirability of multiple interpretations is part of the stock-in-trade of the modern history teacher. Writing more generally about debates on national identities, Miller states

> Very often ... there is a healthy struggle between those who want to hold up a bowdlerised version of the nation's history as an extended moral exemplar ... and those who draw attention to lapses and shortcomings; injustices inflicted on minorities, acts of treachery, acts of cowardice, and so forth. The first group remind us of how we aspire to behave; the second group point to defects in our practices and institutions that have allowed us to fall short.
>
> (Miller 1995: 40)

If schools counterbalanced the liberal account of British history by one emphasising commercial greed and oppression of colonial people, this would both be patently anti-indoctrinatory and might also, apparently paradoxically, help to fill out their picture of their nation as an ethically worthy community. Nationally as well as personally, shame can reinforce positive ideals of how one should live: falling short is falling short of something good.

Is this enough to meet Enslin's challenge? Perhaps not. Indeed, this historical balancing-act may add power to her case. True, it avoids one sort of one-sidedness – but only to embrace another. For both the virtuous and the shameful school histories serve the same end – to associate the nation with positive moral qualities. Myth now reappears at this higher order. British children are subtly being brought to link Britishness with goodness. Although they are encouraged to question the particular histories, the more they enter the debate between them, the more their commitment is likely to be increased to this overarching assumption that the competing histories share, and the less equipped they are critically to reflect on it. Just as a discussion in RE on whether God has this attribute or that can be an effective means of consolidating the background assumption that God exists, so a 'liberal' approach to national history can be a useful vehicle for higher-order indoctrination.

Considerations like this might lead some to conclude that school history should not be harnessed at all to national preoccupations (Lee *et al.* 1992). Apart from anxieties about inculcating national sentiment, there is also the danger that children will end up with a perverted understanding of history as an academic pursuit. History has its own standards. It is above all interested in discovering truth, not in supporting a particular point of view. While school history should obviously connect with pupils' interests, there are many ways of doing this which have the clear purpose of revealing the intrinsic values of history as history. National subject-matter is only one kind among many – and because reliance on it courts the dangers already mentioned, it is best soft-pedalled.

Large issues arise here about the purposes of history teaching. It would be impossible to do full justice to them here. But one thing should be plain. People study and research history for many reasons. Few of them are likely to do so *purely* in order to locate historical truth in some further-value-free way. Among the reasons which have always motivated historians has been the desire to probe the origins of a particular community. This has sometimes been a national community, sometimes something wider, like Islamic culture, sometimes narrower, like civil engineering in Portugal. The more history teachers block out extrinsic purposes, the more they risk purveying a warped conception of what history is.

To come back to civil engineering in Portugal. We can imagine someone from the civil engineering community in that country deciding to research its development to date. (No doubt someone has already done so.) We can imagine, too, that they embark on this out of attachment to the community of which they form a part. They would not do so if they did not feel it was doing valuable work, was a worthy group to which to belong. Although they are scrupulous in following the canons of objective historical enquiry, their work is still coloured by these background values. After them other historians of the same community may challenge their interpretation and place events in, say, a less favourable light, but still against the common background of attachment to a worthwhile enterprise.

There is nothing reprehensible about such proceedings. On the contrary, if attachments to practices and communities play the important part in our identities that most philosophers now recognise, part of this is attachment to an on-going, historically situated phenomenon with a history still to be written about it in the future. Without histories, no communities. We need stories of our own personal lives against which to make sense of who we are. Part of these personal stories are the stories of the various groups to which we belong – our family, professional group, political party, sports club, church, etc.

Should we include the nation among the etcetera'd items? I see no good reason to exclude it. Being Dutch rather than British or Japanese is important in many Dutch people's self-conception. This may prove to be true of Dutch children whose self-identities are still in formation. That is why Dutch history, based, as we have seen, on a possibly tacit belief in the worthiness of the Dutch community, is a necessary item in their education. Without it, they would have a much impoverished sense of who they might be. I say 'might be' rather than 'are', bearing in mind that not all Dutch children might want to define themselves as Dutch. We all come, as has just been said, to have multiple communal affiliations and the way in which we emphasise, and to what degree, is in a liberal society largely up to each of us.

This last point helps meet the challenge thrown down above, that whatever version of national history is taught, whether the bright side or the dark side, reinforces the idea of one's nation as morally worthy. If children were brought up in the thought that they *had* to be Dutch, or Japanese, or whatever, this would be an unjustifiable affront to their autonomy. A vital part of a liberal democratic education is to bring home to children the role of personal choice in establishing one's self-identity. At the same time, there have to be options from which choices can be made. In the modern world, given the place that national membership holds, to a greater or lesser degree, in most people's self-definition, national history, among other sorts of history, must figure significantly in every child's education. Myths and all.

While Penny Enslin's rejection of nation-building as an educational aim may be ill-founded as a universal proposition, she may be right to be suspicious of it as a way forward for the new South Africa. She is in a better position than me to know what makes sense in that context and I have nothing authoritative to add on this.

Just one non-authoritative thought. Enslin accepts that 'reconciliation is urgently required in South Africa, and that education should play a part in this process' (1994: 34). This has to be education for democracy. But she says nothing about the society in which this education should take place, except, by implication, that it will be a society of all South Africans. If so, if all goes well, this will be a society which endures into the future, whose members feel, as reconciliation takes effect, increasingly bonded together. As this happens, just as with Portuguese civil engineers or Taiwanese philosophers of education, hopes and expectations of future flourishing will be accompanied by temporal interest in the reverse dimension – in how this prized phenomenon came into existence. Some historians will concentrate on the bravery of the freedom fighters, others on the inhumanity of the apartheid regime.

What should we call this, if not the creation of a South African nation?

REFERENCES

Anderson, B. (1991) *Imagined Communities*, 2nd edn, London: Verso.

Callan, E. (1991) 'Pluralism and civic education', *Studies in Philosophy and Education* Vol. 11, No. 1.

Enslin, P. (1994) 'Should nation-building be an aim of education?', *Journal of Education (Natal)* Vol. 19, No. 1.

Lee, P., Slater, J., Walsh, P. and White, J. (1992) *The Aims of School History*, London File Series, London: Tufnell Press.

Miller, D. (1988) 'The Ethical Significance of Nationality', *Ethics* Vol. 98.

—— (1989) 'In What Sense must Socialism be Communitarian?' in Frankel Paul, E. *et al.* (eds) *Socialism*, Oxford: Blackwell.

—— (1993) 'In Defence of Nationality', *Journal of Applied Philosophy* Vol. 10, No. 1.

—— (1995) *On Nationality*, Oxford: Clarendon Press.

Tamir, Y. (1992) 'Democracy, Nationalism and Education', *Educational Philosophy and Theory* Vol. 24, No. 1.

—— (1993) *Liberal Nationalism*, Princeton: Princeton University Press.

White, J. (1996a) 'Liberalism, Nationality and Education', *Studies in Philosophy and Education* Vol. 15: 193–9.

—— (1996b) 'Education and Nationality', *Journal of Philosophy of Education* No. 2.

3

EDUCATION, DEMOCRACY AND THE FORMATION OF NATIONAL IDENTITY

Terence H. McLaughlin and Palmira Juceviciene

Two of the most prominent tasks with which education is familiarly charged in liberal democratic societies are those of developing the autonomy of the individual and of laying the foundations of democratic citizenship. Within such societies, in what sense, if any, should education be concerned with questions of national identity? More specifically: in what sense, if at all, should education in a liberal democratic context seek to form a national identity?

There are several ways in which education can aim at the formation of a national identity. An educational institution can form a 'national consciousness' in its students through particular aspects of, and emphases in, its curriculum, through teaching methods and media, and through the ethos and organisation of the institution itself. Further, education more broadly can help to shape a national identity in society as a whole through its wide ranging influence upon culture, the media and political life. In this discussion, rather than engage in any detailed exploration of the broader ways in which education can shape national identity, we shall concentrate upon some questions relating to the formation of a 'national consciousness' in students.

In what sense, and to what extent, should education in a liberal democratic context seek to form a national identity in this way? Our discussion falls into two parts. In the first part we shall consider some matters of general principle relating to this question, derived from reflection upon a conception of education appropriate for a liberal democratic society. In the second part, we shall consider these matters of principle in relation to the specific context of Lithuania, which is currently wrestling with its transformation into a liberal democratic society.

EDUCATION AND DEMOCRACY: THE SHAPING OF GENERAL AND PARTICULAR IDENTITIES

Any conception of education based on liberal democratic principles is suspicious of particularity, especially when the particularity involved concerns the

23

shaping of individuals in ways which presuppose values and commitments which are, from a democratic point of view, significantly controversial. The sort of education attempted in totalitarian societies is seen as objectionable from a democratic perspective on precisely these grounds. In the pre-*perestroika* Soviet Union, for example, education attempted to shape a particular identity in students based on a significantly controversial theory of the good. This education was designed to bring about the sort of unified, detailed, moral formation contained in the notion of *vospitanie*. In this process, individuality, criticism and variety were subordinated to Marxist-Leninist theory, which determined the aims and methods of a monolithic and centralised system of schools. These schools, together with youth organisations and the media, all conspired in a co-ordinated way to develop the ideal communist person, complete with collectivist and atheistic beliefs and qualities of character. (On these matters see, for example, Halstead 1994.)

In contrast, education based on liberal democratic principles seeks to avoid such a particularistic formation. It might be argued, of course, that a 'liberal democratic' form of education is itself based on a theory of the good which is 'particular' and 'significantly controversial'. Such an education, it might be claimed, also tries to shape a certain sort of person, and to impart a 'particular' individual identity. In reply, a proponent of 'liberal democratic' education will argue that, whilst there is some truth in these objections, education based on democratic principles seeks to reduce particularistic influence to a minimum. Further, the proponent will claim that a liberal democratic form of education is committed to an underlying theory of the good which is maximally hospitable to individual autonomy and to differences of view. Whilst a full articulation and evaluation of a 'liberal democratic' conception of education is beyond the scope of this chapter, its general character can be briefly sketched in the following way. (For more detail on these matters see, for example, Gutmann 1987; McLaughlin 1992, 1995.)

The task of education in pluralistic liberal democratic societies is conceptualised in the light of two important realities. First, education of whatever form is inherently value-laden, the values involved being of many different kinds. No form of education can be value-free or value-neutral. The question which arises for education is therefore not *whether* it should be based on, and should transmit, values but *which* values should be invoked. The second reality is the well-grounded, deep-seated and perhaps ineradicable differences of view about many questions of value which are characteristic of pluralistic liberal democratic societies. This is not to suggest that such societies are entirely bereft of value agreement and consensus. If this were so it would be hard to see how these societies could achieve stability and coherence, much less satisfy the value commitments and demands implicit in democracy, such as justice, freedom and personal autonomy. There are, however, large areas of disagreement about many questions, most notably about overall views of life as a whole, or 'comprehensive' theories of the good.

24

In the light of these two realities, public education in pluralistic liberal democratic societies, at least in common schools attended by students from all backgrounds, seeks to base its substantial value influence on principles broadly acceptable to the citizens of society as a whole. This requires that this form of education cannot assume the truth of, or promote, any particular, comprehensive, or all-embracing, vision of the good life. Rather, it aims at a complex two-fold influence. On matters which are widely agreed and which can be regarded as part of the common or basic values of the society, education seeks to achieve a strong, substantial influence on the beliefs of students and their wider development as persons. It is unhesitating, for example, in promoting the values of basic 'social morality' and democratic 'civic virtue' more generally. Involved here is the notion of 'an education adequate to serve the life of a free and equal citizen in any modern democracy' (Gutmann 1992: 14) which includes the notions of both education for a significant form of personal autonomy and for democratic citizenship (McLaughlin 1992). On matters of serious disagreement, however, where scope for a legitimate diversity of view is acknowledged, education seeks to achieve a principled forebearance of influence: it seeks not to shape either the beliefs or the personal qualities of students in the light of any substantial or 'comprehensive' conception of the good which is significantly controversial. Instead, public education is either silent about such matters or encourages students to come to their own reflective decisions about them. One way of expressing in an overall way the nature of educational influence on this view is that it exerts a complex combination of centripetal (unifying) and centrifugal (diversifying) forces on students and on society itself.

On this view, therefore, instead of encouraging students to become committed to any one, substantial, view of life as a whole, education is charged with encouraging students to engage in independent critical reflection and to achieve, at least to a significant extent, an appropriate form of self-directness and personal autonomy consistent with the demands of democratic citizenship. The general or universalistic thrust in the liberal democratic conception of education is well captured in Charles Bailey's insistence that liberal education must lead students 'beyond the present and the particular', including the 'incestuous ties of clan and soil' (Bailey 1984: 20–2).

Education and the significance of particularity

However, education and schooling, though they may seek to transcend particularities, cannot escape from them. Education cannot take place in a vacuum. It is necessarily conducted in particular social, political and cultural contexts. The schools of a liberal democratic society cannot therefore avoid transmitting some norms which are culturally distinctive in that they selectively favour some beliefs, practices and values in ways that go beyond what could be justified from a strictly neutral or 'global' point of view. Amy Gutmann notes that in the USA local communities have been given the democratic right to shape their schools in their own cultural image, within principled liberal democratic constraints (Gutmann 1987: 41–7, 71–5). But within these limits, the shared beliefs and cultural practices which are particular to communities can be transmitted and maintained.

The identity which is developed in students by the educational process is inevitably, therefore, and to a significant extent, concrete and particular, shaped by the specificities of the social, political and cultural context in which this process takes place. Education may seek to transcend these particularities, but they cannot be avoided. Education for citizenship, for example, involves the student coming to understand matters of general democratic principle. But, since there is no abstract 'democratic citizen' who is not the citizen of a particular place, this process cannot be wholly general. This point is well summed up in De-Maistre's remark that 'I have seen, in my times, Frenchmen, Italians and Russians . . . but as for Man, I declare I have never met him in my life ' (quoted in Tamir 1993: 13). The ingredients of a local identity formed by education are wide ranging and include such matters as language, literature, custom and sensibility. The significance of such local and substantial ingredients for personal identity, recognition and flourishing have been acknowledged by many writers, including the communitarian critics of liberalism (on these critics see, for example, Mulhall and Swift 1996, especially part I). Nor can such local and substantial identities be seen as opposed to autonomy and freedom. On the contrary, as Yael Tamir insists, 'no individual can be context-free, but . . . all can be free within a context' (Tamir 1993: 14). Such a context is indeed a prerequisite for freedom.

What appropriate forms of local and substantial commitment should education in a liberal democratic society seek to develop in students? In matters of broadly political identity, it has been suggested that students could be encouraged to develop a certain sort of patriotism focused on an imaginatively enriched concern for the community as a whole (see Callan 1991, 1994). To what extent, however, should the development of a *national* identity be seen as appropriate and defensible?

The nature and value of national identity

David Miller, in his recent philosophical defence of the concept of nationality, offers an account of it which involves eight interconnected propositions (Miller 1993). We present these here in a slightly re-ordered form.

1 National identity may be a constitutive part of personal identity ('may' is important for Miller here, since he does not advance the implausible claim that personal identity *requires* a national identity).

2 Nations are ethical communities in the sense that 'nationality' generates distinctive ethical obligations and expectations. We may have, for example, fuller duties to fellow nationals than we do to human beings as such.

3 National communities are constituted by *belief* – 'a nationality exists when its members believe that it does' (Miller 1993: 6) – rather than simply by any common attribute such as race or language. Examples of the shared beliefs at stake here include a conviction that its members belong together and that they wish to continue their life in common. Miller agrees with Benedict Anderson's claim that nations are 'imaginary' in that they are sustained by acts of the individual and collective imagination (Anderson 1983).

4 Members of a nation must, however, share certain distinctive traits. These may be varied in character, and include cultural features.

5 Nations must embody historical continuity, generating depth of involvement and obligation in ways not found in more transitory groupings.

6 Nations are related to a particular geographical place.

7 Nations are 'active' in the sense that 'they' do things, take decisions and so on.

8 Nations must be, at least in aspiration, political communities. People who form a national community have a good claim to political self-determination, although not necesssarily via a sovereign state. The actions of nations must therefore include at least seeking to control 'a chunk of the earth's surface' (Miller 1993: 7). The validity of this claim has, however, been challenged. Yael Tamir, for example, argues that a nation may be a cultural community without necessarily any political dimensions (see Tamir 1993, Ch. 3).

A number of important distinctions relating to national identity require acknowledgement here. A nation is not to be identified with a state. A state is a legal and political entity with authority of a specific form (sovereignty), resources of power of various kinds and a well-defined territory. Some nations do not have a state, and many modern states, in view of their cultural heterogeneity, cannot be identified with a national society. Many states are multinational in that they contain a number of national communities and cultures. Further, nationality should be distinguished from nationalism. Helpful here is Michael Ignatieff's distinction between 'civic' and 'ethnic' nationalism (Ignatieff 1994: 3–6). Civic nationalism is democratic in character, envisaging the nation as a community of equal, rights-bearing citizens, patriotically attached to a shared set of political practices and values. In contrast, ethnic nationalism sees national identity as based on ethnicity rather than citizenship and law. Whilst civic nationalism can be rational, flexible, pluralistic and morally rich, ethnic nationalism is tempted by irrationality, fanaticism and authoritarianism. It is more likely to be 'nationalistic' in the sense of the term which implies the inherent superiority of one nation over others. The distinction between 'civic' and 'ethnic' nationalism is further illuminated by the distinction which Tamir draws between 'citizenship' and 'nationhood'. Citizenship is a primarily legal concept referring to the relationship between a state and its formal members, embracing such matters as entitlements, rights and liberties. Nationhood involves a sense of membership in an imagined community, and the adoption and practice of a particular imagined cultural and communal identity. In Ignatieff's 'civic' nationalism, 'nationhood' embraces 'citizenship' and does not contradict it.

What is the value of nationality? The general benefits of nationality include affiliation, attachment, embeddedness, belonging and communal identity and solidarity, all of which resonate with the communitarian themes alluded to earlier. Nationality is clearly a significant element in the formation of personal identity.

What, however, is the value of nationality from the perspective of democratic principles and values? The tension between 'ethnic' nationalism and these principles and values is readily apparent. This is less so in the case of 'civic' nationalism. In 'civic' nationalism, democratic principles and values may be 'clothed' by features of nationality, and not submerged by them. It is this sort of nationalism which Miller has in mind in his claim that one of the benefits of nationalism is that it is a *de facto* source of the large-scale solidarity which is needed in complex societies if social atomisation is to be avoided and collective goods secured. Nations can provide an 'overarching sense of community' of the sort which facilitates this. Since in Miller's view national identity has a flexible, because partly mythic, character, it is capable of accommodating a number of different points of political view, and is therefore open to cultural pluralism and to criticism (Miller 1993). These emphases upon flexibility, pluralism and criticism are important features of 'civic' nationalism. It is in the light of considerations such as these that John White argues that the notion of 'British' identity and nationality needs to be re-worked to make it acceptable in terms of democratic criteria (White 1996).

The educational implications of 'civic' national identity

The educational implications of 'civic' nationalism are wide ranging. Although these implications cannot be explored in any detail at this point, education for nationality in the 'civic' sense must clearly be conducted in close connection with education for personal autonomy and for democratic citizenship. With regard to the development of personal autonomy, Tamir notes that 'civic' nationalism is compatible with the 'elective' aspects of our personal identity, which is an important democratic emphasis. Our lives should not be determined by history and fate, and significant possibilities for reflective choice should be insisted upon (Tamir 1993: Ch. 1). With regard to the development of democratic citizenship, the significance of 'civic' nationality for appropriate forms of solidarity are important. One important aspect of the educational development of a 'civic' national identity is the significance of the development in students of capacities for broad critical reflection and understanding, informed by a political and general education of some substance (see, for example, McLaughlin 1992; Williams 1995).

EDUCATION, DEMOCRACY AND NATIONAL IDENTITY IN THE CONTEXT OF LITHUANIA

The general principles outlined in the previous sections relating to education, democracy and national identity require considerable further critical discussion and defence. It is clear, however, that even if they are broadly acceptable as they stand, the principles cannot be applied crudely to any particular societal context. Judgements of great complexity and subtlety are involved both in analysing a particular society with respect to matters of national identity and in bringing to bear principles of the sort discussed. The authors have, however, been trying to explore the implications of these principles for national and nationalistic education in the newly established democracy of Lithuania and it is to this context that we now turn. Three particular questions arise for us:

- What is involved in the notion of a Lithuanian 'national identity'?
- What, if any, are the tensions between Lithuanian 'national identity' and democracy? Can a 'civic' version of Lithuanian 'national identity' be discerned and enhanced?
- In the light of this what features of Lithuanian 'national identity' are valuable and should be particularly promoted in, and preserved by, education and what features are less valuable and should be challenged and weakened by education? What educational means are relevant to these tasks?

A detailed and systematic examination of all of these questions is clearly beyond the scope of this chapter. However, a number of considerations will be explored which will illuminate, at least to some extent, a number of important relevant issues.

As a background to this discussion it is helpful briefly to situate Lithuania in its geographical, historical and political context.

The geographical, historical and political context of Lithuania

Lithuania occupies an area of 65,300 square kilometres adjacent to the Baltic Sea and has a population of 3.72 million people. It is bordered to the north by Latvia, to the east by Belarus, to the south by Poland and to the south west by the Kalingrad region which is Russian territory.

Lithuania has had a complex history. In the thirteenth century its lands were consolidated into a powerful Lithuanian Grand Duchy. Through an alliance with Poland, the Grand Duchy achieved the apogee of its power and, in the fifteenth century, Lithuanian territory extended from the Baltic to the Black

Sea. Eventually, a Polish-Lithuanian Kingdom was created, which gradually weakened and was divided up by Russia, Prussia and Austria. In 1795 Russia absorbed most of Lithuania. In 1863 there was a national uprising against Tsarist rule which led to forced emigration, and to increased repression. Although the uprising failed, it led to a revival of Lithuanian language and tradition.

Lithuania was occupied by Germany in the First World War from 1915. In 1918 Lithuanian independence was declared. During the interwar period, an independent Lithuanian state flourished, although a part of its territory was annexed by Poland. After the signing of the Molotov–Ribbentrop pact by Hitler and Stalin in 1939, Lithuanian independence was brought to an end. During the Second World War, Lithuania was subjected first to Soviet and then to Nazi occupation. From 1944, after the return of Soviet troops, Lithuania was incorporated into the USSR. Over 250,000 Lithuanians were deported to the Gulag. A guerilla war waged by Lithuanian partisans continued until 1953.

Following the emergence of *glasnost* and *perestroika* in the USSR, the Baltic States were prominent in asserting their independence. In 1989, on the fiftieth anniversary of the signing of the Molotov–Ribbentrop pact, over two million Lithuanians, Latvians and Estonians joined hands in protest in a human chain stretching from Vilnius to Tallin. In 1990 the first free elections in Lithuania since 1940 led to an overall majority of pro-independence candidates and to the declaration of Lithuanian independence. After a period of economic blockade by the USSR, and a number of violent incidents – including the tragic killing of fourteen unarmed civilians at the Vilnius television tower by Soviet troops in January 1991 – the independence of Lithuania was accepted by Russia and by the wider world.

Politically, therefore, Lithuania has had to contend with long periods of domination and oppression. In common with many countries in the former USSR, its current process of democratisation has to confront economic realities and imperatives and to be alert to geo-political realities. The instability of Russia in political, economic and ecological terms gives rise to concern. Lithuania's attraction to the EEC and NATO is therefore both economic and geo-political in character. The growth of international crime is also an important reality which demands attention.

The nature of Lithuanian national identity

What is involved in the notion of a specifically Lithuanian national identity? Any brief attempt at an answer to this question cannot do justice to the very wide-ranging and complex historical, cultural, social and political factors which are involved, and to the need for nuanced and appropriately qualified judgement. A tentative sketch is all that can be attempted here.

It is important to note at the outset that many features of Lithuanian national identity are not wholly unique to Lithuania, although they may take a specifically Lithuanian form. The 'particular' Lithuanian national identity that might be sought in education need not be wholly distinct from others.

A number of interrelated elements of Lithuanian national identity can be identified. Lithuanians have traditionally enjoyed a particular sensitivity to nature. This is related to a sense of 'spiritual harmony' embodied in traditions and festivals related to seasonal and agricultural landmarks. This sense of spirituality is rooted in early pagan beliefs and rituals which have been overlaid with Christian beliefs. Lithuania was the last country in Europe to adopt Christianity (in 1387). Another important element in Lithuanian national identity is the rich tradition of Lithuanian folk art, singing and dancing. Certain customs and traditions of behaviour ought also to be mentioned. These include the prominence of the role of the Lithuanian woman as mother and wife and as guardian of Lithuanian traditions in the family. The Lithuanian language is of great significance with respect to national identity. The language has been sustained over the years, sometimes against great odds. In the period 1864–1904, for example, it was forbidden by the Russian Tsar. Lithuanians set up underground schools (*daraktoriu*) where their children were taught to read and write in Lithuanian. It is now the state language and its use is supported and insisted upon in many contexts by law. It is the first language of approximately 80 per cent of the population of Lithuania. The largest of the linguistic minority languages are Russian and Polish (spoken as a first language by around 8 per cent and 7 per cent of the population respectively). Another feature of Lithuanian national identity is a shared sense of national historical memory and a corresponding sense of solidarity (on a number of these features see Grigas 1995; Liubiniene 1996).

In the present, post-Soviet, period it is widely thought that there is something akin to a crisis with regard to Lithuanian national identity. The Lithuanian sociologist Romualdas Grigas has argued that today Lithuania is at the crossroads of 'three ages' (the agricultural age, the capital or industrial age and the knowledge or post-industrial age), each with its associated cultural features. Grigas argues that Lithuanians have lost many of the cultural features associated with the agricultural age (for example, their sense of nature-related spirituality) and, in virtue of the impact of the second age (in both its Soviet and post-Soviet forms), are ill-equipped to move into the last of the three ages (Grigas 1995). Lithuania, he claims, has been led to 'civilisational emptiness', although this is, we contend, something of an exaggeration. Since 1990, in common with other post-Soviet societies in Eastern Europe, Lithuania has had to deal with a disorientating influx of external influences of various kinds.

Lithuanian national identity: ethnic or civic?

There are a number of features of the context of Lithuania which tempt Lithuanians in the direction of an 'ethnic' rather than a 'civic' conception of national identity. The long history of domination and oppression, for example, has heightened rather than diminished Lithuanian national sentiment, which has survived in circumstances of adversity for many centuries. Whilst this has not led to an exaggerated nationalism, it is unfortunate that Lithuania has no experience of democracy prior to 1990. (The independent Lithuanian state in the interwar years cannot properly be said to have been democratic.) A number of the legacies of the Soviet period inhibit the evolution of Lithuania into democracy and into developing a 'civic' national identity. One of these legacies is a lack of confidence in political processes and politicians. Another is the interesting phenomenon of 'double-life' syndrome, where, under Soviet rule, Lithuanians led one life in their families, and another in the public domain. It was only in 1988, for example, that Christmas was celebrated openly in Lithuania for the first time since the end of the Second World War. One of the negative effects of this syndrome is a lack of commitment by individuals to the requirements of civic virtue and the civic domain generally.

There are, however, many reasons for optimism about the development of a 'civic' conception of Lithuanian national identity. One of the historically significant features of Lithuanian national identity has been a stress upon tolerance. Indeed, some scholars claim that it was precisely this spirit of tolerance which led to the destruction of the Grand Duchy of Lithuania (Grigas 1995: 35). Freedom of religion was approved by the *Seimas* (Parliament) in 1563, the first such approval in Europe. There are also strong economic and political forces supporting movements in a democratic and 'civic' direction, and inviting Lithuanians to acquire attitudes and qualities of character to match.

Democracy and Lithuanian national identity: assessment and debate

Conceiving Lithuanian national identity in 'civic' terms involves assessing which elements in the existing sense of national identity need to be promoted and preserved, and which should be challenged and weakened. This assessment, in Lithuania as elsewhere, involves a wide-ranging and informed national debate.

There are no easy answers to the questions at stake. Many people agree that the Lithuanian national historical memory needs to be sustained. There is disagreement, however, about what should be learned from it. There is some feeling that distinctively Lithuanian traditions and lifestyle should be preserved. However, there is disagreement about the salience that they should have in society as a whole. Some feel that these traditions are the preserve of the elderly or peasants, and that the gradual erosion of the agricultural and rural will erode the traditions also. Other Lithuanians seek to preserve the traditions selectively. The reality of the globalisation and homogenisation of culture has led many Lithuanians to adopt an 'ecological' attitude to their local traditions. There is much support for the notion that the Lithuanian community should have more than a geographical and circumstantial reality and that civic bonds should be strengthened, enriched by a distinctively Lithuanian spirit.

The emphasis to be placed on the Lithuanian language gives rise to some interesting questions. As noted earlier, it is an important ingredient in Lithuanian national identity and has been sustained throughout the generations in the face of many threats and obstacles. It is the state language and is legally required as a means of communication in many contexts. Although Lithuanian speakers can be found in neighbouring countries, and in places overseas where there are Lithuanian communities, the language has little functional utility beyond Lithuania. Given the orientation of modern Lithuania to the wider world, the study of foreign languages is therefore stressed in Lithuania, and many students are 'tri-lingual'. Some of the protections given to the national language in the context of education are controversial, however, and require careful consideration. One such protection is the requirement that each study programme in Lithuanian universities should be taught in Lithuanian.

Any adequate debate of the sort for which we are calling must be properly informed throughout by democratic principles and values. This brings the significance of education into focus.

Education, democracy and Lithuanian national identity

A number of recent educational developments in Lithuania should assist in the development in students of an understanding of democratic principles and values, and of a 'civic' conception of national identity. The Science Council of Lithuania is currently encouraging universities to accept the additional responsibility of education for citizenship. Recent initiatives from other quarters convey a similar message to schools. At the turn of the century, there was some reflection upon the nature of Lithuanian national education (Salkauskis 1991). However, during the postwar occupation of Lithuania by the Soviet Union the schooling system was sovietised and russified. Since the end of the occupation, the schooling system has been reconceived. The Lithuanian 'General Conception of Education' was formulated in 1992. This conception, at least at the level of principle, seems markedly similar to the conception of liberal democratic education outlined above (compare Jovaisa 1996). It contains a mixture of 'universal' and 'particular' elements. On the 'universal' side, the principles of the conception stress the freedom and responsibility of individuals and the primacy of democratic aims and values. On the 'particular' side, the principles speak of a commitment to the preservation of Lithuanian culture, identity and historical continuity, whilst emphasising the values of pluralism (in relation, for example, to minority groups) and the need for a critical acceptance of change. This lays the foundation for education for Lithuanian national identity to be seen in 'civic' terms. One expression of the pluralism inherent in this vision is the establishment of schools for minorities (on these schools see, for example, Vysniauskiene and Saugeniene 1996).

Whilst the school is an important context in which a properly focused notion of Lithuanian national identity can be formed, the significance of other agencies of society for this task should not be overlooked. For example, the family is a crucial 'school' in relation to the transmission of national values. It kept alive Lithuanian national identity during the recent period of Soviet occupation. Since Lithuania is a predominantly Catholic country, the church has also an important role to play.

CONCLUSION

We consider that the development of a national identity in students of a 'civic' kind is compatible with, and maybe even required by, the sort of liberal democratic principles which call for education to be concerned with the development of the autonomy of the individual and with democratic citizenship. Further attention to the context of Lithuania should throw light on the many practical implications to which this claim gives rise. It should also illuminate the coherence and justifiability of the claim itself.

REFERENCES

Anderson, B. (1983) *Imagined Communities*, London: Verso.
Bailey, C. (1984) *Beyond the Present and the Particular. A Theory of Liberal Education*, London: Routledge and Kegan Paul.
Callan, E. (1991) 'Pluralism and Civic Education', *Studies in Philosophy and Education* 11, 1.
—— (1994) 'Beyond Sentimental Civic Education', *American Journal of Education* 102.
Grigas, R. (1995) *Destiny of Nation* (in Lithuanian), Vilnius: ROSMA.
Gutmann, A. (1987) *Democratic Education*, Princeton NJ: Princeton University Press.
—— (1992) 'Introduction' in C. Taylor (ed.) *Multiculturalism and 'The Politics of Recognition'*, Princeton NJ: Princeton University Press.
—— (1993) 'Democracy and Democratic Education', *Studies in Philosophy and Education* 12, 1.
Halstead, J. M. (1994) 'Moral and Spiritual Education in Russia', *Cambridge Journal of Education* 24, 3.
Ignatieff, M. (1994) *Blood and Belonging. Journeys into the New Nationalism*, London: Vintage.
Jovaisa, L. (1996) 'The Idea of Universal Education' in Internal Committee of the Conference on the *Upgrading of the Social Sciences for the Development of Post-Socialist Countries. Selected Papers of the International Conference*, Kaunas: Kaunas University of Technology.
Liubiniene, V. (1996) 'Reflection of Gender Roles in Traditional Lithuanian Folk Songs' in Internal Committee of the Conference on the *Upgrading of the Social Sciences for the Development of Post-Socialist Countries. Selected Papers of the International Conference*, Kaunas: Kaunas University of Technology.
McLaughlin, T. H. (1992) 'Citizenship, Diversity and Education: a philosophical perspective', *Journal of Moral Education* 21, 3.

—— (1995) 'Liberalism, Education and the Common School' in Y. Tamir (ed.) *Democratic Education in a Multicultural State*, Oxford: Basil Blackwell.

Miller, D. (1993) 'In Defence of Nationality', *Journal of Applied Philosophy* 10, 1.

Mulhall, S. and Swift, A. (1996) *Liberals and Communitarians*, 2nd edn, Oxford: Blackwell.

Salkauskis, S. (1991) *Pedagogical Writing* (in Lithuanian), Kaunas: Sviesa.

Tamir, Y. (1992) 'Democracy, Nationalism, and Education', *Educational Philosophy and Theory* 24, 1.

—— (1993) *Liberal Nationalism* Princeton NJ: Princeton University Press.

Vysniauskiene, D. and Saugeniene, N. (1996) 'Lithuanian Minority School: History, Present Day Tendencies and Future Perspectives' in Internal Committee of the Conference on the *Upgrading of the Social Sciences for the Development of Post-Socialist Countries. Selected Papers of the International Conference*, Kaunas: Kaunas University of Technology.

White, J. (1996) 'Education and Nationality', *Journal of Philosophy of Education* 30, 3.

Williams, K. (1995) 'National Sentiment in Civic Education', *Journal of Philosophy of Education* 29, 3.

4

MORAL PIETY, NATIONALISM AND DEMOCRATIC EDUCATION

Curriculum innovation in Taiwan

Ching-tien Tsai and David Bridges

苟日新，日日新，又日新…

周雖舊邦，其命維新.

是故君子無所不用其極.

(大學. 第二章釋新民)

If we can renew ourselves, let us do so from day to day,
yea, let there be daily renewal;
The Chou Dynasty was an old nation,
but its leader built a new state.
We too should try to renew ourselves as far as we can.
(Explanation of 'improvement of people' in *Great Learning*
edited by Hsieh, Lee, Lai and Chen 1993: 5)

INTRODUCTION AND HISTORICAL BACKGROUND

On 23 March 1996 the people of the Republic of China (ROC) on Taiwan
voted to choose their first ever directly elected president. This first ever popular selection of a national leader in China's 5,000 year history, along with
three sets of military exercises by mainland China, and the presence of two
American aircraft carriers, all contributed to placing Taiwan in the global
spotlight.

These events reflected the politically changed context in which education
has been developed in Taiwan during the past forty-six years. After the communists took over the mainland in 1949, the national government of ROC
shifted to Taiwan, and Taiwan became culturally and educationally an immigrant society as well as a politically closed one. This was especially the case
during the phase from 1949 to 1978 when there was a military confrontation
between Taiwan and mainland China (Hu 1992b: 26).

A political paternalism was established with a party leadership, which overwhelmingly controlled the systems of legislation, administration, jurisdiction, examination and supervision, i.e. the Executive Yuan, Legislative Yuan, Judicial Yuan, Examination Yuan and Control Yuan in Taiwan. This was headed by Chiang Kai-shek who was elected by the National Assembly. Such a form of government seemed essential to protect the security of Taiwan at this age of revolutionary crisis. This flag-waving democracy was different from western democratic government, and lacked either rule by the people or even a significant level of accountability by the government to its people.

However, the task of the Taiwan government, and the loyal and obedient members of the Kuo Ming Tan (i.e. KMT, the ruling party in Taiwan at that time) who had retreated to the sparsely populated island of Formosa was to survive against the enormous threat posed by mainland China. The survival of Taiwanese society was seen to depend on its members' ability to carry out their duty and serve their society even at the price of their individual rights. The *Ta-wo* (i.e. the greater self or the society) took priority over the *Hsiao-wo* (i.e. the little self or the individual). The individual must be sacrificed to the interests of the society. The overwhelming emphasis on collective interests over the interests of the individual was a fundamental difference between Taiwan and the West in their thinking styles.

Chiang Kai-shek reviewed the situation and claimed that the failure of nationalistic education on the mainland and especially the failure of the young to understand 'San-Ming-Chu-Yi' (i.e. the Three Principles of the People – nationalism, democracy and social welfare: the teachings of the founding father of the ROC Dr Sun Yet-sen) was the reason why the government had been defeated by the communists (Wu 1969). The government could not afford to lose Taiwan as its last haven, and therefore, the most important social value was to achieve security supported by national identity and allegiance in Taiwan.

NATIONAL SPIRIT EDUCATION/CHINESE-ISATION – THE SOCIAL STUDIES CURRICULUM OF THE 1950s

'Min-Tsu-Ching-Sheng-Chiao-Yu' or 'national spirit education' (i.e. the development of national consciousness) in Taiwan has been not just about national pride, but also about the spiritual and moral values which the country stood for and which have made it different from other countries. These values included, in particular, the Eight Moral Virtues, i.e. *Pa Te* taught by Confucius. The Ministry Of Education in Taiwan argued the importance of the Eight Moral Virtues as the essence of Confucianism:

> In our education, common courses shall be based both on the teachings of Dr Sun Yat-sen and on the Eight Chinese Moral Virtues: loyalty,

filial piety, mercifulness, love, faithfulness, righteousness, harmony, and peacefulness.

(Ministry of Education 1992: 3)

The political ideologies of the Three Principles of the People – Confucianism, patriotism and obedience to government – were brought together as 'national spirit education' in which pupil citizens were to be indoctrinated. It was clear that the school was to become a 'symbolic battlefield' (Paquette 1991: 2) in the fight against communism.

Furthermore, to standardise the academic level of schools of the same category, the Ministry of Education prescribed the '*Ko-Cheng-Piao-Chun*' which translates roughly as 'curriculum specifications'. This is a formal government statement of the prescribed curriculum expressed in educational administrative regulations and requirements specified by the Ministry of Education.

In the revised 'curriculum specifications' of 1975, the social studies curriculum in the elementary schools was an integrated subject with elements of history, geography and civics. Social studies in the elementary schools was clearly seen as the subject which was most important to the fulfilment of the aims of elementary schooling in Taiwan, because it was the only part of the formal curriculum for which the government provided '*Chiao-Hsueh-Chin-Yin*' (instruction directions), '*Chiao-Ko-Shu*' (textbooks) and '*Hsueh-Sheng-Hsi-Tso*' (pupil practice booklets) aimed at enabling pupils to understand the society in which they lived and at celebrating the inherited national values. Thus, the social studies curriculum was a kind of 'national spirit curriculum' (Tsai 1996). The government (Ministry of Education 1992: 3) argued:

Our education requires that geography and history be taught so as to build the sense of nationalism, that lessons on social life and conduct be taught to demonstrate the operation of democracy, and that vocational skills be offered to form the base of the principle of livelihood.

The definition of the curriculum based on the 'curriculum specifications' was published by the Ministry of Education, and the supporting materials included textbooks and 'instruction directions' which were all edited by the National Institute under the authority of the Ministry (National Institute 1993: 3).

In order to transport Chinese culture, especially 'national spirit education', from mainland China to Taiwan and to make Chinese Taiwanese society culturally and educationally Chinese, all the politicians who acted as successive Directors of the National Institute in Taiwan were 'mainlanders' (i.e. people who had come over from mainland China with the national government around and since 1949). The Chairperson of the Committee, Sun Tan-yueh, and Tusung Liang-tung and all the members of the Editorial and Reviewing Committee for the social studies textbooks appointed by the National Institute were also mainlanders. Those mainlanders were more familiar with and consequently emphasised mainland China rather than Taiwan, and there was only one unit of content relating directly to Taiwan in elementary history textbooks of the 1950s and this unit aimed to establish Taiwan as a base of the Three Principles of the People to recover the mainland (Tu 1991: 24). One member of the Editorial and Reviewing Committee recalled:

> The policy of 'recovery of the mainland' had an important impact on the design of social studies curriculum. We followed this policy and selected and emphasised the negative effects of Chinese Communism in the textbooks.
>
> (Sze 1995: 1)

Social studies was the core of a curriculum designed to implement nationalistic education and to implement the government's policy of 'anti-communism and recovery of the mainland' (National Institute 1993: 4). The importance of 'national spirit education' allocated to social studies was so great that Chiang Kai-shek himself reviewed and corrected the content of social studies textbooks and emphasised the contribution of Dr Sun Yat-sen and the importance of the national flag and the national anthem to the Republic (Sze 1992: 78).

The social studies curriculum was designed to transmit traditional social beliefs and values to the next generation and to pursue cultural consensus (Gong 1966: 2; Sze 1990b: 2) and thus to ensure the continuity of the nation (Schug and Beery 1987: 8). This instruction emphasised the importance of the morality of traditional Chinese Confucianism, the virtues of obedience, loyalty and devotion to family, friends and teachers. However, the Taiwan government extended this to include the 'nation' or even the 'government', and Confucianism was thus distorted by political paternalism.

There were bronze statues of Dr Sun Yet-sen and President Chiang Kai-shek on the campuses and photographs of Great Leaders hung on the walls in classrooms. Teachers talked to pupils about the origins and meaning of national holidays, especially those related to the establishment of the Republic, and pupils were asked to draw pictures, to write compositions or calligraphy whose content was about these national holidays, to bring the national flag to join a congregation, to celebrate and shout slogans. Furthermore, the official language used was Mandarin. Taiwanese dialect was prohibited in schools, and if pupils used Taiwanese dialect to communicate then they would be punished. Those activities were used to increase their sense of national identity and patriotism.

The social studies curriculum in the 1950s was seen as an essential form of social control in Taiwan designed to equip and to arm the thinking of its next generation in an age of military confrontation between Taiwan and mainland China. The head of the textbooks department in the National Institute emphasised (Hsieh 1995: 8):

That was a particular age when we had a particular political situation and social environment.... However, if you want to evaluate this curriculum, you have to understand its particular social background and political situation ... patriotism and national spirit education were necessary in national compulsory education and the editing of textbooks had to follow these principles.

However, as time moved forward and the survival of Taiwanese society has been secured to some extent, needs changed: 'The principles we applied in editing textbooks at that time are no longer appropriate nowadays' (Hsieh 1995: 8).

Educators in Taiwan pointed out that the social studies curriculum should not only set out the facts to be learned, but should also raise the level of cognition to analysis, synthesis and evaluation, and that it should have concern for the continuity, sequence and integration of pupils' experiences (Chin 1989a: 105; Perng 1972: 2). Alternative approaches to curriculum development in social studies were beginning to emerge in Taiwan.

THE BEGINNING OF EDUCATION FOR DEMOCRACY/ WESTERNISATION – THE SOCIAL STUDIES CURRICULUM SINCE THE 1970s

The context for curriculum changes in social studies was a period of political innovation in Taiwan. After the death of Chiang Kai-shek in 1975, his son Chiang Ching-kuo was elected to take over as president. He began to undo his father's paternalism. The government believed that Taiwan in the 1980s would be a liberal society in which those in authority espoused a preference for procedures that encouraged the exploration of issues affecting the lives of its citizens. The assistant Minister of Education argued:

The assumption is that the society is changing all the time, so each proposed solution is a hypothesis to be tested. The structure of this society is temporary, multiple, dynamic, and the evolution of a great variety of value systems increase the severity of educational misconceptions. There are different ideas and values emerging in an open society, and education has an important and practical role to play in clarifying those values.

(Wu 1989: 6)

In 1979, the Taiwan Provincial Institute for Elementary School Teachers' In-service Education (the Taiwan Institute) was requested by the Ministry Of Education in Taiwan to conduct a 'Wen-Sze-Chiao-Hsueh-Shih-Yen', i.e. an inquiry teaching experiment in the social studies curriculum. It was interesting that the term 'Shih-Yen' (experiment) was preferred by the Taiwan Institute in this Taiwanese context because they claimed that the idea that they were engaged in an experiment came from the quasi-scientific American model of curriculum development which they were following, even if the process of 'experimentation' in the pilot schools would more accurately be described as 'trials' and it could not really claim the kind of scientific approach which that name implied. The concept of 'inquiry learning' rather than 'inquiry teaching' (*Wen-Sze-Chiao-Hsueh* cf. *Tan-Chiu-Chiao-Hsueh*) is more familiar to western ears. But the choice of words was significant. This Taiwanese preference for 'inquiry teaching' indicated that in this form of pedagogy the teacher was still very much in control of the learning process and its outcomes. It corresponded to what in an Anglo-American context is usually referred to as 'guided discovery learning'.

The curriculum aims in this experimental social study curriculum had two functions: one was to develop individual interest and ability and to pursue individual happiness; and the other one was to cultivate patriotic citizenship. The curriculum aims represented a fusion of tradition and modern spirit, with its legacy from the 1950s and its new spirit borrowed from the US. The aims of this experimental curriculum were:

> to cultivate pupils' manners, behaviours and habits of good living; to cultivate basic knowledge and ability to adapt to modern social life; to practice excellent traditional morality; to help them to be active pupils and patriotic citizens.
>
> (Taiwan Institute 1987b: 7)

Meanwhile, Chiang Ching-kuo abandoned martial law on 15 July 1987 in order to promote democracy in Taiwan. Taiwan has taken steps over the past years to reduce the risk of confrontation with mainland China, including its announcement to end the national mobilisation period for the suppression of the Chinese communist rebellion (Hu 1992b: 26). When martial law in Taiwan was abandoned, the criticisms of education, especially of textbooks, were also made public, and there were vigorous debates about the bias of textbooks regarding issues of the aboriginal group in Taiwan, and inspired by awareness of feminism and the ethnocentrism of mainland China. The textbooks developed by the National Institute were severely criticised and there was a demand for them to be revised.

Unfortunately, Chiang Ching-kuo died in 1988 before the reforms took root, and it fell to Lee Teng-hui – Taiwan's first native-born president – to continue to build Taiwan as 'a model of emerging democracy, with a free press, free elections and human rights protections' (China News 1995b: 1). With the development of democracy in Taiwan in the form of multi-party politics (seventy-six parties) and freedom of speech (361 daily newspapers) and with the expression of a multiple value system in the society, there was a developing pressure for major revisions in the curriculum. This message was echoed by the President of Taiwan who declared that:

education reform is the one of the important tasks after political reform...
pluralism, the abilities of critical thinking and problem-solving should
be emphasised in the school curriculum.

(Central Daily News International Edition 1994: 2)

It was to be expected that this would make a major impact on the design of the
school curriculum and approaches to curriculum development in primary
school social studies. Under such conditions, the Ministry Of Education
issued an order and asked the National Institute to revise their textbooks
based on the criteria of rationality and suitability (Lu 1994: 59). This innovation in the 1980s introduced a number of significant changes in social studies
education in Taiwan. There were changes in the curriculum aims, curriculum
content, learning and teaching styles.

First, the director responsible for the development of this innovation
pointed out change in the curriculum *aims* (Huang 1995: 2):

> We emphasised the concept of sound self in the curriculum aims; this
> was never emphasised before because in the past we emphasised the
> greater self (i.e. Ta-wo) rather than the little self (Hsiao-wo) or the indi-
> vidual. However, if the individual does not have a sound self, then
> neither sound inter-personal relationships could be established, nor the
> greater self of society.

Another member of the project team pointed out:

> The curriculum was developed to help pupils to understand how to make
> rational decisions and to take social action based on a values system, to
> deal with social problems which pupils encountered, and to help pupils
> become reflective and responsible members in society, and thus, to
> improve social life.

(Ou 1991: 9)

Social studies aimed to teach and enable children to be familiar with the structured knowledge and enquiry methods of social science, and further to clarify
values, to make rational decisions, and to take action which was based on
rational decisions (Ou 1991: 10).

Second, there were also changes in the curriculum *content* areas. The content of social studies was not limited to history, geography and civics, but
was expanded to include sociology, cultural anthropology, politics, economics
and psychology (Liu 1987: 69; Lin 1989: 55). It was a kind of knowledge defined
by social scientists which could be used as the framework for a social studies
curriculum that aimed to understand society (Steering Committee 1990: 54).
However, how this related to all the new ideologically laden aims about
democracy, autonomy, etc. was not mentioned in this model.

The third set of changes introduced were changes in the pupils' *learning
style*. Pupils were expected to learn the rules of social science within which

they could construct cognitive systems of understanding. Pupils would discover concepts and 'generalisations' just as social scientists research answers to their questions in social science. In this process, pupils would use scientific methods, understand the process of knowing and develop a scientific attitude to understanding society. Members of the innovation team explained:

> Pupils were encouraged to find answers from incomplete information. It would need pupils to organise the evidence and discover the systematic order of knowledge.
>
> (Lee and Sue 1990: 211)

PROBLEMS AND CHALLENGES

The Taiwanese experience raises a number of important issues for a more general discussion of the way in which political principles impinge on educational practice. First it reveals how problematic the notion of national identity, let alone nationalistic education, can be in a particular context. One of the major divisions in Taiwanese politics is between (i) those who see themselves as Chinese, sharing an identity with the people of mainland China, resident in a province of China which is temporarily isolated from the rest; (ii) those who see themselves as the heirs to a true national Chinese identity which has been destroyed by communists on the mainland but which will eventually be restored to the mainland; (iii) those who see themselves as the people of a new independent nation which is called Taiwan. These different views of what it is to be Taiwanese result in different views of the cultural sources of national identity and the kind of educational programmes which will support that identity.

Second it shows how integral to national identity can be certain kinds of moral values. National or nationalistic education is not just a form of political education: moral education is at its core. For some Taiwanese, to be Taiwanese is to be Chinese, which meant historically that one would act in accordance with the principles of moral piety embodied in Confucian teaching and practice. For those seeking to establish a new identity based on (largely imported) democratic principles, democracy requires an apparatus of values and practice (personal autonomy, critical enquiry, challenge to authority, open discussion, equality between the sexes) which sits uncomfortably with some of those traditional Chinese values. As education is expected to take the lead in promoting the democratic values of modern Taiwan and as curriculum developers draw on western practice as the source for democratic education, the classrooms of Taiwan look set to be the battleground on which the struggle for Taiwan's identity will be fought.

Third, and unsurprisingly in this context, it is the teachers who find themselves grappling, not always successfully, with the burden of educational and social innovation. One teacher describes her problems in trying to introduce group discussion into a class long accustomed to a heavily didactic mode of instruction.

> There were difficulties in group discussion. Pupils' presentation was not good enough and it was very demanding for the pupils to conduct discussion because in the other subject lessons there was no group discussion. When pupils had group discussion in the social studies lesson, they became very noisy and it was very difficult for teachers to control discipline in discussion. Therefore, teachers tried their best to avoid discussion. Furthermore, in order to carry out group discussion, pupils had to move all the desks and chairs around and this created a turbulence in the classroom and a lot of noises for the next door classroom, and the other teachers complained.
>
> (Chen 1995: 1)

In practice, some teachers treated textbooks as the main teaching media and even expected pupils to memorise the content. A teacher educator describes the disarray among teachers called upon to introduce an innovative new social studies programme:

> Some lazy teachers used traditional methods to teach the new curriculum and they taught to the textbooks. Some teachers did not find the right answer in the textbook or when there were too few words in the textbook. Some teachers even photocopied the content of the teaching programmes and asked pupils to read the process of teaching activities set out in the Teachers' Handbook and carried out this kind of teaching by reading the text of the Teachers' Handbook in the classroom.
>
> (Hsu 1995: 1)

However, some were more optimistic about the capacity of the schools and the new social studies curriculum innovation to establish the foundations of a new democratic order in Taiwan:

> The chaos in Taiwan (especially the fight in the Legislative Yuan) was the result of different voices which had been prohibited in the past. This was a transformative period. When our pupils grow up and participate in society, the whole situation will change. Our pupils were encouraged to participate in discussion under due procedure to present their argument with the understanding of the pros and cons, and they were educated to respect democracy and law, and they were equipped with competence to present their argument. They would not keep silent in public debate without complaining after the meeting. This would be a great contribution to the establishment of a democratic society in Taiwan. If our citizens were educated in line with this good curriculum

and trained by good methods and good materials, they would establish democratic habits and there would be no such chaos in this society.

(Chen 1995: 3)

Finally, the problems facing Taiwan's schools, however, are not just the practical and pragmatic problems associated with adjustment to change. They reflect in microcosm the fundamental uncertainties which are a product of Taiwan's extraordinary circumstances. Its political, military and commercial relations with the west and the entrepreneurial success of its people in the commercial domain have opened Taiwan to a positive embrace of democratic principles and procedures, but the social and political imperatives which derive from the threats from its enormously powerful neighbour remain as strong as ever, as do, though perhaps year by year more weakly, the cultural imperatives associated with a history and identity which is Chinese.

Such unique circumstances will almost certainly call for unique solutions at the level of national politics and educational policy, solutions which will extend rather than replicate the current repertoire of democratic politics and educational principles and practice largely developed to meet the needs of people in a different hemisphere.

REFERENCES

Bruner, J. (1966) *Toward a Theory of Instruction*, Cambridge: Harvard University Press.

Central Daily News, International Edition (1994) 'We should work hard to carry out educational reform', 30 September, p. 2.

Central Daily News, International Edition (1994) 'Thirty Black Organisations are going to be withdrawn by the Administration Yuan', 27 October, p. 8.

Chen San-hui (1995) Interview by C. T. Tsai regarding social studies in Taiwan, 27 February.

Cherng, Jiann-jiaw (1991) *Research of Elementary School Social Studies Teaching*, Taipei: Wuu-nan Publisher.

Chin, Pao-chi (1989a) 'Final Evaluation Report of the Fourth Grade Social Studies Experimental Curriculum', *Journal of Elementary Education* 2, pp. 73–105.

Chin, Pao-chi (1989b) 'Introduction of Curriculum Development in Pan-chiao Model', *Modern Education* 4 (2), pp. 29–39.

Chin, Pao-chi (1989c) 'An Introduction of the Curriculum Development in the Pan-chiao Model', *Modern Education* (4) 2, pp. 29–39.

China News (1995a) 'Vincent Siew explained the issue of representation of China', 5 May, p. 2.

China News (1995b) 'President Lee departed on a landmark trip to the US', 8 June, p. 1.

Ellis, A. K. (1981) *Teaching and Learning Elementary Social Studies*, Boston: Allyn and Bacon.

Gong, Bao-shann (1966) *Research and Practice of Social Studies Teaching*, Taipei: Jenq-chung Bookstore.

Hsieh, Ping-ying; Lee, Hsieh-yu; Lai, Yan-yuan and Chen, Man-ming (eds) (1993) 'Great Learning', Chapter Two. Explanation of 'improvement of people', *New Translation of the Four Books*, Taipei: San-ming Bookstore.

Hsieh Fu-sheng (1995) Interview by C. T. Tsai regarding Chou-shan Model, 10 March.

Hsu, Hsueh-hsia (1995) Interview by C. T. Tsai regarding social studies in Taiwan, 28 March.

Hu, Jason C. (1992a) *A Brief Introduction to the Republic of China*, Taipei: Kwang Hwa Publishing Co.

Hu, Jason C. (1992b) *Republic of China at a Glance*, Taipei: Kwang Hwa Publishing Co.

Huang, Ping-huang (1995) Interview by C. T. Tsai regarding Nan-hai Model, 6 March.

Lee, Shiuh-wu and Sue, Hui-min (1990) *Social Studies Teaching Material and Method*, Taipei: Wuu-nan Publisher.

Lin, Ju-jung (1989) 'Developmental Trend and Implication of Social Studies Curriculum in Elementary Schools', *Modern Education 4* (2), pp. 53–67.

Liu, Te-sheng (1987) *Curriculum Structure and Content of Social Studies in Elementary Schools*, Ko-hsiung: Fu-wen Bookshop.

Lu, Jo-yu (1994) *A Research in the Curriculum Development of Social Studies*, an unpublished MEd thesis, Taipei: National Taiwan Normal University.

Ministry Of Education (1992) *Education in the Republic of China*, Taipei: Bureau of Statistics in the Ministry Of Education.

Ministry Of Education (1993) *Curriculum Standard for the Primary Social Studies Curriculum*, Taipei: Ministry Of Education.

National Institute for Compilation and Translation (1993) *Profile of National Institute for Compilation & Translation*, Taipei: National Institute for Compilation and Translation.

Ou, Yong-sheng (1991) *Research of Social Studies Teaching in Elementary School*, Taipei: Shi-ta Bookshop.

Ou, Yong-sheng (1995) Interview by C. T. Tsai regarding Nan-hai Model, 7 March.

Paquette, J. (1991) *Social Purpose and Schooling: Alternatives, Agendas and Issues*, London: Falmer Press.

Perng, Jiah-shing (1972) *Social Studies Teaching Material and Method for Elementary School*, Taipei: Taiwan Bookshop.

Schug, M. C. and Beery, R. (1987) *Teaching Social Studies in the Elementary School: Issues and Practices*, London: Scott, Foresman and Company.

Steering Committee of Humanistic and Social Science Education (1990) *Research Report about Social Science Teaching Outlines*, Taipei: Steering Committee of Humanistic and Social Science Education in Ministry Of Education in Taiwan.

Sze, Chi (1990a) 'Postscript' in Steering Committee of Humanistic and Social Science Education *Research Report about Social Science Teaching Outlines*, Taipei: Steering Committee of Humanistic and Social Science Education.

Sze, Chi (ed.) (1990b) *Research and Practice of Social Studies Teaching*, Taipei: Fuh-shing Bookstore.

Sze, Chi (1992) 'Things That Have Come to Pass in the Editing of Primary School Social Studies Textbook', *The Memory of the 60 Anniversary of the National Institute for Compilation & Translation*, Taipei: National Institute.

Sze, Chi (1995) Interview by C. T. Tsai regarding Chou-shan Model, 6 March.

Taiwan Provincial Institute for Elementary School Teachers In-service Education (1987a) *The Introduction of the Taiwan Provincial Institute for Elementary School Teachers' In-service Education*, Taipei: Taiwan Provincial Institute for Elementary School Teachers In-service Education.

Taiwan Provincial Institute for Elementary School Teachers In-service Education (1987b) *The Research Plan of Experimental Social Studies Curriculum in Elementary School: Summary Report in First Stage*, Taipei: Taiwan Provincial Institute for Elementary School Teachers In-service Education.

Tsai, C. T. (1996) *Approaches to Curriculum Development: Case Studies of Innovation in the Social Studies Curriculum in the UK and Taiwan*, unpublished PhD thesis, University of East Anglia.

Tsuei, Jian-chyi (1987) 'Preface' in *The Research Plan of Experimental Social Studies Curriculum in Elementary School: Summary Report in First Stage*, Taipei: Taiwan Provincial Institute for Elementary School Teachers In-service Education.

Tu, Ping-tsun (1991) 'Social Studies of Elementary School in the past Forty Years of Taiwan', *Educational Anthology* 16, pp. 19–50. The National Institute of Educational Materials ROC.

Tu, Ping-tsun (1995) Interview by C. T. Tsai regarding Chou-shan Model, 7 March.

Wang, Hao-po (1989) 'Textbooks and Political Socialisation: An Analysis of the Political Socialisation Function in the Experimental Social Studies Curriculum', *Journal of Elementary Education* 2, pp. 107–25.

Wu, Ching-ji (1989) 'The School Teachers' Role in An Open Society', *Journal of Elementary Education* 2, pp. 1–22.

Wu, Jih-pyng (1969) *The Educational Thought of President Chiang Kai shek*, Taipei: Jenq-chung Bookshop.

5

INDIVIDUALISM, COLLECTIVISM AND EDUCATION IN POST-TOTALITARIAN EUROPE

Felisa Tibbitts

INTRODUCTION

The unitary and collectivist outlook that largely pervaded education in the former Soviet Union prior to 1990 has been met with a reaction of 'individualism'. Just recently, this impulse appears to be tempering. This 'too and fro' in the educational system mirrors the political and philosophical complexities that characterise the region as it struggles to grasp a notion of individualism that rejects collectivism but embraces living in community and tolerance.

In this chapter, I overview developments in political education in schools between 1990 and 1996, relying on my experiences as a project director for national civic and human rights educational projects in Romania, Albania, Estonia and Ukraine, and with broad exposure to the region. I also interviewed educationalists from Romania, Russia, Albania, Slovakia and Lithuania directly on the topics of individualism and collectivism in the classroom.

The reforms of the social sciences in the post-totalitarian countries of Central and Eastern Europe provide a microcosmic lens for examining philosophical and ideological struggles that may well be evident in other circles: academic, political and the artistic. Each of these areas will evidence such struggles in their own way. The educational sector is particularly revealing because the philosophical struggles (a) are semi-public, (b) demand timely resolution (in terms of textbook development and other educational policies), and (c) suggest a country or region's view about what constitutes ideal citizenship in the long run.

This chapter merely introduces some of the core issues surrounding a very complex relationship between outlook, habit and need. Though the treatment of this rich and important topic is somewhat superficial, it at least provides an opportunity to introduce this subject as an area deserving further attention.

PRE-1989 COLLECTIVISM IN THE SCHOOLS

All countries organise schools to conduct political education, which may be defined as the development of competencies in thinking and acting in political arenas, both governmental and non-governmental in nature (Gillespie 1981). During the Soviet period, the countries of what are now known as Central and Eastern Europe, the Baltics and the Newly Independent States, experienced a special form of political education. A collectivist world view, one of Marxism-Leninism and national constitutions, pervaded not only the social and political sciences, but also the ideological orientation of schooling overall. No doubt this collectivist outlook was attempting to create 'ethno-linguistic territorial "national administrative units" i.e. "nations" in the modern sense where none had previously existed' (Hobsbawm 1992: 166).

Schools were overtly used as the main instrument for converting children to the communist cause (Fischer-Galati 1952). Marxism-Leninism was represented in all texts, and new vocabularies reinforced this. In Romania, 'popular democracies' was substituted with 'triumph of popular-democratic and socialist revolutions' (Capita 1992). School assemblies celebrated Soviet and communist anniversaries and Pioneer organisations prepared youth to eventually join the Communist Party.

In the classroom, collectivism and a unitary outlook were promoted using 'transmission models' of teaching. An open, critical approach to learning was absent, since student self-expression and a plurality of perspectives was threatening to ideological homogeneity and a collectivised world view. This had direct implications for the ways that classrooms were organised. Students and teachers alike were rewarded for assent to the 'correct view', a didactic orientation that was reinforced, no doubt, by an historically traditional, teacher-centred approach in the classroom. Open-ended discussions, experimental content and instructional practices were all impeded within a highly centralised curriculum controlled by the Ministry of Education, in conjunction with the Central Party.

A group of Russian pedagogical specialists summarised the collectivist values that were taught in schools:

- concern for the common good;
- the power of the group;
- conformism;
- helping one another;
- think first of your homeland, then yourself.

(Interstudie conference 1996)

Certain features of collectivism were undoubtedly attractive, as a political system organised in this way provided support and protection, while personal responsibility was low. Two of the consequences, however, were a lack of self-expression and a lack of individual responsibility for results. 'We didn't have choice, but we weren't responsible for anything', a Russian headmaster confessed. This statement, and the one that follows, reveals the complex orientation to the collectivist approach, seen retrospectively by citizens of the region:

> Totalitarianism would not have held on as long as it did or swept so many individuals along in its wake if it were as alien to ordinary human aspirations as we would like to believe today. What were its secret attractions? ... Communist society strips the individual of his responsibilities – 'they' always make the decisions; but responsibility is often a heavy burden to bear.
>
> (Todorov 1990: 25)

According to Russian philosophy and pedagogy, individualism was a negative phenomenon; collectivism was the only possible system for interpersonal relations and useful for education (Golovatenko 1994).

RETURN TO INDIVIDUALISM

With the movement towards democracy, educational systems in these regions were forced to revise political, moral and other forms of normative education. A period of de-ideologisation in the early 1990s meant that formal references to Marxism-Leninism and the former communist system were struck out of curricula. Mandates for new civics, ethics and sociopolitical classes were called for to replace the former Marxism-Leninism subjects. At all levels of the educational communities, there was a broad, general acceptance in principle that classes that addressed democratic education and human rights themes needed to be developed.

One impulse, borrowed largely from the west, but influenced by previous knowledge about humanist psychology and 'classical pedagogues', was to focus on individualism. This theme was fed both by a knowledge about good teaching practice, which sought to promote individual development and recognised diverse learning styles, and a reaction against the collectivism that had landlocked schooling in previous years.

Across subject areas, there was an interest in reclaiming 'individualism' as the operating educational paradigm, rather than the notion of the individual whose identity is wrapped up in group membership. This movement, called 'humanism' in some countries, recognised the unique personality and potential of each student, and the opportunities that individuals have to influence society's development (Golovatenko 1994). This philosophical reclamation of individuality dovetailed with a surge of interest in adapting certain western pedagogical methods that employ activity-based, cooperatively-oriented and constructivist instructional techniques.

Individualism was demonstrated in post-totalitarian texts in many ways. Progressive, new civics and human rights texts for schools in Romania, the Czech Republic, Albania and Estonia presented lessons on self-identity, creative self-expression, moral dilemmas, children's rights, debate and conflict resolution. Critical analyses of everyday social and sometimes political situations are also encouraged. Not all these changes are able to be tracked, of course, since they are so numerous. The text examples presented below are representative of the changes one could find in the 'reform minded' approaches to political education.

The Citizen Project in the Czech Republic introduced an alternative civics curriculum for Forms 5–9, and included school-wide efforts, including the development of a school parliament, a school board, a school newspaper, and a school constitution. The objective of the project was 'to educate youngsters about their rights and responsibilities, to encourage them to think independently and to make responsible decisions, to become knowledgeable of human rights and democratic laws, and be aware of the fact that their country is an integral part of the whole world' (Ondrackova and Tibbitts forthcoming).

In Albania, primary level human rights activity books introduced individual, group work and role playing. The goals for the students included the development of self-expression, listening skills and conflict resolution in the classroom, acceptance of differences, empathy and awareness of rights and duties. There was an emphasis both on children's rights and responsibilities. A text development leader explained that they wanted children to be 'active participants in a democratic society, to contribute and to know that they are responsible for their own rights, and also the rights of others in the community' (Tibbitts forthcoming).

In Ukraine, a 9th Form course on the state and law took up a basic definition of human rights; civil society and the rule of law; international standards of and international mechanisms for securing human rights; and practical aspects of protection by Ukrainian citizens of their rights, among other topics (Ukrainian Centre for Human Rights 1995). Numerous other examples exist in the region.

In Romania, an alternative civics text developer explained her philosophical assumptions:

> In Romania, there was a mass society. The individual was not taught that he was an individual with rights and responsibilities. Everybody was taught that they were part of a collective, with collective rights. . . . I start from the perspective of human rights and man as seen as a 'person.' The emerging perspective is the person in the first article of the Declaration of Human Rights, which is inspired from the Kantian perspective. What is a human being? The human being is an end and not a means. . . . A person is a person, with reason and consciousness. . . . We all look for our own identity, and from here we look to others, and try to understand differences in people.
>
> (Tibbitts 1994: 368)

In the Romanian alternative civics text, students were asked questions about slavery, and the ways in which this social phenomena was consistent or inconsistent with Kant's view of the human being. This philosophical starting point enabled the curriculum developers through discussion questions to raise a variety of human rights values. These values included respect for self and others, the multi-dimensional nature of personhood, and tolerance. Teachers were invited through lessons in the text to move into an inquiry-oriented approach through discussion and listening techniques, self-expression, empathetic awareness and conflict management.

Some local reformers talk about teachers 'being drunk on the possibility for exercising their will, needs and values' in the classroom. However, when such freedom is used superficially or incompletely, these new methods and topics can be interpreted as reinforcing a unitary world view, as in former times. In Lithuania, some teachers have started to use the new teaching methods, such as group work, short-term projects and out-of-school activities. A guide developed for teachers provides examples for the use of mass media, table games, photographs and cartoons, drama and conflict resolution for teaching human rights. Yet, one of the persons involved in this training pointed out that 'these methods promote collective work. . . . It means promoting of the collective style of thinking [may not be] dead in the Lithuanian schools' (Duoblys 1996: 1).

In fact, what these changes have asked of teachers is nothing short of a change in world view. The 'return to individualism' with its complexity of perspectives on epistemology, political philosophy, psychology and instruction is more like a paradigm shift than a change in approach. In fact, without such a paradigm shift in the political education field, it is doubtful that teachers would have undertaken any significant change. From the perspective of students, how different is human rights teaching from the previous political education classes, if human rights are presented as facts to be learned in a classroom atmosphere where critical thinking is discouraged and authority and decision-making are not shared with the teacher?

This paradigmatic shift in teaching is a shift in the core belief system about the teaching and learning process. In this new view, resources brought to the political education classroom include not only the teacher's ability in the subject area, but the students' previous knowledge, abilities and potentials. Knowledge is partly fixed, and partly discovered. As in a democracy, both teacher and students are responsible to each other for a successful learning process. The goals for instruction include the development of the intellectual, emotional and value domain and in political education, also the ability to take action. Teaching methods are varied, based on knowledge about the complexity of the learning process, and especially learning specific to a discipline. (Teaching history, for example, involves modes different than teaching civics or music.)

EARLY RESULTS

There are some early results to these first attempts by school systems to promote individualism and a new form of political education. First, the new approaches have rarely been implemented. Besides a general lack of access to new, experimental materials, deeply held teaching traditions and belief systems are personal barriers for teachers. Many educators remain comfortable with the 'transmission mode' of teaching and continue to believe in the infallibility of the ideas and values sanctioned in texts. This uncritical view is preferred even when the ideas concern democracy and human rights. Thus, some teachers find students' open expression confrontational, disrespectful and difficult to bear. Critical thinking is equated with unhealthy criticism.

A German political scientist has noted:

> Even the most radical process of political change and economic progress could not in the short term erase the traces which the authoritarian legacy has left in the political mentality. It must therefore be accepted that many people will come to terms with current and future problems using a mechanism which we have identified and presented as an authoritarian substitute solution.
>
> (Fritzsche 1992: 2)

At this moment, only a small segment of history and civics teachers are genuinely interested in or capable of changing their outlook and method of education. Moreover, their own experimentation points to the difficulty of making the 'paradigm shift' in the face of tradition and a fluid political and social environment. Collective responsibility remains better understood than individual responsibility. A Romanian teacher recognised this as a special moral problem for her country, where avoidance of 'becoming involved' was a survival tactic until recently. Although individual opportunity has been linked with economic entrepreneurship, individual responsibility to the community through creative civic and social action has no familiar antecedent.

Moreover, collectivism has sometimes persisted in a new form, that of aggressive nationalism or, in some cases, xenophobia. As social and economic security have disintegrated for many in the post-Soviet period, there has been an impulse to identify 'the community of the innocent' as well as the guilty (Hobsbawm 1992: 174). Within the political education field, a line has emerged separating those who would promote internationalism, integration with Europe and western educational methodologies with those supporting a strong emphasis on the nation-state, reference to a glorious, often more ethnically homogeneous past, as well as traditional teaching methods. In this struggle over the politics of identity, the first approach is more forward looking and critical in outlook; the second looks back, in search of a sanctified, more certain, historically-based image.

In the classroom, teachers have expressed confusion about the new interactive rules of classroom instruction, especially around the use of small groups. Sometimes, co-operative and group work is seen through an old lens, where participation in groups implied self-denial in relation to the greater good. The group can still be seen as an entity in and of itself, as opposed to a collection of individuals. It is difficult for some educators to understand that co-operative learning for children does not diminish individuality but in fact enhances it through increased opportunity for participation, at the same time that skills that enhance relationships with other individuals in the group, such as communication, decision-making and conflict resolution, are also practised.

Sometimes local cultural traditions can also undermine group co-operation. A Russian researcher who has focused on the implementation of role play in the school found that breaches of role play rules happened very frequently. Students did not see this violation as serious,which the researcher traced to the Russian predisposition to value power over the rule of law (Tibbitts forthcoming).

Another area of difficulty lies with the students. Some young people take individualism and individual freedom to mean that they do not need to follow rules or compromise with others. One Romanian teacher explained how this had led her to believe that she had over-emphasised individuality.

> Myself, having a strong anti-collectivist attitude, I couldn't stop stressing individualism. . . . I even refused radically anything that sounded 'collectivist.' I got very close to the classical liberalism idea. What is bothering me now could be a kind of result of what I was promoting in my discourse with them. . . . Even decision-making in small groups isn't going easily. Children aren't willing to compromise. . . . They don't even obey every time the results of the votes [in the group].
>
> (Ivan 1996)

The following definitional list of attributes was developed by the group of Russian educationalists referenced before. To them, individualism is a 'mixed bag' meaning:

- what is right for me;
- maximum self-demonstration;
- insensitivity to other people's feelings;
- nonconformism;
- things that are important for others are not necessarily important to me;
- freedom for yourself.

(Interstudie conference 1996)

Those educators throughout the region who have been open to this 'shift in paradigm' have had to work against a system whose logic, culture and accountability measures serve to reinforce a much narrower, content-driven form of instruction. They are creating new meanings for individualism that are embedded in classroom practice. In this new terrain, there are inevitable misunderstandings, hurts and uncertainty.

A NEW SOLUTION

Despite the unevenness of these reforms, those teachers who are genuinely searching for a new mode through 'the new individualism' can be seen as experiments for further innovation in political education. They have taken this idea, sought to implement it in the classroom and on this basis are reformulating its meaning on a daily basis. In conversation, many of these teachers are pointing to a new direction, one that focuses on both the individual and community, but not the collective. A Slovakian reformer commented that there is a chance to reconstruct the notion of 'union' so that it is based on the individual, without denying a quality of relationships with the community as a whole (Kviecinská 1996). This community is ideally inclusive and heterogeneous.

In this broader view, knowledge and practice of individual rights are balanced with the knowledge and practice of responsibility to community. This idea, although not foreign to civic education in other places, has been rediscovered in the region through grounded experience in an emerging democracy. Although these notions were never absent from the first wave of political education reform in Central and Eastern Europe, the Baltics and NISs, they were somewhat overlooked. Either 'community' was interpreted through the former 'collectivism' lens, or the enthusiastic message of individualism drowned out the parallel message of responsibility. This same group of Russian educators recognised that the concept of 'community' absorbs both the positive and negative features of individualism and collectivism, but mediates the extremes. Community was defined as meaning:

- a goal that is larger than the self;
- a group that takes into account all of its members' interests;
- a group whose members have different 'life standards';
- individuals have responsibilities to the group (as a condition for remaining in the group, like a social contract);
- communities have different sub-groups with different aims.

(Interstudie conference 1996)

This new understanding of individualism among the initial reformers recognises that there should be individual freedom within the community based on universally accepted values, while personal responsibility should remain high. Individualism and community-building would be mutually beneficial, with the core being social responsibility. In political education, individualism would be presented alongside the notion of community.

I think that what is needed is a balance where the value of 'individualism' will be accepted as the right to initiative and flexibility, which can support in the most efficient way the pursuit of common goals of a community. I think that the sense of community represents the translation of 'individualism' to a 'collective' scale.

(Georgescu 1996)

With this view in mind, interactive instructional methods would be understood as supporting both the individual personality of students and teachers but also the sense of belonging to a community. Group work would be understood as opportunities for individuals to express themselves at the same time that they would be following a common purpose in a group task. The introduction of such teaching methods would not preclude the use of other well-known techniques, such as lecturing and whole group discussion, but they would help to ensure that multiple perspectives are expressed in the classroom.

What has happened for those teachers who have implemented the progressive approaches is that they have made a personal discovery about the need for balance between individualism and community. These ideas are already core to democratic thought, but have had new life breathed into them. The educationalist John Dewey pointed out that, in a democratic society, moral principles must be self-accepted rather than uncritically imbibed, freely chosen rather than externally imposed. This needs to be done in the light of the awareness of the collective good of the community, with individualism tailored to communal responsibility (Giroux 1988).

The struggles that have taken place in the political education sectors in the region are suggestive of the difficulties that members of the larger population are facing in the workplace, home and political sector. The vast majority are caught between the 'grand shifts' promised by an emerging democracy and economic structure and the persistent realities of everyday life. Amidst the 'politics of displacement' (Elshtain 1995: 41) individuals must resist the temptation to associate with a new national identity that excludes all but one's most immediate ethnic, linguistic, religious, cultural and/or geographic reference group. It may be that all citizens of these emerging democracies will need to discover their own personal meaning of individualism – good, bad or indifferent – in what will be an inevitable movement away from collectivism. Given the difficulty of changing lenses, a love affair with individualism may be requisite for coming to know and embrace community in a new way. This path, however, is neither smooth nor straight.

REFERENCES

Capita, L. (1992) 'Post-War History and Unification of Europe in Textbooks: The Romanian Experience', unpublished paper presented at the European seminar 'Post-War History and Unification of Europe in Textbooks: Prospects After the End of the Cold War', Berlin, June.

Duoblys, G. (1996) Personal correspondence with author (Lithuania).

Elshtain, J.B. (1995) *Democracy on Trial*, New York: Basic Books.

Fischer-Galati, S.A. (1952) 'Communist Indoctrination in Rumanian Elementary Schools', *Harvard Educational Review* Vol. XXII, No. 3.

Fritzsche, K. P. (1992) 'Human Rights Education after the Collapse of Communism', unpublished paper presented at the conference 'Human Rights and Human Rights Education in the Process of Transition to Democracy', 2–6 November, Praha.

Georgescu, D. (1996) Personal correspondence with author (Romania).

Gillespie, J.A. (1981) 'Introduction' in D. Heater and J.A. Gillespie (eds) *Political Education in Flux*, London and Beverly Hills: Sage Publications.

Giroux, H.A. (1988) *Schooling and the Struggle for Public Life*, Minneapolis: University of Minnesota Press.

Golovatenko, A. (1994) 'Education for Democracy, Social Responsibility, and Creative Activity in Russia Today' in B. Reardon and E. Nordland (eds) *Learning Peace*, Albany: State University of New York Press.

Hobsbawm, E. J. (1992) *Nations and Nationalism since 1780: Programme, Myth, Reality*, Cambridge: University of Cambridge Press.

Interstudie conference (1996) 'Educating for Social Responsibility', comments of Russian participants in workshop 'Individualism and Collectivism' facilitated by author, 26–27 September, Arnhem, The Netherlands.

Ivan, A. (1996) Personal interview with author, 21 May, 1996 (Romania).

Kviecinská, J. (1996) Personal correspondence with author (Slovakia).

Ondrackova, J. and Tibbitts, F. (forthcoming) 'Human Rights and Citizenship Education – A Czech Classroom Experience' in H. Starkey and F. Tibbitts (eds), *Human Rights Education in Schools*, Strasbourg: Council of Europe.

Tibbitts, F. (1994) 'Human Rights Education in Schools in the Post-Communist Context', *European Journal of Education* Vol. 29, No. 4, pp. 363–76.

Tibbitts, F. (forthcoming) 'Research and Evaluation in the Service of Human Rights Education' and 'Albania: Text Development at the Primary School Level' in H. Starkey and F. Tibbitts (eds), *Human Rights Education in Schools*, Strasbourg: Council of Europe.

Todorov, T. (1990) 'Post-Totalitarian Depression', *The New Republic*, 25 June.

Ukrainian Centre for Human Rights (1995) 'Topical framework for 9th form', *The State and Law of Ukraine Basic Course*, Kiev: Ukrainian Centre for Human Rights.

Part II

EDUCATION, DEMOCRACY AND THE MARKET

6

AUTONOMY, CITIZENSHIP, THE MARKET AND EDUCATION

Comparative perspectives

Robert Cowen

INTRODUCTION

One of the major bodies of literature which exists in educational studies, and which has grown voluminously in the last fifty years, has been the literature on development. The literature has concerned itself with questions of economic modernisation and, occasionally, the question of values and the survival of cultures. The literature has centred on the development of the 'Third World', and for the most part has been constructed in the 'First World' – in Paris, New York, San Francisco, London and so on (Anderson and Bowman 1966; Alavi and Shanin 1982).

In the work of the international agencies, such as UNESCO, the International Institute of Educational Planning and the World Bank, the classical question addressed was how to vitalise Adam Smith's factors of production (land, labour and capital) to produce economic growth (Simmons 1980). For scholars in universities an important theme in this analysis was how education – notably formal schooling – might contribute to these processes of economic growth, not least by the formation of a skilled labour force. Thus much of the work dealt with upper secondary and first cycle higher education, especially the improvement of provision in applied science, technology and technical services. At the level of the lower secondary school, a major question addressed was the balance of general and vocational education and how to break the dichotomy between academic and vocational education so strongly embedded in the colonial models of education introduced into parts of the 'Third World', by Britain and France in particular (Altbach, Arnove and Kelly 1982).

The question was framed by a distinction in the world economy: countries such as the United States, Britain, Germany, France and so on had been economically successful. Other countries, in Africa, in Latin America, in Asia were 'underdeveloped'. There were, apparently, clear reasons for this – corruption, political instability, rigid social structures and values (Buddhism, Hinduism, Confucianism, and even Catholicism as in Southern Europe) which were inappropriate. Economic growth would follow if these 'variables' were changed – preferably towards patterns of values which it was known would lead to 'modernity'. For example, the dichotomous pattern variables of Talcott Parsons stressed, as favourable to the construction of modernity, the appointment of persons to important positions through criteria of achievement (rather than ascription) and the performance of tasks on the basis of self-orientation (rather than a concern with a collectivity such as an extended family) (Parsons 1961). For economic modernisation there were certain value patterns that were dysfunctional.

Of course there were various practical problems which would need attention in the reform of the educational systems of the Third World to produce economic modernity, such as the preparation of planners and administrators, increased financial allocations to education (especially higher education and science) and the improvement of various sub-systems of education, such as curriculum, information management, teacher education and so on. There remained also questions about sectoral balances in investment in education, for example, the correct strategies for investment in elementary education and literacy on the one hand, and higher and technical education on the other. But these were tactical issues – on which there was massive technical expertise in the international agencies and indeed in the universities of the major cities of the First World (Simmons 1980).

However, the strategy of solution to the problems of economic modernity was clearly delineated. The major actor in the construction of modernity would be international skills and international capital available in the First World for the improvement of the Third World. The major 'domestic' actor would be the state (of Brazil, Ghana, India) through its expatriate-educated technical elites. The major sociological question was how to disturb irrational stratification patterns (based on unequal patterns of land and capital ownership) and value patterns which were pre-modern and stressed cosmic and social relationships (through Buddhism etc.) rather than the secular virtues of economic efficiency. Tradition – traditional patterns of social stratification, traditional value systems, traditional dysfunctional economic practices, and traditional (often colonial) educational practices – was what had to be disturbed.

It is suggested here that this version of the modernity problematique has collapsed. It is further suggested that this version of the modernity problematique has reversed. Modernity or at least late modernity is our problem and we – the former First World – are deeply ambivalent about how to deal with this particular cuckoo that has come rather noisily to roost.

In more formal language, then, it will be suggested that the traditional modernity problem, based centrally in how to replicate the organisation of 'advanced' societies around industrialisation including its associated educational forms, has collapsed and that we have a new puzzle about the nature of 'advanced' societies and their associated educational systems. It will be suggested, second, that the learning relationship of some parts of the First and

Third Worlds has reversed: it is, or it should be now our concern to understand from countries which were formally 'the problem', how to maintain our tribal traditions – notably our western tribal definitions of autonomy, citizenship and concern for the other.

MODERNITY AND EDUCATION REVISITED

The relationship between modernity, identity and education was inserted into the literature of comparative education most fully in the mid-1970s, especially through the work of Carnoy (1974) and Altbach and Kelly (1978). Working from slightly different perspectives these authors asked questions about the role of formal education in the construction of cultural imperialism and neo-colonialism. They traced, in case studies, the ways in which western educational models (most notably the British and French, but also the American) had formed new identities among those exposed to 'modern' schooling in, for example, India or Vietnam, or through 'internal colonialism', and the formation of minority identity, in the US. Central to the work are the themes of oppression, 'dependency' and neo-colonial identities. The work remains fascinating and it has been subsequently extended. But here the important point is how late it was that the theme emerged in the literature. It was a most valuable counterpoint, and an oppositional view, to the work on modernity by scholars such as Inkeles and Smith (1974), Parsons (1961) and McLelland (1972). By drawing on the literature from the 'Third World', notably dependency theory from Latin America and writers from the Maghreb, the theme of identity was inserted into the agenda of analysis of modernity. The paradox is that even this new literature addressed a problem which in the non-academic world had been visible for at least 100 years.

The Japanese were among the first countries to acknowledge the problem publicly, that is how to modernise while simultaneously retaining cultural identity. Their ambition in the period of the Meiji Restoration – after 1868 – was to balance their acquisition of 'western technique with eastern morality'. Granted the technological gap, represented by the 'black ships' of Admiral Perry, between Japan and those powers insisting on the incorporation of countries on the western rim of the Pacific into the world economy, the Japanese had little choice. They needed knowledge of modern metallurgy, medicine, communication systems, military arts and education. But, amid furious debates and even armed insurrections, a balance was gradually struck. The new useful western knowledge was to be acquired within a central value system that remained Asian, i.e. Confucian, Buddhist and Shintoist, and which in the Japanese case was legitimated in the name of the Emperor-God of Japan. Even the insistence that the most pragmatic of skills – literacy – be acquired by all households and all individuals began with an edict from the Emperor: 'Know ye our Subjects . . .' (Passin 1965).

The final formation of the Japanese educational system in the late nineteenth century, through the plans of Education Minister Mori, produced an educational system which was deliberately schizophrenic. It was simultaneously hierarchical and egalitarian, Confucian and practical, collectively oriented but with pockets for the acquisition of individual autonomy and useful knowledge. Thus the main thrust of the system was toward using the schooling system as a ladder of meritocratic selection through education, but the social values expressed in the daily rituals of schools were those of Confucian hierarchical obligation and social order. However, simultaneously at the higher levels of the education system in the vocational schools and colleges which became the Imperial Universities, the acquisition of 'modern knowledge' was encouraged not least by the use of expatriate teachers from the US, Germany, Britain and so on, as well as by sending large numbers of young Japanese overseas.

What is striking about the Japanese initiative, in retrospect, is its success: the delivery of modernity at least until the pathology of militarism in the interwar period (Horio 1988). It is this successful implementation which distinguishes the Japanese case from the cultural resistance movements marked in other countries by the Boxer Rebellion in China, the Slavophile movement in Russia, the Ghandian or Freirian responses in India or Brazil or the Mao period in China of the 1960s. It should perhaps be noted that the process continues – it is not merely a historical oddity of the late nineteenth and early twentieth centuries. Iran is a contemporary representative of the tensions between modernity and cultural identity, as was Tanzania. The case of Algeria remains moot, while Belarus, Latvia and Russia (again) are going through extreme contemporary versions of the problem.

These 'socialist' countries – countries of the 'Second World' – had also gone through an earlier crisis of modernity and identity. The Soviet experiment from 1917 to 1990 (see also on this the chapter by Nikandrov in this volume) offered a solution to the problems of balancing western knowledge and a version of 'eastern morality'. In economic and political terms it was as extreme as the Japanese solution – the legal abolition of feudal aristocracies and land-owning groups, new political structures, the imposition of a rigid central value system, the insistence on mass educational provision, and the organisation of a 'modern' industrial economy. Like the Japanese educational system, the Soviet education system was schizophrenic. Useful knowledge, especially of natural science, applied science and technology, was to be acquired within a political socialisation stressing hierarchy (i.e. subordination to the leadership of one Communist Party) (Price 1977). Loyalty to a vision of a single future was demanded, parallelling the Japanese vision of 'defend the nation, enrich the nation' and, for that matter, revere a leader.

As in the Japanese case, there were careful Soviet limitations placed, socially and educationally, on the development of individual intellectual autonomy. As in the Japanese case, there was a very detailed Soviet cultural specification of the duties of citizenship. And as in the Japanese case, there was a carefully nurtured definition of the care of others – in the Soviet case, socialist citizens and revolutionaries on a world-wide basis. In the Japanese case, those messages were constructed with very great care for transmission by school rituals, e.g. uniforms, school behaviour codes, and collective assemblies in which messages from an actual or quasi-Emperor were read out. Thus, the traumas of economic modernization were, in both countries, socially framed, were made explicable, and the terms of individual autonomy, the obligations of citizenship and a culturally specific version of caring for others – in each case, a unique social contract – were defined in the daily social control processes of the schools.

There are a number of points which could be extracted from the preceding analysis – for example that both the Japanese and Soviet systems tipped into failure. The messianic visions, compounded by international isolation and not domestically limited by political checks and balances, went out of control (in the military period of Japan and in the actual collapse of the USSR as a political unit). The point could also be made that Japan of the period 1868 to 1945 and the Soviet Union are merely extreme examples of social mobilisation processes undertaken in Singapore, Taiwan and Malaysia in the last thirty years – how to combine western technique with eastern morality while defining carefully in the central value system and in the schools the detailed behaviours through which individual autonomy, citizenship and care for others are limited and culturally understood. (See also on this the chapters by Bridges and Tsai and by John Phillips in this volume.)

Here it is more logical in terms of the overall argument to stress two other points: the changed nature of the modernity problem and its 'reversal'.

LATE MODERNITY AND EDUCATION

There is now a major literature on the nature of late modern or even post-modern societies. Not only are the socio-economic configurations of 'advanced' societies judged to be changing but they are doing so in a world economy characterised by mobility of sites of production, international capital flow and increased international mobility of highly educated labour. Variations of the concept of 'globalisation' are being energetically analysed in the literature (Waters 1995). Following the thinking of authors such as Reich (1992) and Porter (1990), the terms of international economic competition are changing, and this idea has begun to influence the thinking of major international organisations and governments. The terms of international economic competition will, it has been suggested, shift to competition within a world 'knowledge economy', that is, competitive advantage and wealth will depend on advances in and control of a knowledge base in such complex languages as bio-technology, information and communication technology, and management skills.

Such a scenario throws up, of course, a number of routine comparative puzzles. How may vocational technical sectors of education be strengthened – can the German system be borrowed? How may higher education systems be changed – is an American community college a useful international exemplar? How may education in the inner cities be strengthened – does the American magnet school provide a model for City Technical Colleges? What if 'whole-class' teaching is borrowed from Taiwan? The questions are as careless and the answers as frenetic as those asked and answered in the last flurry of anxiety about industrialisation and its relation to schooling in the period 1890 to 1914. Snipping bits from other people's educational gardens without fundamental knowledge from a range of social sciences is the sociological equivalent of cut and burn agriculture; except it is more expensive. The routine puzzles of governmental and advocacy comparative education are then at best alarming distractors. But there is a problem, and it is an interesting one, which can be opened up by four arguments.

First, redefining educative processes to meet the exigencies of a putative 'knowledge economy' is a novel challenge. The educational borrowing which was, by volition or by *force majeure*, undertaken by Algeria, Brazil, India, Japan, the People's Republic of China, the USSR and Zambia (etc.) is not an option. The immediate problem is not to adapt 'a borrowing', but to invent. Second, invention has taken place. Australia, Canada, New Zealand, the United Kingdom and the United States have experimented and are experimenting with new modes in the transmission of education. Third, in this invention, the problem has become how to combine western technique with western values. Fourth, the counterpoint for reflection (though not the arena for 'learning lessons') becomes the earlier experiments of the 'Third World' in mixing western technique and eastern morality.

It is not possible to demonstrate, without a major funded research project, that policy makers in Australia, Canada, New Zealand, the United Kingdom and the United States arrived independently and more or less simultaneously at the view that the twenty-first century world economy would be a 'knowledge economy'. It is, however, possible to identify publicly signalled crises, of a nation's international competitiveness, and attention to the national education system as something which, with dramatic reform, would assist in increasing international economic competitiveness. In each of these countries, national reports, the statements of new parties in office, and educational legislation (Cowen 1996) mark the coupling: reform education to recover international competitive advantage. In each country there has been a specification of routine puzzles: improve vocational-technical education or lower cycle higher education; reform curriculum and evaluation and (national) testing; improve teacher education; make universities more efficient; define 'effective' schools.

These routine puzzles are however embedded in two fresh strategic stances, both ideological (i.e. concealing class and economic interest within a broader legitimation). Of the two fresh strategic stances, one involves major institutional reforms and the other involves the specification of a new mission for educational systems.

The first strategy is institutional reform. The institutional rearrangements, with national variation, involve the construction of educational institutions as a double market. That is, educational institutions will compete with each other within an 'internal' market (for pupils or students, for scores on tests, for market niche). Educational institutions will also compete with each other in an 'external' market – they will seek community financial support, business financial support, support from (research) foundations and governmental financial support which may be conditional on explicit performance criteria.

Thus what we have seen in the last twenty years in these systems of education is a major rearrangement of modes of control in the schooling system. With local variations, the powers of consumers of education – parents, business, governments – have been increased. The power of professional groups – teachers, advisers, local authorities – has diminished. The justification for reform has been offered in the vocabularies of 'choice', 'responsiveness', 'flexibility', 'parental power', 'evaluation and assessment' and 'effectiveness' (Bondi 1991; Grace 1991; Kenway *et al.* 1992; Lawton 1992). Of the examples, the English one has perhaps been the most extreme. Standardisation and thus comparability of educational result has been guaranteed by a new national curriculum, new national school level testing procedures and a national Research Assessment for the universities. Financial alertness in educational institutions has been increased by locating control of finance much more at individual school level, by limiting local educational authorities' rights over their educational budgets, and by deliberately reducing the proportion of state finance of university budgets. Consumer influence has been increased by strengthening the role of parents in school governing councils (and reducing teacher union representation) (Edwards and Whitty 1992; Whitty 1989). The central state is now the consumer of trained teachers and the control of teacher education is in the hands of a state-dominated Teacher Training Agency. It is business and a reformed Department for Education and *Employment* that has a major role in defining vocational-technical education.

However, while England is the most extreme and dramatic contemporary example of a shift to what may be called 'market-driven' educational systems, the other countries mentioned above have embarked on approximately similar reforms, taking the vagaries of political party victories and the specific initial conditions of historical circumstance into account. There has in other words been a shift in the role of the State in the provision and definition of an educational service. The state (in the US, Britain, Canada, Australia) used education as part of nation-building in the nineteenth century (Green 1990). Now the state is the agent which defines the terms of competition in an imperfect or quasi-market, and which in particular defines the terms in and on which the education service will be evaluated. It defines educational 'effectiveness'. It is this ideological redefinition of the point and purpose of education which constitutes the second, ideological, strategy of the state as the organiser of education in market driven systems.

This strategy is the construction of the idea of 'performativity'. This is a political project, and a deliberate one. It involves defining and measuring and publicising the 'results' of education in quantative terms. Paradoxically the concept and the project has probably affected the universities of the US, Canada, Australia, Britain and so on more dramatically than other sectors of education – the universities had further to go. Historically, they had been their own judges. Thus the careful assembly by 'management' in the universities of indices of performance is now a routine exercise (Peters 1992). Measures of publication output, major academic honours, funded research, PhD graduation rates are now not merely part of the American experience, but have been institutionalised with varying degrees of state control in the other countries. The Australian example is more a self-evaluation model than the British, but the Canadian, Australian and New Zealand measures of performativity are, *de facto*, rather similar to the state-mandated measures of university research profiles in the United Kingdom (Cowen 1996).

The consequence is at least a double one. Schools and universities are now comparable on performativity criteria. 'Consumers' can choose; the market is operationalised. The second consequence is that what counts as 'educational transmission' is altered. As 'performativity' is constructed, older tribal values come into question, are displaced, and are sometimes destroyed. In my university now, for example, a book is operationally defined for purposes of 'performativity' (the UK Research Assessment) as something, no doubt within a unitary cover and published commercially, that is 76 pages long. Through such simple signals mighty messages are carried.

AUTONOMY, CITIZENSHIP AND SOCIAL CONTRACTS

The 'western' educational systems of the 1950s through to the 1970s were easy to understand in comparative terms. The educational patterns captured well the socio-economic stratification systems of a straightforward division of economic labour linked to a simplistically viewed industrial and agricultural occupational pattern. Thus with local variation, the Gymnasium, the *Realschule* and the *Hauptschule* (or the English grammar, secondary technical and secondary modern schools) led into white collar, skilled labour and other labour occupational hierarchies. The 'common secondary school' movement of the 1950s to 1970s, whether in Scandinavia or by the late 1970s in Spain, mainly succeeded in deferring this selection process to upper secondary education. University systems were generally small, offering an education to something less than 20 per cent of the age cohort; more typically less than 10 per cent. The United States was partially an exception – but there educational selection and social stratification occurred also. It was mainly done later (at about 18 years of age) through guidance and counselling and curriculum choice. Gender and ethnic stratification remained, for the most part, issues whose salience was only just beginning to be negotiated. Control of evaluation was primarily in the hands of professional groups, such as teachers, private testing services or university influenced school leaving or university entrance examinations – with the notable exception of examinations in Europe at the age of 10, 11 or 12 for admission to secondary education.

These differentiations in socio-economic selection and alternative educational futures were parallelled by differential socialisation into moral futures and messages about political possibilities in Europe. In the French *lycée* the languages of 'philosophy' and mathematics provided possibilities for individual intellectual autonomy (as well as the acquisition of a Cartesian canon of rationality). In Germany, in the Gymnasium, the Humboldtian vision of *Bildung* and *Wissenschaft* provided not only an intellectual formation but a moral vision of the disinterested pursuit of truth. In the English grammar school, the Lockean curriculum of high specialisation (a 'few essential subjects') provided a general intellectual formation (through a transfer of training argument) which, with the hierarchical arrangement of pupils into 'senior prefect', 'prefect' and 'sub-prefect' roles, provided access to a moral universe. That universe was intellectually hierarchical (Latin was better than metalwork) and being appointed a prefect confirmed a present and probably a future leadership role. Outside such academic schools in Europe the moral socialisation was more ambiguous and less crisply defined. In the United States, school cultures also replicated domestic adult political processes (elections for leadership positions): moral education was primarily socialisation into American identity through the informal curriculum of schools.

All of these transmissions of moral messages were differentiated, including in the United States where, at least until 1954, and the *Brown v Tokepa* legal decision, racially segregated schools were within the law. However, the American emphasis in schools on the construction of a common American identity brought the American model closer to the universal stress on citizenship emphasised in Japan and the USSR. In France, also, the emphasis on republicanism and especially the strong conception of a French *culture générale* provided a national sense of identity (somewhat to the discomfort of regions such as Brittany) (Barnard 1969).

In the north-west European educational formations of the 1950s through to the 1970s, individual autonomy for a select group of academically able pupils – a sense of empowerment and potential control over parts of the social world – came from immersion in and attachment to an intellectual subject. The sense of self was disciplinary based, taking its definition from access to difficult languages (French, philosophy, mathematics, Greek or Latin or the separate sciences). The model was divisive: the intellectual power to claim autonomy through public displays of academic cleverness was limited to a small fraction of the age cohort. In the USSR and in Japan academic achievement and conventional schooling success were also valued, but personal autonomy was highly constrained by a social ethic stressing service, obligation, hierarchy and loyalty (in different cultural forms).

In the European educational formations, citizenship roles were also differentially distributed. In France following not so much the principles of liberty, equality and fraternity of the French Revolution and Condorcet, but rather the technocratic elite selection of Napoleon (marked by the *grandes écoles*) it is possible to identify a self-confident putative elite whose claim to govern was based on intellectual selection. In England, the powerful educational network of the public schools, the grammar schools and the metropolitan universities (notably Oxford and Cambridge) produced another self-confident elite whose identity had been reinforced in schools by both the formal and informal curriculum. In contrast, in the United States elite formation was typically the job of particular graduate schools – and even there populist motifs in American life and social selection produced a surprisingly permeable political, business and administrative elite. However, the American common school – in Horace Mann's word, 'the social balance wheel' – created an emphasis on almost universal citizenship. The exception was the caste-like educational systems of the Southern United States. As a consequence, there emerged multiple versions of the social contract, the idea that (wo)men willingly construct systems of governance of their own freewill which draw their conditional loyalty.

In the United States, the Jeffersonian model was taken to its extremes: a suspicion of big government, a confident assertion of the rights of citizenship based in the Constitution (a belief which the National Association for the Advancement of Coloured Peoples was to use to great effect) and a weak sense of welfare rights and obligations. The facet of the immigrant experience stressed in public discourse (except in the eugenics movement) was economic success and social mobility. In France, the social contract had been violently affirmed in the Revolution, and the educational modifications of the Napoleonic period merely produced a particular version of how to implement the social contract: through the leadership of technocratic philosopher kings. In England this leadership motif – including the continued formal presence in the ruling class of an hereditary aristocracy – was modified by the Beveridge vision of a welfare estate and a reformist Labour Party that implemented this vision after 1945.

Retrospectively, and with the advantage of hindsight, it may be suggested that these moral visions of social contract, citizenship and a confident sense of autonomy (constructed through attachment to a discipline) begin to unravel in north-west Europe with the common secondary school movement. In Norway and Denmark, the Netherlands and Belgium strong, locally rooted conceptions of social democracy slowed dramatically the confusion over the balance of elitism and egalitarianism in social and educational terms but elsewhere, in Germany, France and England, the common school movement was an uneasy innovation, contradicted by the retention of older forms of examination structures or strongly defined vocational tracks as well as disagreements among political parties (or Länder) (Husen, Tuijnman and Halls 1992). The final cancellation of the egalitarian theme is marked by the shift to market-driven patterns of education systems. There is a clear entitlement to compete (internationally, institutionally and individually) but in a market-driven educational system, 'western' tribal values of autonomy, citizenship and social caring are deleted from the public agenda.

Notions of intellectual autonomy, based in the acquisition of a disciplinary subject, are replaced by the models of the acquisition of modules, courses or transferable credits. Redefinition of curricula in terms of competencies and skills packages, deliberately oriented to occupational utility, reinforce the notion of schooling as personal consumption and anticipated economic production. The moral messages (about the nature of truth) embedded in Lockean, Cartesian and Humboldtian notions of education disappear. In the emphasis on the potential economic utility of education, conceptions of political citizenship are displaced: the concern for a common social identity is subordinated to the acquisition of differentiated economic identities through mastering core curriculum skills or pragmatically useful knowledge 'modules'. The adaptation of educational systems to the pressures of economic globalisation has created a visible vacuum over the terms of social cohesion in these societies for which it is temporarily difficult to envisage a solution.

The 'Asian' solution – in Japan, Singapore, Malaysia, Taiwan – to the problems of the shift into a modern society (*Gesellschaft*) while maintaining elements of a (national) community (*Gemeinschaft*) manifestly had and has unpleasant, even hysterical, elements (Lee 1991). The social and educational visions of a Mori, a Lee Kwan Yew or the inheritors of Chiang Kai-shek sit uneasily as exemplars to rescue the social visions of Jefferson, Thomas Paine or John Locke. But the problem is more complex than this issue of the transfer of messianic nationalist visions, despite contemporary debates in England about what is good school literature or good school history.

There are two key problems. In a world of economic globalisation there are at the present moment only partial visions available of an educational system that is not constructed around the two nineteenth-century ideals of nationalism and economic modernisation (Lister 1995). There is a gap between the world view of the major religions and the secular visions of the nation, as politically coherent or economically successful, which defined the nature of schooling systems between 1890 and 1990. There are no immediate socio-educational practical visions – not even in Asia – of a world which celebrates multiple 'others'; their otherness specified by differences in nationality, language, gender (Coulby and Jones 1995). There is no clear operational vision of multiple citizenships.

The second gap is just as frightening. Educational studies – through their location in market-driven universities – have become increasingly fragmented, technocratic and pragmatic. Some of the important older sources of critical reflection and visionary alternatives, such as departments of philosophy of education, are themselves being eroded. Educators, as a scholarly research community, are an endangered species. As researchers, efficient, organised, plugged-in, they are in danger of becoming too immediately useful.

REFERENCES

Alavi, H. and Shanin, T. (eds) (1982) *Introduction to the Sociology of 'Developing Societies'*, London: Macmillan.

Altbach, P, Arnove, R. and Kelly, P. (eds) (1982) *Comparative Education*, New York: Macmillan.

Altbach, P. and Kelly, G.P. (eds) (1978) *Education and Colonialism*, London: Longmans.

Anderson, A. and Bowman, M.J. (eds) (1966) *Education and Economic Development*, London: Frank Cass.

Barnard, H.C. (1969) *Education and the French Revolution*, London: Cambridge University Press.

Bondi, I. (1991) 'Choice and diversity in school education: comparing developments in the United Kingdom and the USA', *Comparative Education* 27, 2: 125–34.

Carnoy, M. (1974) *Education as Cultural Imperialism: A Critical Appraisal*, New York: David McKay.

Coulby, D. and Jones, C. (1995) *Postmodernity and European Education Systems: Cultural Diversity and Centralist Knowledge*, Staffordshire, England: Trentham Books.

Cowen, R. (ed.) (1996) *The Evaluation of Higher Education Systems: World Yearbook of Education 1996*, London: Kogan Page.

Edwards, T. and Whitty, G. (1992) 'Parental choice and educational reform in Britain and the United States', *British Journal of Educational Studies* 40, 2: 101–17.

Grace, G. (1991) 'Welfare Labourism and the New Right: the struggle in New Zealand's education policy', *International Studies in Sociology of Education* I: 25–42.

Green, A. (1990) *Education and State Formation: The Rise of Education Systems in England, France and the USA*, London: Macmillan.

Horio, T. (1988) *Educational Thought and Ideology in Modern Japan: State Authority and Intellectual Freedom*, Tokyo: University of Tokyo Press.

Husen, T., Tuijnman, A. and Halls, W.D. (1992) *Schooling in Modern European Society: A Report to the Academia Europaea*, Oxford: Pergamon Press.

Inkeles, A. and Smith, D.H. (1974) *Becoming Modern: Individual Change in Six Developing Countries*, London: Heinemann.

Kenway, J. with Bigum, C. and Fitzclarence, L. (1992) 'Marketing education in the postmodern age', *Journal of Education Policy* 8, 2: 105–22.

Lawton, D. (1992) *Education and Politics in the 1990s: Conflict or Consensus?*, London: Falmer Press.

Lee, W.O. (1991) *Social Change and Educational Problems in Japan, Singapore and Hong Kong*, London: Macmillan.

Lister, I. (1995) 'Educating beyond the Nation', *International Review of Education* 41, 1–2; 109–18.

McClelland, D. (1972) *The Achieving Society*, New York: The Free Press.

Parsons, T. (1961) *The Social System*, London: Routledge and Kegan Paul.

Passin, A. (1965) *Society and Education in Japan*, New York: Teachers' College Press.

Peters, M. (1992) 'Performance and accountability in "post-industrial society": the crisis of British universities', *Studies in Higher Education* 17, 2: 123–39.

Porter, M. (1990) *The Competitive Advantage of Nations*, London: Macmillan.

Price, R. (1977) *Marx and Education in Russia and China*, London: Croom Helm.

Reich, R.B. (1992) *The Work of Nations: Preparing Ourselves for 21st Century Capitalism*, New York: Vantage Books.

Simmons, J. (ed.) (1980) *The Education Dilemma: Policy Issues for Developing Countries in the 1980s*, Oxford: Pergamon.

Waters, M. (1995) *Globalization*, London: Routledge.

Whitty, G. (1989) 'The New Right and the national curriculum: State control or market forces?', *Education Policy* 4, 4: 329–41.

7

SAVING EDUCATION FROM THE 'LURCHING STEAM ROLLER'

The democratic virtues of markets in education

James Tooley

Only limited government can be decent government . . . a single omnipotent 'legislature' . . . is wholly incapable of pursuing a consistent course of action, lurching like a steam roller driven by one who is drunk.

(Hayek 1982 Vol. III: 11)

INTRODUCTION

Carr and Hartnett (1996) argue that 'any vision of education that takes democracy seriously cannot but be at odds with educational reforms which espouse the language and values of market forces and treat education as a commodity to be purchased and consumed' (p. 192); in particular, there will be contrasting interpretations of autonomy by those who espouse markets in education and those who espouse 'democratic education'. On the contrary, I argue that markets in education are *not* incompatible with democratic education at all, nor are they incompatible with conceptions of autonomy which purportedly embody democratic principles. Indeed, it may be that a 'democratic' conception of autonomy is better served by markets than by democratic control of education, paradoxical though this may sound.

Carr and Hartnett are certainly not alone in this position (a selection from the ubiquitous examples include Green 1991, Hillcole Group 1991, Ball 1990, 1993, Ranson 1990, 1993, 1995, White 1988, Whitty 1989); their recent, strongly argued case for the need to resist moves towards markets in education for 'the struggle for democracy' will be used as a springboard into the discussion. The second section outlines their argument, bringing in definitions of democracy, autonomy and markets in education. It then sets out why markets in education are not incompatible with democratic education. The next section looks at some objections to this position, while the fourth explores whether a stronger case can be made about the desirability of markets in education to promote democratic ends. Finally, the last section summarises the issues.

DEMOCRATIC EDUCATION AND MARKETS IN EDUCATION

Carr and Hartnett (1996) could not be less unequivocal. Democratic education is opposed to markets in education. Their argument rests on a series of dichotomies between what I will term an *individualist* and a *deliberative* perspective on society. These bring differences in the way autonomy, democracy and hence democratic education are conceived.

The individualist view stresses that people are 'emphatically not social or political animals' (p. 47); hence, it endorses a view of *autonomy* as a 'commitment to developing the capacity of individuals to . . . determine and pursue their own version of the "good life" for themselves, free from . . . external pressure and constraints' (p. 47). In contrast, the deliberative perspective, influenced by Dewey, specifies a view of *autonomy* 'recast' in the 'public sphere' (p. 186). This 'democratic' autonomy requires a commitment of individuals to 'a form of practical reasoning that requires collective deliberation aimed at realizing the common good' (p. 65).

Considering *democracy*, Carr and Hartnett (1996) distinguish the 'contemporary' and 'classical' interpretations, the former linked with my individualist, and the latter the deliberative, perspective. The former assumes that people only form social relationships to satisfy personal needs, and thus, on whom there is 'no obligation to participate in political decision-making' (p. 43). The latter, on the other hand, assumes that people are 'essentially political and social animals who fulfil themselves by sharing in the common life of their community' (p. 41). Three important features about Carr and Hartnett's favoured conception of democracy is that it allows *deliberation* in the public sphere, ensuring *accountability*, and that it endorses *equality*, ensuring that all are able to partake in these deliberations.

These different conceptions furthermore 'entail' different conceptions of *education*: fitting in with the individualist conception is an education 'that prepares . . . the mass of ordinary individuals for their primary social roles as producers, workers and consumers in a modern market economy' (p. 44); the deliberative conception, however, endorses 'democratic education', which 'seeks to empower its future members to participate collectively in the processes through which their society is being shaped and reproduced' (p. 43).

While much could be challenged in these categories as ideal types, this is not my quarrel here with these authors. I will accept their characterisation of the 'deliberative' conception of society, and the desirability of this, as a rough and ready formula, to see what follows from it. However, I fundamentally disagree with the authors' classification of markets in education as belonging in the *individualist* category, hence as opposed to the *deliberative* mode. This misunderstands the potential adaptability of markets. Neither the 'deliberative' conception of autonomy, nor the 'classical' conception of democracy, nor the educative vision of the learning society is incompatible with markets in education; those who favour markets in education do not have to have foisted upon them the self-centred rational autonomy, amoral democracy or a divisive and hierarchical notion of education. To help explain, we need further conceptual clarification of 'democratic education' and 'markets in education'.

Democratic education is education *within* and *for* democracy. It is within democratic control, but there is nothing in the favoured conception of democracy which implies that democratic control of education will be unlimited. For unlimited democratic control of education could lead to education which was not favourable to democratic expression. Carr and Hartnett (1996) recognise this problem, and propose, as a 'specifically *democratic* response' to it (p. 187), that democratic decision-making *must be limited* 'in order to prevent educational decisions from being made which would prevent the next generation of citizens from acquiring the knowledge, virtues and dispositions that their participation in the [democracy] requires' (p. 190). To this end, they endorse Gutmann's (1987) principles of limits to democratic decision-making, of 'non-repression' and 'non-discrimination'.

Non-repression prevents the use of education 'to restrict rational deliberation of competing conceptions of the good life and the good society' (Gutmann 1987: 44). *Non-discrimination* means that 'all educable children must be educated' (p. 45), and in particular, that no child who is 'educable' may be excluded from an education adequate for participation in the democracy. Together, Gutmann argues, these principles 'are necessary and sufficient for establishing an ideal of democratic education' (p. 93). Carr and Hartnett (1996: 193) unreservedly endorse these principles.

Hence democratic education equips people to behave in the 'deliberative' autonomous fashion, through a 'learning society'; it is protected from the arbitrariness of democratic control by two principled limits on decision-making.

I work towards a definition of *markets in education* by starting from the three ways – regulation, provision and funding – in which governments can intervene in education (Barr 1993: p. 80). Governments can regulate supply (e.g. through a national curriculum), as well as demand (e.g. through compulsory schooling). Intervention in provision can involve the state itself producing the goods and services (e.g. by building schools and/or employing teachers), while state intervention in funding can be either 'direct' or 'indirect'. Direct funding involves government subsidy of the price of the good (e.g. 'free' schooling), while indirect funding would come through income transfers by the state (e.g. vouchers or cash handouts).

Now the important features of *markets* is that they have competing suppliers and open competition for new entrants to the supply-side; and that demand is expressed through a price mechanism (Tooley 1996: ch. 6). Hence I define 'markets in education' as pertaining when government is *at most* only one competing supplier of educational *provision* (with no advantages in this regard simply because it is the government), and any government *funding* is, again *at most,* of an indirect kind (i.e. of vouchers or cash handouts) operating within a genuine price system; *regulation* of any kind which is consistent with these principles is tolerated within this definition.

This definition brings in two difficulties. The first is that, in much of the literature, the outcomes of 'school choice' reforms (e.g. the Education Reform Act in England and Wales), are described as 'markets' in education. But these do not fit my definition, given that there is no genuine price system operating, and the supply-side is dominated by government. Refusing to go along with current fashion in labelling these as 'markets' would not matter particularly, except for our second difficulty: it might be that Carr and Hartnett (1996), and the myriad other authors cited above, are actually arguing against these current 'so-called' market reforms only, and hence that the discussions here will miss their target.

However, usefully, it does seem that many of the authors have in mind that that their arguments will apply *a fortiori* against these more full-blooded markets in education (e.g. Carr and Hartnett 1996: 192 specifically object to education with a price mechanism operating). Moreover, the debate about current educational reforms is ultimately about the nature and extent of government involvement in education, so it is worth taking the debate towards its limits, whatever the commentators cited think on this issue, where it will encounter markets in education as we have defined them here.

Now, with this conceptual framework, we can ask: where is the incompatibility between markets in education and democratic education, both as defined above? There is none. In the democracy, *deliberation* and *accountability* can be exercised in deciding upon the regulation of the curriculum and ethos of educational settings; Gutmann's principle of *non-repression* could govern these regulations just as easily whether they are to apply to markets in education or to state education. Similarly, *equality* so that all can participate in the democracy and *non-discrimination* in democratic education can be ensured, where necessary, through funding of those who otherwise could not afford educational opportunities and compulsory schooling for those unwilling to partake of the opportunities offered. Neither require the full gamut of state funding and provision with which we are so familiar.

Although often stated, the supposed incompatibility between educational reforms which 'treat education as a commodity to be purchased and consumed' and democratic education cannot be found here. What seemed counter-intuitive has simply disappeared in a puff of conceptual clarification. Because the bare bones of supply and demand mechanisms can be regulated, and because the state can step in if necessary to provide a funding and regulatory safety-net, markets in education are completely compatible with 'classical' democracy, with the 'deliberative' notion of autonomy, and with the educative learning society. I take some comfort in the fact that John White seems to have arrived at a similar stance recently, although not known for his affection towards markets, and as one who would endorse something like the 'deliberative' notion of autonomy (White 1990). Elsewhere he writes: 'I can see no reason of principle why the State must own and run its own schools. . . . The crucial thing is not who owns a school, but whether the school conforms to certain criteria of adequacy – . . . for instance . . . as regards aims and curricula' (White 1994: 122).

DEMOCRATIC ARGUMENTS AGAINST MARKETS IN EDUCATION

White's endorsement notwithstanding, there is a vast literature condemning markets in education on democratic grounds. Chief among relevant objections are those arguing that 'markets' are inequitable because they reinforce class and ethnic inequality (e.g. Ball 1993, Edwards and Whitty 1992 and in this volume, Gewirtz *et al*. 1993, 1995). I have argued elsewhere that these objections certainly target something unfair about current 'choice' systems, but that these problems could be alleviated with 'more authentic' markets. In particular, I have disputed that markets are unfair because they inevitably and only reward attributes of certain privileged classes; on the contrary, I suggest that markets do reward the desirable quality of 'educational responsibility', but that those who do not have this quality can, in a 'one tier' private system, 'free ride' on the responsibility of others (Tooley 1996, 1997a).

Other important democratic objections relevant here concern the issue of education as 'a public good' and the 'commodification' of education (Grace 1989, Winch 1996), the prisoner's dilemma and the problem of collective action (Jonathan 1990, Ranson 1993, 1995, Winch 1996), and the problem of positional goods (Jonathan 1990, Miliband 1991, Ranson 1993). Elsewhere I have challenged these objections, suggesting that if we distinguish 'education' from 'the delivery of educational opportunities' then the problem of 'commodification' disappears (Tooley 1997b); and just because education is a public good does not mean that it needs to be publicly provided – indeed, public provision might well undermine desirable educational aims (Tooley 1994, 1995b). Moreover, the prisoner's dilemma is unlikely to satisfactorily characterise the problem of educational provision under market conditions, because education is both a public *and* a private good; but in any case, even if educational provision could be modelled in this way, there are co-operative and assurance solutions to the prisoner's dilemma which vindicate education outside of state control (Tooley 1992, 1995b, 1997b). Finally, while the positionality of education *does* present a problem for equity and democracy with markets in education, it is equally a problem for state education (Tooley 1995b, 1996).

None of these objections, if the discussion elsewhere holds, succeeds in showing that markets in education undermine any of the aims of democratic education. However, before moving on to consider whether a case can be made for markets in education actually being *preferable to* democratic education, it is incumbent on me to address one set of objections which I have not covered elsewhere: Gutmann (1987) has been influential on Carr and Hartnett (1996), and hence on the discussion here; her objections to markets in education will now be considered.

Gutmann (1987) argues that a voucher proposal exhibiting similar features to our 'markets in education' is incompatible with the democratic principles of non-discrimination and non-repression. Her argument tackles the two principal democratic justifications given by proponents of the voucher scheme.

First, there is the consequentialist argument: 'The democratic virtue of parental empowerment is based on a consequentialist calculation: that schools will improve – they will better serve their democratic purposes – if the guardians of their clients are less captive' (p. 66). Now, she confesses that there is a difficulty in knowing how to weigh up the possible evidence here:

> Were citizens to agree on what consequences count it would be very difficult to predict the consequences of a thoroughgoing voucher plan versus an improved [state] school system. But we do not agree, nor is it likely that we shall ever agree. . . . On consequentialist grounds, the question of whether to institute a constrained voucher plan or to improve public schools by decentralization . . . is inherently indeterminate.
>
> (1987: 67)

But if this is the case, it is very odd that she should then argue for the *status quo*, of great governmental control over education, just because that is what happens to be in place now, particularly as the *status quo* was not introduced in accordance with her democratic principles. At the least, by her own argument, Gutmann should be in favour of experiments to determine what the possible advantages and disadvantages of a voucher system were in practice, so that the 'indeterminacy' noted will be less problematic. Gutmann's argument is not a satisfactory rebuttal of the consequentialist position at all.

Second, there is the argument that since in our democratic deliberations we will not be able to agree on common standards, 'publicly supported education should reflect the diversity of our values by imposing only a minimal set of common standards' on schools (p. 67). Gutmann challenges those who put forward this type of argument thus: 'having admitted the . . . necessity . . . of imposing a set of collective standards on schools, [the protagonists] can no longer rest the case for vouchers on the claim that such plans avoid the need for settling our disagreements over how citizens should be educated' (p. 68). But why is it inconsistent to argue that disagreement is likely over many educational issues, but to concede that there will be some 'minimal set of common standards' which could be agreed upon? She argues that 'The more room voucher plans make for regulation, the less room they leave for parental choice' (p. 69); but this trade off between choice and regulation is obvious to all who put forward market models, and surely cannot be a valid objection to them. Furthermore, she argues that 'The problem with voucher plans is not that they leave too much room for parental choice but that they leave too little room for democratic deliberation' (p. 70). But this simply does not follow: In our education markets, there is considerable room for democratic deliberation to decide the regulation of educational settings (subject to the limiting principles), *and* within this framework, for parental choice; both are possible within markets in education.

Perhaps Gutmann would argue that the education 'adequate for participation in democracy' would simply be too demanding for regulation to accommodate, or that there would be great difficulties in making private schools comply? (Although wisely she points out that this could be true of public schools too, p. 112.) The desired education requires 'the intellectual skills and the information ... to think about democratic politics and to develop ... deliberative skills and . . . knowledge through practical experience' (p. 147). But with this specified, and bearing in mind the experience of curricula in private schools, and the wealth of opportunities for 'education for democracy' through other private media, there does not seem to be any *a priori* reason why the desired curriculum could not be met through a regulated market.

Gutmann's objections to markets in education do not seem convincing. In conjunction with the counters to other objections rehearsed elsewhere, I suggest then that there is no incompatibility between markets in education and democratic education.

A 'DEMOCRATIC' CASE FOR MARKETS IN EDUCATION?

I have argued that markets in education are *compatible* with democratic education, but can a stronger case be made than this? Is it possible that a 'deliberative' democracy *might actually favour* markets in education rather than democratically controlled state funded and provided schooling? This section presents three arguments which could inform the democratic deliberations, and which could, in combination, lead to a democratic endorsement of markets in education, in preference to state schools.

The historical case

I have already noted how odd it is that Gutmann should accept the *status quo* of state education, given its oppressive origins. Indeed, a case can be made that state intervention was, and still is, destructive of communitarian impulses of people, and that leaving space for markets in education would be a desirable *democratic* alternative. We can draw on the historical excursions of Carr and Hartnett (1996) to reinforce this conclusion.

First, they point out that state schooling had inauspicious origins in the 'absolutist monarchies of eighteenth century Europe', used there as 'a powerful instrument for promoting political loyalty amongst the people and for creating a cohesive national culture after the image of the ruling class' (p. 77); similarly, in England and Wales, state involvement in schooling was explicitly for reasons of 'social control', to inculcate in 'working-class children their social duties; a modicum of useful knowledge; a respect for authority; and a belief in religion' (p. 80). They also note – and decry – the prejudices against working-class education of those seeking to introduce state education (pp. 80ff). Curiously, however, they do not seem to be able to move away from taking these prejudices at face value, and it is only through such a move that the case here can be made.

For example, they apparently endorse Tawney's 'observation' that in the nineteenth century Britain was one of 'the most illiterate and under-educated' nations of western Europe (p. 75); similarly, they uncritically accept the conclusions of the Taunton Report of 1868, which condemned 'the majority of private and grammar schools' for employing 'untrained teachers' and for 'poor' pedagogy (p. 88). But are either of these sources true, or simply a state-ment or later reiteration of the prejudices that led to state intervention in the first place? For they also note that Gardner (1984) shows that working-class private schools were a 'ubiquitous presence, both in town and country at least up to the 1870s' (quoted in Carr and Hartnett 1996: 83) and that this gave working-class parents some 'degree of power and control over both the content and organisation of education, which was entirely absent in the pub-licly provided alternative'. Moreover, they mention the Newcastle Commis-sion report of 1861 (pp. 84–5), but curiously ignore its findings that the vast majority of young people were in schooling *before the state got involved* for an average of 5.7 years (West 1994). They cite the arguments of Andy Green (Carr and Hartnett 1996: 83), but omit to mention that, *pace* Tawney, he argued that England's relative position in the mid-nineteenth century was *better than France's* as regards the percentage of the population receiving schooling (Green 1990: 15) and with regard to adult literacy (p. 25). Moreover, noticeable by its absence is any discussion of the arguments of West (e.g. 1975a, 1975b, 1983, 1994), who has thoroughly catalogued the extent of working-class education without the state and how the state intervened to eliminate it.

The point is that governments got involved in education not for benign reasons, but for reasons of social control; and that in order to do this, it is at least arguable that they had to undermine both the efforts of working-class people themselves and of outside philanthropy (see e.g. Green 1993, Whelan 1996). Carr and Hartnett (1996) note that one of the impediments of 'the devel-opment of a national system of education' in the nineteenth century was 'the belief that state-provided education would undermine the moral responsibility of individual parents for the education of their children and so replace self-reliance by state dependency' (p. 80); in their view such 'self-reliance' conjures up negative images of 'excessive individualism' (p. 80), and is directly counter to their favoured notions of deliberative autonomy and democracy. However,

if this 'self-reliance' was at least in part 'community self-help', and if it was supplemented from outside the poorer communities by altruistic philanthropy,
as these sources suggest, then it is clear that state intervention historically
had the effect of displacing activity which was desirable on *democratic*
grounds. If this argument could be defended – and provided that there
remained a safety-net satisfying the principle of non-discrimination – then
this would be a strong argument to relax state intervention in education, to
give room for these non-state activities to be revived within an education
market. (Note in this connection how Samuel Smiles regretted the title of his
Self-Help because this led to it being judged as 'a eulogy of selfishness', but
that this was the 'very opposite of what ... the author intended it to be ... the
duty of helping one's self in the highest sense involves the helping of one's
neighbours', Smiles [1866] 1996: xii.)

This historical case suggests that state provision and funding could undermine desirable aspects of a deliberative democracy; the next two arguments
strengthen the democratic case for markets in education.

Gutmann's case

Gutmann's (1987) case is simple. She points out that, by implication, a necessary condition for schools to bring democratic education to young people is
that they are able to perform adequately, with adequate resources, and so on.
She notes that many state schools clearly do not reach these adequate standards at present, and that there is a 'seductive logic' about the argument that
market incentives could make them improve to the standards of better private
schools:

> The idea of empowering all parents to choose among schools for their
> children is in this sense democratic: it increases the incentive for schools
> to respond to the market choices of middle-class and poor as well as
> rich parents.

> (1987: 65)

She takes this argument no further, having dismissed the arguments for markets on the grounds given above; however, finding those reasons unsatisfactory
here, it is at least a possibility that markets in education could be *democratically* preferable to state schools if they simply perform a better educational
job. In which case, even the purely 'selfish' choices of parents for these private
educational settings would better fit democratic impulses, if these were better
able to deliver the democratic curriculum. We do not have sufficient evidence
as yet that they would do this; but rather than Gutmann's acquiescence in the
status quo, we suggest that the gathering of suitable evidence should be a democratic priority, to enable us to better make the appropriate judgement.

Hayek's case

Markets in education, I have argued, can be regulated in accordance with the democratic principles of non-repression and non-discrimination. State schools, however, would be subject not only to these regulations, but also presumably to whatever additional controls the democracy deemed fit, assuming that these principles were not offended. The two preceding arguments suggested that such additional intervention in education may contribute to the displacing of desirable democratic impulses in the community, and may also undermine the success of the educational enterprise. Hayek's case offers a further, more general argument, for seeking to limit the extent of democratic control, which could be applied to reinforce the democratic argument for markets in education. (It could also be used to offer a stronger argument against even the sort of regulation embodied in Gutmann's two principles: such an argument is beyond the scope of this essay, but see Tooley 1996: ch. 5.)

Hayek (1982) argues that, although democracy is 'an ideal worth fighting for . . . one of the most important safeguards of freedom' (Vol. III: 5), this does not imply that the democracy should have unlimited power. For it is illegitimate to move from accepting that '*only* what is approved by the majority should be binding for all' (p. 6), to argue that *everything* that is approved by the majority should also be binding for all. It may seem an insignificant step, yet it signals

> the transition from one conception of government to an altogether different one . . . from a system in which through recognised procedures we decide how certain common affairs are to be arranged, to a system in which one group of people may declare anything they like as a matter of common concern and on this ground subject it to these procedures.
>
> (1982: 6–7)

Hayek has three main arguments for this position. The first points to technical problems with voting, for it is little known that 'different but equally justifiable procedures for arriving at a democratic decision may produce very different results' (p. 35), and voting procedures can sometimes produce results which 'are in fact not desired by a majority, and which may even be disapproved by a majority of the people' (p. 6). Riker (1982, 1986) is an excellent source on these sorts of technical difficulties, which undermine the notion that 'the common good' can be the outcome of democratic voting procedures, since the outcome will often be quite arbitrary.

Second, Hayek points to the dangers of 'log-rolling', the 'I'll scratch your back, if you'll scratch mine' process in political bargaining (see Tullock 1976). Hayek describes it thus:

> Each group will be prepared to consent even to iniquitous benefits for other groups out of the common purse if this is the condition for the consent of the others. . . . The result of this process will correspond to

nobody's opinion of what is right, and to no principles; it will not be based on a judgement of merit but on political expediency.

(Hayek 1982 Vol. III: 9)

Log-rolling distorts the political process, to arrive at outcomes which are not necessarily desirable and can be exceedingly harmful to the democracy at large.

Finally, Hayek gives an argument for limits to democratic control on the grounds of political selfishness; he argues that there is:

> no more reason to believe in the case of the majority that because they want a particular thing this desire is an expression of their sense of justice, than there is ground for such a belief in the case of individuals. In the latter we know only too well that their sense of justice will often be swayed by their desire for particular objects.
>
> (1982: 7)

Individuals are taught to 'curb illegitimate desires', and when they don't, authority is there to restrain them. Political majorities, however, are not taught to be 'civilised' in this way, and hence require restraints over what they may legitimately have power.

We can see that this sort of argument could inform the democratic deliberations in society. Perhaps education is one of those areas which will be particularly subject to log-rolling, or to the selfish desires of particular interest groups? Perhaps this is an area in which agreement will be hardest to reach, and minorities most vulnerable or most easily influenced? Perhaps Gutmann's principles will not be enough to protect the education system from corruption, distortion or complacency? These kinds of considerations could lead to a decision to insulate as far as possible education from the reach of over-ambitious democratic control.

In combination, the 'historical' case, and Gutmann's and Hayek's cases, could be powerful inputs into the democratic deliberations. If state provision displaces voluntary community self-help and altruism; if markets in education can better deliver education for democracy; and if greater democratic control brings the danger of selfish corruption of the political process; then the democratic deliberations in society might well arrive at an endorsement of markets in education, an endorsement very much on democratic grounds.

CONCLUSION

It is the accepted wisdom that markets in education are opposed to 'democratic education', and that those who support markets in education must be in favour of a narrow 'individualist' autonomy, a sterile conception of democracy, and an education solely oriented towards capitalism. By contrast, those who 'struggle' against markets in education uphold an autonomy which contexualises individuals within the 'public sphere' of deliberative democracy, enjoying a rich education in the 'learning society'. Carr and Hartnett (1996) explicitly argue this; others rally around similar claims. I have argued that this mis-characterises markets in education. Markets in education are not incompatible with democratic education within a deliberative democracy at all. For markets can be regulated – hence educational opportunities delivered within them can be within democratic safeguards – and supplemented with a funding and regulatory safety-net, for the sake of equity.

However, not only is there no incompatibility, but there are significant arguments which should form part of the democratic deliberations about the role of the state in education, which could lead to an endorsement of markets in education, *in preference to* state schooling. Of course, those taking part in the democratic deliberations might not find these arguments ultimately persuasive; and it is not for us here (in contrast to Carr and Hartnett) to decide at what conclusions a deliberative democracy will arrive. But suffice it to suggest that the arguments do not all go the way of those opposing markets in education; nor is there a clear run for those who would seek for education to be subject to the vagaries of the 'lurching steam roller'.

REFERENCES

Ball, S. J. (1990) *Markets, Morality and Equality in Education* (Hillcole Group Paper 5), The Tufnell Press, London.

Ball, S. J. (1993) 'Education markets, choice and social class: the market as a class strategy in the UK and the USA', *British Journal of Sociology of Education* 14, 1, 3–19.

Barr, N. (1993) *The Economics of the Welfare State*, 2nd edn, Weidenfeld and Nicolson, London.

Carr, W. and Hartnett, A. (1996) *Education and the Struggle for Democracy: The Politics of Educational Ideas*, Open University Press, Buckingham and Philadelphia.

Edwards, A. and Whitty, G. (1992) 'Parental choice and educational reform in Britain and the United States', *British Journal of Educational Studies* 40, 2 101–117.

Gardner, P. (1984) *The Lost Elementary Schools of Victorian England: The People's Education*, Croom Helm, London.

Gewirtz, S., Ball, S. J. and Bowe, R. (1993) 'Parents, privilege and the education marketplace', *Research Papers in Education* 9, 1, 3–29.

Gewirtz, S., Ball, S. J. and Bowe, R. (1995) *Markets, Choice and Equity in Education*, Open University Press, Buckingham and Philadelphia.

Grace, G. (1989) 'Education: commodity or public good?', *British Journal of Educational Studies* 37, 207–211.

Green, A. (1990) *Education and State Formation*, Macmillan, Basingstoke.

Green, Andy (1991) 'The structure of the system: proposals for change' in Chitty, C. (ed.) *Changing the Future: Redprint for Education* (The Hillcole Group), The Tufnell Press, London.

Green, D.G. (1993) *Reinventing Civil Society: The Rediscovery of Welfare Without the State*, London: Institute of Economic Affairs.

Gutmann, A. (1987) *Democratic Education*, Princeton University Press, Princeton.

Hayek, F.A. (1982) *Law, Legislation and Liberty*, Routledge & Kegan Paul, London.

Hillcole Group (1991) 'Critique of Alternative Policies' in Chitty, C. (ed.) *Changing the Future: Redprint for Education* (The Hillcole Group), The Tufnell Press, London.

Johnson, R. (1979) 'Really useful knowledge: radical education and working class culture, 1790–1848' in Clarke, J., Critcher, C. and Johnson, R. (eds) *Working Class Culture: Studies in History and Theory*, Hutchinson, London.

Jonathan, R. (1990) 'State education service or prisoner's dilemma: the 'hidden hand' as source of education policy', *British Journal of Educational Studies* 38, 116–132.

Miliband, D. (1991) *Markets, Politics and Education: Beyond the Education Reform Act*, Institute for Public Policy Research, London.

Ranson, S. (1990) 'From 1944 to 1988: Education, Citizenship and Democracy' in Flude, M. and Hammer, M. (eds) *The Education Reform Act 1988: Its Origins and Implications*, The Falmer Press, Lewes.

Ranson, S. (1993) 'Markets or Democracy for Education', *British Journal of Educational Studies* 41, 333–352.

Ranson, S. (1995) 'Public institutions for co-operative action: a reply to James Tooley', *British Journal of Educational Studies* 43, 35–42.

Riker, W. (1982) *Liberalism Against Populism*, W.H. Freeman, San Francisco.

Riker, W. (1986) *The Art of Political Manipulation*, Yale University Press, Newhaven and London.

Smiles, S. ([1866] 1996) *Self-Help*, Institute for Economic Affairs, London.

Tooley, J. (1992) 'The prisoner's dilemma and educational provision: a reply to Ruth Jonathan', *British Journal of Educational Studies* 40, 118–133.

Tooley, J. (1994) 'In defence of markets in education', in Bridges, D. and McLaughlin, T. (eds) *Education and the Market Place*, Falmer, London.

Tooley, J. (1995a) 'Markets or democracy for education? A reply to Stewart Ranson', *British Journal of Educational Studies* 43, 1, 21–34.

Tooley, J. (1995b) *Disestablishing the School*, Avebury, Aldershot.

Tooley, J. (1996) *Education without the State*, Institute of Economic Affairs, London.

Tooley, J. (1997a) 'Choice and diversity in education: a defence', *Oxford Review of Education* 23, 1, 103–16.

Tooley, J. (1997b) 'The family, the child and the state: Winch on the 'neo-liberal' critique of markets in education', *Journal of Philosophy of Education* forthcoming.

Tullock, G. (1976) *The Vote Motive*, Institute of Economic Affairs, London.

West, E.G. (1975a) 'Educational slowdown and public intervention in 19th-century England: a study in the economics of bureaucracy', *Explorations in Economic History* 12, 61–87.

West, E.G. (1975b) *Education and the Industrial Revolution*, London, Batsfords.

West, E.G. (1983) 'Nineteenth-century educational history: the Kiesling critique', *Economic History Review* 36, 426–434.

West, E. G. (1994) *Education and the State*, 3rd edn, Liberty Fund, Indianapolis.

Whelan, R. (1996) *The Corrosion of Charity: From Moral Renewal to Contract Culture* Institute of Economic Affairs, London.

White, J. (1990) *Education and the Good Life*, Kogan Page, London.

White, J. (1994) 'Education and the limits of the market' in Bridges, D. and McLaughlin, T. (eds) *Education and the Market Place*, Falmer, London.

White, P. (1988) 'The New Right and parental choice', *Journal of Philosophy of Education* 22, 195–9.

Whitty, G. (1989) 'The New Right and the National Curriculum: state control or market forces?', *Journal of Education Policy* 4, 329–341.

Winch, C. (1996) *Quality and Education*, Blackwell, Oxford.

8

SCHOOL AUTONOMY AND PARENTAL CHOICE

Consumer rights versus citizen rights in education policy in Britain

Geoff Whitty

THE RISE OF NEO-LIBERAL EDUCATION POLICY

In Britain, during the period of so-called social democratic consensus following the Second World War (CCCS 1981), all but a small minority of children were educated in state schools maintained by democratically elected local education authorities (LEAs). From the 1940s until the mid-1970s, one of the emphases of social democratic policy was on state intervention to ensure access and entitlement to a standard model of education for all, together with a degree of positive discrimination in order to enable disadvantaged groups to take advantage of it.

For the neo-liberal politicians who have dominated educational policy making in Britain since the 1980s, however, social affairs are best organised according to the general principle of consumer sovereignty (Ashworth *et al.* 1988), which holds that individuals are the best judges of their own needs and wants, and of what is in their best interests. The preference for introducing market mechanisms into education is derived partly from a predilection for freedom of choice as a good in itself. But it is also grounded in the belief that competition produces improvements in the quality of services on offer which in turn enhances the wealth producing potential of the economy, thereby bringing about gains for the least well-off as well as for the socially advantaged.

In so far as it is accepted at all that markets have losers as well as winners, the provision of a minimum safety net rather than universal benefits is seen as the best way to protect the weak without removing incentives or creating a universal dependency culture. But it is also sometimes claimed that the market will actually enhance social justice even for the least well-off, by placing real choice in the hands of those trapped in neighbourhood comprehensives in the inner city rather than, as before, having a system where only the wealthy or the knowing could get choice of school by moving house even if they could not afford a private school.

In an attempt to break what they saw as an LEA 'monopoly' of education dominated by producer interests, the Thatcher and Major governments introduced policies to enhance parental choice and grant more autonomy to individual schools. In a strictly economic sense, these quasi-market policies cannot be regarded as privatisation of the education system, but they do require public sector institutions to operate more like private sector ones and families to treat educational decisions in a similar way to other decisions about private consumption. Such reforms have been widely criticised from the Left because they seem to embody a commitment to creating, not a more equal society but one that is more 'acceptably' unequal. There is no aspiration towards a rough equality of educational outcomes between different social class and ethnic groups, it being argued that such a target has brought about a 'levelling down' of achievement, and has been pursued at the expense of individual freedom. To those on the Left, it seems that individual rights are being privileged at the expense of the notion of a just social order.

However, although such reforms can be seen as a typical neo-liberal crusade to stimulate market forces at the expense of 'producer interests', that is only one way of looking at it. Part of their wider appeal lies in a declared intention to encourage the growth of different types of school, responsive to needs of particular communities and interest groups. This argument is especially appealing when it is linked with the claim that diversity in types of schooling does not necessarily mean hierarchy and, in this context, the new policies have gained some adherents amongst disadvantaged groups. Potentially, they also link to notions of decentred identity and radical pluralism and can thus seem more attractive than uni-dimensional notions of comprehensive schooling and, indeed, uni-dimensional notions of citizenship.

Thus, the espousal of choice and diversity in education seems superficially to resonate with notions of an open, democratic society as well as with a market ideology. Put in those terms, the new policies have a potential appeal far beyond the coteries of the New Right. The American commentators Chubb and Moe (1992) have identified the neo-liberal aspects of the British approach as 'a lesson in school reform' that other countries should follow. The rhetoric of the British government's 'five great themes' – quality, diversity, parental choice, school autonomy and accountability (DFE 1992) – is already becoming increasingly familiar in many other countries with different political regimes (Whitty 1997).

A POSTMODERN PHENOMENON?

In the final chapter of *Specialisation and Choice in Urban Education* (Whitty *et al.* 1993), Edwards, Gewirtz and I considered how far the British reforms might be part of a movement that is much broader and deeper than the particular set of policies that have come to be termed 'Thatcherism'. In particular, we considered how far these shifts in the nature of education policy reflected broader changes in the nature of advanced industrial societies, that is the extent to which they could be seen as a response to shifts in the economy, or more specifically patterns of production and consumption, often described as post-Fordism; and how far they might be an expression of broader social changes that are sometimes taken to signal the existence of a 'postmodern' age.

First, we noted that some observers suggest that the reforms can be understood in terms of the transportation of changing modes of regulation from the sphere of production into other arenas, such as schooling and welfare services. They have pointed to a correspondence between the establishment of markets in welfare and a shift in the economy away from Fordism towards a post-Fordist mode of accumulation which places a lower value on mass individual and collective consumption (Jessop et al. 1987). Various commentators, such as Ball, have claimed to see in new forms of schooling a shift from the 'Fordist' school of the era of mass production to the 'post-Fordist school' (Ball 1990). The emergence of new and specialised sorts of school may be the educational equivalent of the rise of flexible specialisation driven by the imperatives of differentiated consumption, and taking the place of the old assembly-line world of mass production. These 'post-Fordist schools' are designed:

> not only to produce the post-Fordist, multi-skilled, innovative worker but to behave in post-Fordist ways themselves; moving away from mass production and mass markets to niche markets and 'flexible specialization' . . . a post-Fordist mind-set is currently having implications in schools for management styles, curriculum, pedagogy and assessment.
>
> (Kenway 1993: 115)

So, it is argued, the new policies not only reflect such changes, they help to foster and legitimate them.

However, there were problems about assuming a correspondence between education and production, as well as with the notion of post-Fordism as an entirely new regime of accumulation. We urged caution about concluding that we were experiencing a wholesale move away from a mass-produced welfare system towards a flexible, individualised and customised post-Fordist one. In the field of education, it is certainly difficult to establish a sharp distinction between mass and market systems. The so-called 'comprehensive system' in Britain was never as homogeneous as the concept of mass produced welfare suggests, being always a system differentiated by class and ability. Neo-Fordism was a more appropriate term for recent changes than post-Fordism, which implied something entirely distinctive. However, we might actually be witnessing an intensification of social differences and a celebration of them in a new rhetoric of legitimation. In the new rhetoric, choice, specialisation and diversity replace the previous language of common and comprehensive schooling.

Second, in commenting on wider changes in the nature of modern or post-modern societies, we noted that, for commentators such as Kenway (1993), the rapid rise of the market form in education was best understood as something much more significant than post-Fordism; she therefore terms it a postmodern phenomenon. In her pessimistic version of postmodernity, 'transnational corporations and their myriad subsidiaries ... shape and reshape our individual and collective identities as we plug in ... to their cultural and economic communications networks' (Kenway 1993: 119). Her picture is one in which notions of 'difference', far from being eradicated by the 'globalization of culture', are assembled, displayed, celebrated, commodified and exploited (Robins 1991).

But there are also other accounts of postmodernity where the rhetoric of 'new times' offers more positive images of choice and diversity. In this context, the reforms are regarded as part of a wider retreat from modern, bureaucratised state education systems. Such systems are perceived as having failed to fulfil their promise, and now seem inappropriate to the heterogeneous societies of the late twentieth century. Thus, moves towards diversity in schooling may reflect the needs of particular communities and interest groups brought into existence as a result of complex contemporary patterns of political, economic and cultural differentiation, which intersect the traditional class divisions upon which common systems of mass education were predicated.

In so far as these new divisions and emergent identities are experienced as real, they are likely to generate aspirations that will differ from traditional ones – hence some of the attraction of current policies mentioned earlier. The more optimistic readings of postmodernity regard it as a form of liberation from the oppressive uniformity of modernist thinking, in which the fragmentation and plurality of cultures and social groups allow a hundred flowers to bloom (Thompson 1992). Some feminists have therefore seen attractions in the shift towards the pluralist models of society and culture associated with postmodernism and postmodernity (Flax 1987). Possibilities for community-based welfare, rather than bureaucratically controlled welfare, are also viewed positively by some minority ethnic groups. Some aspects of the new policies did seem to connect to the aspirations of groups who had found little to identify with in the 'grand master' narratives associated with class-based politics. Support for schools run on a variety of principles might, we said, be viewed as a rejection of totalising narratives and their replacement by 'a set of cultural projects united [only] by a self-proclaimed commitment to heterogeneity, fragmentation and difference' (Boyne and Rattansi 1990: 9).

THE RECORD TO DATE

However, there is now considerable empirical evidence that, rather than benefiting the disadvantaged, the emphasis on parental choice and school autonomy in the British reforms is further disadvantaging those unable to compete in the market by increasing the differences between popular and less popular schools on a linear scale – reinforcing a vertical hierarchy of schooling types rather than producing horizontal diversity. The result is a system which, far from being variously differentiated through the 'free' interplay of market forces, is increasingly stratified. In this situation, there is likely to be a disproportionate representation of socially advantaged children in the most 'successful' schools, and of socially disadvantaged children in those schools identified as 'failing'. Similar findings have emerged from much of the research on devolution and choice in the US and New Zealand (Whitty 1997).

In our book (Whitty *et al.* 1993), we pointed out that in Britain such tendencies could have disastrous consequences for some sections of the predominantly working-class and black populations living in the inner cities. We conceded that these groups never gained an equitable share of educational resources under social-democratic policies, but the abandonment of planning in favour of a quasi-market seemed unlikely to provide a fairer outcome. For most members of disadvantaged groups, as opposed to the few individuals who escape from schools at the bottom of the status hierarchy, the new arrangements seemed to be just a more sophisticated way of reproducing traditional distinctions between different types of school and between the people who attend them.

To regard the current espousal of heterogeneity, pluralism and local narratives as indicative of a new social order seemed then to mistake phenomenal forms for structural relations. Marxist critics of theories of postmodernism and postmodernity, such as Callinicos (1989), who reassert the primacy of the class struggle, certainly take this view. Even Harvey, who does recognise significant changes, suggests that postmodernist cultural forms and more flexible modes of capital accumulation may be shifts in surface appearance rather than signs of the emergence of some entirely new post-capitalist or even post-industrial society (Harvey 1989). At most, current reforms would seem to relate to a version of postmodernity that emphasises 'distinction' and 'hierarchy' within a fragmented social order, rather than one that positively celebrates 'difference' and 'heterogeneity' (Lash 1990) as implied by the rhetoric.

Although current education policies may seem to be a response to changing economic, political and cultural priorities in modern societies, it would be difficult to argue, at least in the case of Britain, that they should be read as indicating that we have entered into a qualitatively new phase of social development – or experienced a postmodern break. Despite new forms of accumulation, together with some limited changes in patterns of social and cultural differentiation, the continuities seemed to us just as striking as the discontinuities.

Nevertheless, there clearly have been some changes in the state's mode of regulation. Quasi-autonomous institutions are now operating alongside, and increasingly in place of, collective provision by elected bodies with a mandate to cater for the needs of the whole population. Similar reforms have been introduced into the health and housing fields. With the progressive removal of tiers of democratically elected government or administration between the central state and individual institutions, conventional political and bureaucratic control by public bodies is replaced by quasi-autonomous institutions with devolved budgets competing for clients in the marketplace – a system of market accountability sometimes assisted by a series of directly appointed agencies, trusts and regulators. These administrative arrangements for managing education and other public services can be seen as new ways of resolving the problems of accumulation and legitimation facing the state in a situation where the Keynesian 'welfare state' is no longer deemed capable of doing so (Dale 1989).

Such quasi-autonomous institutions, state-funded but with private and voluntary involvement in their operation, appear to make education less of a political issue. The political rhetoric accompanying the educational reforms in Britain certainly sought to suggest that education had been taken out of politics as normally understood. However, Weiss (1993) doubts that such reforms will be successful in deflecting responsibility for educational decision-making from the state to market forces and atomised individuals and units operating within civil society. In practice, anyway, recent education reforms in Britain are as much to do with transferring power from the local state to the central state as with giving autonomy to the schools. Nevertheless, governments can make cuts in education expenditure and blame the consequences on poor school management practices. This is a characteristic feature of how the new public administration actually works in practice, while appearing to devolve real power from the state to the market and agencies of civil society.

For this reason, I would now want to say that, although the extent of any underlying social changes can easily be exaggerated by various 'post-ist' forms of analysis, both the discourse and the contexts of political struggles in and around education *have* been significantly altered by the reforms. Not only have changes in the nature of the state influenced the reforms in education, the reforms in education are themselves beginning to change the way we think about the role of the state and what we expect of it. In his important historical study of *Education and State Formation* in England, France and the US, Green (1990) has pointed to the way in which education has not only been an important part of state activity in modern societies, but also played a significant role in the process of state formation itself in the eighteenth and nineteenth centuries. Current changes in education policy may also be linked to a redefinition of the nature of the state and a reworking of the relations between state and civil society.

THE STATE AND CIVIL SOCIETY

The growing tendency to base more and more aspects of social affairs on the notion of consumer rights rather than upon citizen rights involves more than a move away from public-provided systems of state education towards individual schools competing for clients in the marketplace. While seeming to respond to critiques of impersonal over-bureaucratic welfare state provision, this also shifts major aspects of education decision-making out of the public into the private realm with potentially significant consequences for social justice. Atomised decision-making within an already stratified society may appear to give everyone formally equal opportunities but will actually reduce the possibility of collective struggles that might help those least able to help themselves. As Giroux and McLaren (1992: 103) put it, 'competition, mobility, getting access to information, dealing with bureaucracies, providing adequate health and food for one's children are not simply resources every family possesses in equal amounts'. Because of this, the transfer of major aspects of educational decision-making from the public to the private sphere undermines the scope for defending the interests of disadvantaged individuals and groups and thereby potentially intensifies those groups' disadvantage.

As the new education policies foster the idea that responsibility for welfare, beyond the minimum required for public safety, is to be defined entirely as a matter for individuals and families, then not only is the scope of the state narrowed, but civil society will be progressively defined solely in market terms. Foucault reminded us in one of his interviews that one of the many origins of the concept of civil society was the attempt by late eighteenth-century liberal economists to protect an autonomous economic sphere in order to limit the growing administrative power of the state (Kritzman 1988). Political radicals would have shared this wish for a set of social relations not prescribed by state regulation, but would have had a different conception of civil society, regarding it as a context in which common, as opposed to individual, interests can expressed in social movements – the realm, if you like, of active citizenship. However, Meehan (1995) suggests that, by the mid-twentieth century in Britain, the establishment of political democracy had led to a view that state bureaucratic regulation itself might serve as a tool to improve the collective life of society.

More recently, as responsibilities have been devolved from the state to an increasingly marketised civil society, and consumer rights prevail over citizen rights, the opportunities for democratic debate and collective action have become severely restricted. McKenzie (1993) argues that education has progressively been excluded from the public sphere in Britain, though she also suggests that it has never been firmly established within a popular discursive arena. The contrast between the popular response to attacks on publicly-provided education in Britain and France perhaps demonstrates that, under certain conditions, a stronger tradition of citizen rights in education can help to counter the trends in education policy outlined in this paper.

Green (1994) does not see the 'neo-liberal' or 'postmodern turn' in education policy as having much appeal in countries with effective state educational systems, including Japan and much of continental Europe, nor does he foresee those nations abandoning the key role of planned education systems in fostering social solidarity and national cohesion. However, social solidarity and national cohesion are not the same thing as democratic citizenship rights. Even in Britain, certain aspects of state intervention have been maintained, indeed strengthened, by a National Curriculum. Yet, through its particular selection of content and modes of assessment, this itself serves to promote an individualistic, hierarchical and nationalistic culture rather than an open and tolerant society.

So, it is not merely that the state has devolved responsibility for educational decision-making to a re-marketised civil society. In the British case, it may have abdicated some responsibility for ensuring social justice by deregulating major aspects of education, but in increasing a limited number of state powers it has actually strengthened its capacity to foster particular interests while appearing to stand outside the frame. McKenzie (1993) claims that British governments have increased their claims to knowledge and authority over the education system whilst promoting a theoretical and superficial movement towards consumer sovereignty. While some aspects of education have been 'privatised' in the sense of transferring them to the private sphere, others have become a matter of state mandate rather than democratic debate. These education policies in Britain can thus be seen as part of that broader project to create a free economy and a strong state (Gamble 1988). In other words, as far as democratic citizenship is concerned, probably the worst of both worlds.

Foucault warned us against the Manicheaism of seeing the state as bad and civil society, the sphere of voluntary association, as good (Kritzman 1988). We also have to be careful not to reverse that evaluation now that civil society is being marketised. There is sometimes a tendency for those of us who have criticised the role of the state in education in the past suddenly to present the state as the solution to the inequities of the market. Furthermore, a Gramscian view of civil society would warn us against seeing even non-marketised versions of civil society as purely the repository of citizenship rights and an effective counterbalance to the state. However, if all social relations become accommodated in the notion of the strong state and the free economy, then *neither* the state *nor* civil society will be the context of active democratic citizenship through which social justice can be pursued.

TOWARDS A NEW PUBLIC SPHERE

So, in the current context, the reassertion of citizenship rights in education would seem to require the development of a new public sphere *between* the state and a marketised civil society, if you like, in which new forms of collective association can be developed. Even Chubb and Moe (1990), who argue that equality is better 'protected' by markets than by political institutions, have to concede that choice of school cannot be unlimited and should not be unregulated. In Britain, far too much is being left to the market, to be determined by the self-interest of some consumers and the competitive advantages of some schools. Adler (1993) suggests that there is an urgent need to strike a better balance between the rights of parents to choose schools for their children and the duties of public authorities to promote the education of all children. However, those public institutions that might provide a context for adjudicating between different claims and priorities on behalf of the wider community have been progressively dismantled by New Right governments.

In this context, creating a new public sphere in which educational matters can even be debated – let alone determined – poses considerable challenges. Foucault points out that what he called new forms of association, such as trade unions and political parties, arose in the nineteenth century as a counter-balance to the prerogative of the state, and that they acted as the seedbed of new ideas (Kritzman 1988). We need to consider what might become the contemporary versions of these collectivist forms of association to counter-balance not only the prerogative of the state, but also the prerogative of the market.

Part of the challenge must be to move away from atomised decision-making to the reassertion of collective responsibility without recreating the very bureaucratic systems whose shortcomings have helped to legitimate the current tendency to treat education as a private good rather than a public responsibility. We need to ask how can we use the positive aspects of choice and autonomy to facilitate community empowerment rather than exacerbating social differentiation. In England, the Left has done little yet to develop a concept of public education which looks significantly different from the state education that some of us spent our earlier political and academic careers critiquing for its role in reproducing and legitimating social inequalities (Young and Whitty 1977). Even if the social democratic era looks better in retrospect, and in comparison with current policies, than it did at the time, that does not remove the need to rethink what might be progressive policies for the next century.

If new approaches are to be granted more legitimacy than previous ones, what new institutions might help to foster them, initially within a new public sphere in which ideas can be debated, but potentially as new forms of democratic governance themselves? Clearly, such institutions could take various forms and they will certainly need to take different forms in different societies. They will no doubt be struggled over and some will be more open to hegemonic incorporation than others. Some may actually be created by the state, as the realisation dawns that a marketised civil society itself creates contradictions that need to be managed. Thus, there are likely to be both 'bottom-up' and 'top-down' pressures to create new institutions within which struggles over the control of education will take place.

Community Education Forums have sometimes been favoured by the Labour parties in England and New Zealand, but we will need to give more careful consideration to the composition and powers of such bodies if they are to prove an appropriate way of reasserting democratic citizenship rights in education in the late twentieth century. If we wish to replace the role of unaccountable individuals, agencies and private consultants in educational decision-making with representatives of demonstrably legitimate interests, what forms of representation should we be calling for? Who are the appropriate constituencies through which to express community interests in the late twentieth century? What do we mean by communities? What forms of democracy can express their complexity? If, as Mouffe (1992) suggests, a radical pluralist conception of citizenship involves creating unity without denying specificity, how can this actually be expressed? We have to confront these difficult questions as a matter of urgency since, at the level of rhetoric (though not reality), the recent reforms of the New Right *have* probably been more responsive than their critics usually concede to those limited, but nonetheless tangible, social and cultural shifts that have been taking place in modern societies.

BEYOND SOCIAL DEMOCRACY

A straightforward return to the old order of things would be neither feasible nor sensible. Social democratic approaches to education which continue to favour the idea of a common school are faced with the need to respond to increasing specialisation and social diversity. As Connell (1993: 19) reminds us:

> justice cannot be achieved by distributing the same amount of a standard good to children of all social classes . . . That 'good' means different things to ruling class and working class children, and will do different things for them (or to them).

Yet, while recognising specificity, we also have to be careful not to deny our potential commonality.

Hargreaves (1994) argues that we should be happy to encourage a system of independent, differentiated and specialised schools, but that we should also reassert a sense of common citizenship by insisting on core programmes of civic education in all schools. My own view is that Hargreaves pays insufficient attention not only to the effects of the neo-liberal reforms in exacerbating existing inequalities between schools and in society at large, but also underestimates the power of the *hidden curriculum* of the market to undermine any real sense of commonality. The very exercise of individual choice and school self-management can so easily become self-legitimating for those with the resources to benefit from it and the mere teaching of civic responsibility is unlikely to provide an effective counter-balance.

Most crucially, in view of what I have been saying here, Hargreaves' analysis fails to recognise that the changing nature of modern societies not only requires changes in the nature of schools for the next century but also changes in the manner in which decisions are made about schools. If we are to avoid the atomisation of educational decision-making, and associated tendencies towards the fragmentation and polarisation of schooling, we need to create new contexts for determining appropriate institutional and curricular arrangements on behalf of the whole society. This will require new forms of association in the public sphere within which citizen rights in education policy – and indeed other areas of public policy – can be reasserted against current trends towards both a restricted version of the state and a marketised civil society. If we want equity to remain on the educational agenda, we should certainly be looking to find new ways of making educational decision-making a part of democratic life and a legitimate public sphere, rather than colluding with the death of public education or even merely critiquing its demise.

ACKNOWLEDGEMENTS

Parts of this chapter draw upon work carried out with Tony Edwards and Sharon Gewirtz with support from the Economic and Social Research Council. A longer version of this chapter was presented at the International Conference on Autonomy and Education, National Taiwan Normal University, 14–16 March 1995.

REFERENCES

Adler, M. (1993) *An Alternative Approach to Parental Choice*, London: National Commission on Education, Briefing Paper 13.

Ashworth, J., Papps, I. and Thomas, B. (1988) *Increased Parental Choice,* Warlingham: Institute of Economic Affairs Education Unit.

Ball, S. (1990) *Politics and Policy Making in Education: Explorations in Policy Sociology*, London: Routledge.

Boyne, R. and Rattansi, A. (eds) (1990) *Post Modernism and Society*, London: Macmillan.

Callinicos, A. (1989) *Against Post Modernism: A Marxist Critique*, Cambridge: Polity Press.

Centre for Contemporary Cultural Studies (CCCS) (1981) *Unpopular Education*, London: Hutchinson.

Chubb, J. and Moe, T. (1990) *Politics, Markets and America's Schools*, Washington: Brookings Institution.

Chubb, J. and Moe, T. (1992) *A Lesson in School Reform from Great Britain*, Washington: Brookings Institution.

Connell, R. W. (1993) *Schools and Social Justice*, Toronto: Our Schools/Our Selves Education Foundation.

Dale, R. (1989) *The State and Education Policy*, Milton Keynes: Open University.

Department for Education (DFE). (1992) *Choice and Diversity: A New Framework for Schools*, London: HMSO.

Flax, J. (1987) 'Post modernism and gender relations in feminist theory'. *Signs* 12, 4: 621–43.

Gamble, A. (1988) *The Free Economy and the Strong State*, London: Macmillan.

Giroux, H. and McLaren, P. (1992) '*America 2000* and the Politics of Erasure: Democracy and Cultural Difference under Siege', *International Journal of Educational Reform* 1, 2: 99–109.

Green, A. (1990) *Education and State Formation*, London: Macmillan.

Green, A. (1994) 'Post modernism and State Education', *Journal of Education Policy* 9, 1: 67–84.

Hargreaves, D. (1994) *The Mosaic of Learning: Schools and Teachers for the Next Century*, London: Demos.

Harvey, D. (1989) *The Condition of Post Modernity: An Enquiry into the Origins of Cultural Change*, Oxford: Basil Blackwell.

Jessop, B., Bonnett, K., Bromley, S. and Ling, T. (1987) 'Popular capitalism, flexible accumulation and left strategy', *New Left Review* 165: 104–23.

Kenway, J. (1993) 'Marketing education in the postmodern age', *Journal of Education Policy* 8, 1: 105–22.

Kritzman, L.D. (ed.) (1988) *Foucault: Politics/Philosophy/Culture*. New York: Routledge.

Lash, S. (1990) *Sociology of Post Modernism*, London: Routledge.

McKenzie, J. (1993) 'Education as a Private Problem or a Public Issue? The Process of Excluding "Education" from the "Public Sphere"', paper presented at the International Conference on the Public Sphere, Manchester, 8–10 January.

Meehan, E. (1995) *Civil Society*, Contribution to an ESRC/RSA seminar series on 'The State of Britain', Swindon: Economic and Social Research Council.

Mouffe, C. (ed.) (1992) *Dimensions of Radical Democracy: Pluralism, Citizenship, Democracy*, London: Verso.

Robins, K. (1991) 'Tradition and translation: national culture in its global context', in J. Corner and S. Harvey (eds) *Enterprise and Heritage: Crosscurrents of National Culture*, London: Routledge.

Thompson, K. (1992) 'Social pluralism and postmodernity', in S. Hall, D. Held, and T. McGrew (eds) *Modernity and Its Futures*, Cambridge: Polity Press.

Weiss, M. (1993) 'New guiding principles in educational policy: the case of Germany', *Journal of Education Policy* 8, 4: 307–20.

Whitty, G. (1997) 'Creating quasi-markets in education: a review of recent research on parental choice and school autonomy in three countries', *Review of Research in Education* 22: 3–47.

Whitty, G., Edwards, T. and Gewirtz, S. (1993) *Specialisation and Choice in Urban Education: The City Technology College Experiment*, London: Routledge.

Young, M. and Whitty, G. (eds) (1977) *Society, State and Schooling*, Lewes: Falmer Press.

9

MORALITY, WORK AND COMPETENCE

Social values in vocational education and training

Terry Hyland

Perhaps the single most important goal for a teacher to work towards has to do with the basic attitude towards work.

(Jarrett 1991: 206)

VALUES AND VOCATIONALISM

Since the early 1970s there has been a 'vocationalisation' of education (Hyland 1991) at all levels in response to rising youth unemployment, economic global-isation of markets and post-Fordist industrial re-structuring (Esland 1990). Vocationalism – in the sense of the reinforcement of the economic utility and job preparation functions of schools and colleges – is now a 'world-wide trend' and a 'common thread which runs across the education and, increas-ingly, the employment policies of every country, whatever its level of develop-ment, political system or geographical location' (Skilbeck et al. 1994: 7). Moreover, such developments have had an impact, not just on the traditional spheres of vocational education and training, but on all sectors and domains of education, from schools (Moon 1990) to universities (Neave 1992). Educa-tion and training have become commodities to be sold or bartered in the marketplace.

This so-called 'new vocationalism' (Esland 1990) has, however, been domi-nated by a one-dimensional, technicist approach to VET represented by the competence-based education and training (CBET) strategies popularised through the National Council for Vocational for Qualifications (NCVQ) in Britain (Wolf 1995) and Australasia (Gonczi 1994) and widely established in the United States. This excessively technicist approach to vocational educa-tion and training (VET) has been described as 'morally impoverished' (Fish 1993: 10). If it allows for the discussion of values at all, it generates a largely uncritical and mechanistic approach in which something called 'moral com-petence' (Wright 1989, Hyland 1992) is recommended largely as a means of

99

ensuring that young workers develop the values, attitudes and personal qualities required by employers.

Within the framework of work-related outcomes, even supposedly 'autonomous' and 'independent' learning comes to be interpreted in this mechanical, behaviouristic manner. Jessup (1991) tells us that CBET strategies help promote the 'autonomous learner' because the 'learner is regarded as the client and the model is designed to provide him or her with more control over the process of learning and assessment' (1991: 115). In a similar vein, NCVQ supporters claim that the system can provide teachers with more control over curriculum matters (McAleavey and McAleer 1991) and are conducive to 'flexible learning' (FEU 1992, Thomas 1995).

There is, however, a yawning gulf between rhetoric and reality in these claims and a wilful abuse of values and the concept of autonomy. The NCVQ competence system and other technicised and 'mercantilised' (Lyotard 1984) approaches to education and training – in addition to their equivocal conceptual bases and ambiguous epistemological foundations (Hyland 1994) – are informed by behaviourist learning theory which devalues knowledge, understanding and learning processes. Moreover, CBET approaches are seriously at odds with the cognitive and experiential tradition – linked to learner empowerment and autonomous learning through Kolb's (1993) strategies – which runs through British and European further, adult and higher education. They promote instead a conception of VET which is 'inappropriate to the description of human action or to the facilitation of the training of human beings' (Ashworth 1992: 16).

Such technicist approaches are part and parcel of the 'McDonaldisation' process identified by Ritzer (1993) to refer to the increasingly technical rationalisation of all aspects of social life. Values, ideals and learning are all rendered subordinate to the agenda of the 'corporate State' (Ranson 1994) and concerned exclusively with economic competitiveness, behaviourist outcomes, and input/output accountability. Along with the marginalisation of learning processes and the devaluing of knowledge and experience, such rationalisation leads to a serious distortion of the notions of educational autonomy and flexible learning. Flexibility is reconstructed as an aspect of 'post-Fordism, strategically arranged to normalise a view of the future of work' in which 'persons will be disciplined into certain forms of behaviour and more readily managed within a social formation of structural inequality' (Edwards 1993: 185).

Autonomous and independent learning strategies are replaced by a McDonaldised 'fake fraternisation' (Hartley 1995) in education and training which – through learning contracts, needs analysis, action plans and pre-packaged modules (Collins 1991) – is designed to persuade learners that they are in control of their own learning. In reality, however, post-Fordist 'flexibility' may actually entail a more stricter control over work-related learning (Field 1993) and what Brown and Lauder (1995) call a form of 'neo-Fordism' which 'can be characterised in terms of a shift to flexible accumulation based on the creation of a flexible workforce engaged in low-skill, low-wage, temporary and often part-time employment' (1995: 20). Such conceptions of work, employment and VET are inconsistent with any normally accepted interpretation of autonomy and with the shared values which are necessarily central to the induction of people into any form of genuinely social practice (MacIntyre 1981).

The goal of developing autonomy and associated values relating to, for example, democratic accountability and social justice (Jarrett 1991) applies as much to vocational education and training (VET) as to more general or academic spheres of education. It is a serious mistake to think that technical, vocational or occupational pursuits are in some sense value-free or value-neutral (Halliday 1996). Concepts such as work, labour, toil and employment are too often conflated, resulting in an excessively technicist and instrumental conception of VET (Green 1968) which neglects the 'shared values' which underpin our common 'understanding of why productive work is a fundamental condition of human life' (Skilbeck et al. 1994: 50) or indeed our understanding of the wider quality of life, including work, which we want to cultivate and support.

I prefer to start with Dewey's broad conception of vocational education (Hyland 1993) as a process which transcends the vocational–academic, liberal–technical divide and 'stresses the full intellectual and social meaning of a vocation' (Dewey 1966: 316) and I shall propose an 'education for work' core component for VET in which values are centrally placed and which is conducive to the idea of autonomous learning and development outlined above. Such a core dimension builds on Corson's conception of 'studies in work across the curriculum' (1991: 173), and locates this within a context of general education for all students which is meant to be supportive of any vocational – whether broad-based or occupationally-specific – elements of 14–19 education and training.

I suggest that a programme concerned with autonomy, values and work could profitably incorporate the following elements (a) work and social values; (b) work, labour and *eudaimonia*; (c) work, jobs and community. I will offer a sketch of each of these areas in turn.

WORK AND SOCIAL VALUES

In attempting to answer the question 'What are the ingredients of the good life in pursuit of which we undertake to educate people?', Mary Warnock (1977) outlines a programme which contains three elements: 'virtue, work and imagination' (1977: 129) What she has to say about 'work' provides a useful starting-point for a discussion of the place and value of work in human life.

In agreeing with those educators who point to the dangers of narrowly-focused vocationalism, Warnock maintains that work is, and must always be an important ingredient of the good life; that a life without work would always be less good than a life which contained it; and that to be totally unemployed is indeed a dreadful fate.

(Warnock 1977: 144)

This forthright account of the role and positive value of work is based upon and justified by a number of presuppositions. First, there is the idea that, even though a job that is boring, pointless and alienating can be regarded as no more than a necessary evil, it is still 'better to have it than not, and probably better to work hard at it than less hard' since 'money earned is better than money handed out as a right, divorced from any work done'. Second, work can be regarded as a basic human need and motivation to action; in a Nietzschean sense the 'will to power is perhaps identical with the will to work', and it is 'certain that all work is effort to make or change things or reduce them to order, and that all these efforts are worth making' (Warnock 1977: 144–5).

The notion of money earned through work being superior to that received in 'charity' might be regarded as a form of revised Protestant work ethic – suitably modified to fit the current neo-liberal agenda (Hyland 1992). This was recently reincarnated in the form of the 'enterprise culture' (Heelas and Morris 1992) which informed the new vocational initiatives of the 1970s and 1980s. It was a theme running throughout many of the state-sponsored Technical and Vocational Education Initiative (TVEI) and youth training schemes in this period (Shilling 1989), and played a key role in the British National Curriculum Council 'Education for Citizenship' initiative (NCC 1990).

The general flavour of this approach is well summed up in the National Curriculum Council document in a section called 'Work and Leisure' in which teachers are asked to stress the 'importance to the society and the individual of wealth creation'. Later on we read that students should learn that 'public services depend for their scope and effectiveness on the generation of wealth – they are not free' (NCC 1990: 8–9). Beneath the superficial veneer of the apparently commonsensical and unexceptionable nature of such sentiments are unarticulated values about enterprise, economic individualism and the nature of society and community relationships. There is nothing here about the darker underside of the enterprise culture in terms of the massive increases in relative poverty, homelessness, un/underemployment, de-skilling of occupational roles, and the now undisputed findings pointing to the fact that 'income inequality has increased more rapidly in the United Kingdom in the 1980s than in other western countries' (Atkinson 1996: 15).

In the interests of fostering rational autonomy in vocational students (if not avoiding overt indoctrination!), the neo-liberal triumphalism of the enterprise culture surely needs to be balanced by an examination of alternative perspectives. Some of these point to the fact that, over the last decade or so, 'incomes have been redistributed, against earlier post-war trends, in favour of the propertied, and a culture has developed in which wealth has been celebrated and rendered apparently free from guilt and responsibility' (Rustin 1994: 76). The vacuous inadequacy of such a relentless and unremittingly individualistic value system is demonstrated with superb clarity and imaginative insight in Martin Amis' satirical novel *Money*. The central character of the novel, John Self, is portrayed as an egotistical, money-obsessed and essentially amoral product of the late twentieth century whose philosophy is well summed up by his observations on one of his business friends who, Amis tells us,

> uses money to buy and sell money. Equipped with only a telephone, he buys money with money, sells money for money. He works in the cracks and vents of currencies, buying and selling on the margin, riding the daily tides of exchange. For these services he is rewarded with money. Lots of it. It is beautiful, and so is he.
>
> (1985: 120)

Perhaps more significant than the moral bankruptcy of such unalloyed materialism is the clear and obvious danger that any such one-sided perspective is bound to produce a distorted vision of the nature of society and the values which regulate human relationships. What is missing from such an account is the crucial domain of 'social values' and the acknowledgement that any set of 'guidelines for the government of the learning society need to begin by celebrating education as a public good' (Ranson 1994: 113). Any introduction to the nature and value of work needs to make reference to the 'moral basis of economic activities and the balance between individualist and communitarian values in the national culture' (Thompson 1992: 274). In democratic communities it is essential that work is firmly located within the framework of what Marshall (1950) called 'social citizenship' which accords a certain status that gives every member of society a claim upon all the rest for help and support in the contingencies of life.

WORK, LABOUR AND EUDAIMONIA

Also absent from Warnock's justification of work is a clear articulation of the differences between work and labour or toil, and, given that it is the latter which is realistically the common experience of most of the human race, some attempt to locate this within a context of principles, values, and human interests and motivations. Herbst (1973) uses a distinction brought out in the writings of Hannah Arendt to mark differences between work and labour which are of the first importance for education.

Although the concepts have much in common – both consume the time and energies of people, for example, and can be done more or less efficiently – work can be said to have some intrinsic value (the work is integrally related to its end product) whereas labour essentially has extrinsic or utilitarian value (it is generally done for purposes beyond itself). It is, therefore, more properly 'toil'. Labour is 'hardship . . . the price we pay for whatever advantages the rewards of labour will buy' (Herbst 1973: 59). Another way of expressing the key difference is by saying that 'work, unlike labour, must have a point which the workman [*sic*] can endorse, and a purpose with which he can associate himself' (1973: 61). Ainley (1993) highlights similar distinctions in his historical review of changing conceptions of skill and the division of labour, and makes much of the evolution of 'artisanship' (1993: 6ff) through a combination of the activities of workers and artists.

Such an account seems to offer a far more meaningful description than that of Warnock who, though recognising the menial and often futile nature of much so-called work, does tend to over-emphasise the creative work of artists and professionals. Against this, Wringe (1991) rightly points out that 'some kinds of work are not at all constitutive of the good life and are at best a necessary evil' (1991: 37). Wringe has in mind here the sort of work which tends to be boring and repetitive (i.e., 'labour' under Herbst's description) and suggests that, to a greater or lesser degree, most humans will have to face tasks of this kind at some stage in their lives.

The fostering of autonomy must, therefore, take into account such vicissitudes which may inhibit the goal of human flourishing which is at the heart of *eudaimonism.* Indeed, as Kekes' (1995) account of moral wisdom explains, the 'agonistic' element of *eudaimonism* insists that 'living a good life is recognised as being hard, requiring constant struggle against serious adversity' (1995: 2).

There is some evidence to suggest that school pupils are only too aware of these basic facts of working life. The working-class 'lads' observed and interviewed by Willis (1977) were almost fatalistically reconciled to their future lives in dead-end and menial jobs, and research in Australia by Walker (1991) produced similar findings. Shilling's (1989) work with youngsters involved in TVEI and other vocational schemes in British schools was graphically realistic in this respect. After their experience of working in a large factory, the majority of students had developed negative attitudes and remarked on the mechanical and tedious nature of much of the work. For these students, any positive factors (such as easy work or good money) were 'not sufficient compensation for the labour process they would have been subject to'. Furthermore, 'far from making students more open to the possibilities of working in industry, this part of the course had alienated the majority from working in a large factory' (Shilling 1989: 124–5).

Nevertheless, much of positive educational value can be gained from examining work in the light of such realistic experiences and expectations. If work of this kind is, for many people, a necessary evil, then to 'undertake one's share of this evil, and consequently to undertake such learning as will enable one to do so . . . may be a universal obligation as well . . . as being in itself an educative experience' (Wringe 1991: 37). Indeed, the heightened realism of practical wisdom may demand that we move beyond the rather bourgeois notion (stemming from the 'gentleman ideal' in British education; Hyland 1993) that only professional or creative occupations can be intrinsically valuable, satisfying or self-affirming.

Part of the 'morality of work' for Wringe is to insist that

> work does not have to be sublime or spectacular . . . to be worthwhile. Many relatively mundane jobs can be challenging and varied and involve standards of logic, efficiency, integrity, judgement and so on.
>
> (1991: 38)

With these considerations in mind, Green (1968: 25) goes as far as to say that the 'meaningfulness of a task lies not in the work, but in the worker' and that 'some people may find even cosmic significance in a task that, to others, would seem mean and inconsequential'. As Jarrett (1991) suggests, all such discussions are essentially concerned with moral questions relating to values, attitudes, motives and dispositions. The values connected with Buddhist 'mindfulness' – the seventh branch of the eight-fold path which seeks to wean us 'away from our usual habit patterns' in a way which 'sharpens and intensifies our powers of direct perception; it gives us eyes to see into the true nature of things' (Snelling 1987: 61) – are worthy of a special emphasis in the field of vocational or technical pursuits in which activities are often mistakenly undervalued (Williams 1994). A particularly vivid illustration of the application of such values to the world of work is provided with penetrating insight, wit and imagination in Pirsig's *Zen and the Art of Motorcycle Maintenance* (1974). Pirsig's central character at one point makes the following observation:

> Precision instruments are designed to achieve an *idea*, dimensional precision whose perfection is impossible. There is no perfectly shaped part of the motorcycle and never will be, but when you come as close as these instruments take you, remarkable things happen, and you go flying across the countryside under a power that would be called magic if it were not so completely rational in every way . . . I look at the shapes of the steel now and I see *ideas* . . . I'm working on *concepts*.
>
> (Pirsig 1974: 102)

On perhaps a less idealistic or mystical plane, Corson calls for a consideration of work as 'craft . . . pursued for its own ends . . . as unconstrained occupational work . . . similar to recreational work in having a value for its own sake' (1991: 171). In order to realise such (essentially Deweyan) ideals of occupational work, Corson suggests a framework for learning – perhaps incorporating principles of craftsmanship of the sort generally admired in the German *'Berufsprinzip'* system (Reuling 1996) – designed to reinforce the 'value that students see in their work and the significance of that work for themselves and for their society' (Corson 1991: 171–2).

In the absence of such conditions, however, education still has a vital role to play in helping students to make sense of the less than ideal world in which toil is a commonplace experience. Wringe (1991) has two principal proposals to make in relation to the 'morality of toil and the division of labour'. First, since 'toil, regular, serious toil cannot itself be a necessary part of the good life', the 'facts of human existence are such that a preparedness to undertake it may be regarded as a necessary part of a life that is just'. Second, if 'toil is a necessary evil, training which enables it to be done more efficiently . . . or enables it to be replaced by a more challenging or worthwhile form of work seems morally desirable' (1991: 40).

In the light of such observations, both vocational (technical) and moral education (concerning the values of work and craftsmanship) are necessary components of an 'education for work' curriculum, as, indeed, are those aspects of general education (art, humanities, science, sport) which give meaning to those aspects of life not taken up with work or toil.

WORK, EMPLOYMENT AND COMMUNITY

Warnock's argument that 'if children are educated in such a way that they can get jobs, it is reasonable that someone must try to work out roughly what kind of jobs there will be for them' (1977: 146) was written just prior to the onset of massively increased youth unemployment and, with hindsight, can perhaps be forgiven for a certain naivety. Moreover, there is also, as critics of the new vocationalism of the 1970s and 1980s point out, a dangerous over-simplicity in thinking that education and training can either supply what employers need or predict future industrial requirements. Although economic vicissitudes since the 1970s have generated a whole range of 'ritualistic' (Stronach 1990) responses in the form of providing youngsters with job-specific, flexible or enterprise skills, there is scant evidence of any links between these activities and actual employer requirements (Finn 1990, Avis et al. 1996). Much rhetoric has been built around what a recent Employment Policy Institute (EPI 1995) study called the 'skills mirage', but there is very little evidence to support a skills/industrial productivity link and even less justification for a belief in the efficacy of manpower planning (White 1990).

Certainly, any approach to vocational training which moved away from what Lee et al. (1990) called the 'immorality' of youth training which, under the guise of the all-purpose 'enterprise' slogan, sold 'unemployment relief as training' (1990: 195) would be greatly welcomed. Notwithstanding the inadequacies of industrial skills planning, there is still a vital educational need for comprehensive careers advice and educational counselling. As Taylor (1991) has observed, although some form of careers advice service is a requisite of the 1973 UK Employment Training Act, this has always been unsystematic, and even this minimal provision is now threatened by economy measures. Drawing on the work of Watts (1984), Taylor recommends a careers counselling programme which includes 'survival skills' and encompasses an awareness of the psychological impact of un/underemployment and familiarity with the support services available in society.

Values programmes in vocational education and training need to move beyond the learning society rhetoric and the slogan of 'learning pays' (Bennett *et al.* 1992) to incorporate a critical exploration of rights and benefits in relation to work and employment. Although it is difficult to sustain any natural or legal 'right to work' (Coope 1994), there is still much to be examined at the level of social justice and the changing nature of work and employment. Linking the values of work with self-respect, autonomy and basic liberty, Smart (1985) has argued that 'deprivation of work is an attack on one's status as an adult' which can reduce people to the 'status of the chronically sick' (1985: 37–8).

Similarly, it will be important for students to examine the nature and causes of changing work and employment patterns and the growth of un/underemployment on a global scale since the 1950s. There was a tendency for the 'new vocationalism' of the 1980s to 'juvenalize and personalise' (Stronach 1990: 157) the problem of unemployment by implying that this was somehow caused by the deficiencies of young people. Instead of the personalisation of such problems, students might be informed about the crises and difficulties which have beset most modern economies since the bubble of the post-war boom was pierced by the 'capitalist crisis of over-accumulation' (Armstrong *et al.* 1984: 235) in the early 1970s. Moreover, it needs to be emphasised that, in spite of the globalisation of the recession, some countries with 'extensive social policies' (Denmark, Belgium, Japan) have coped rather better than others such as Britain and the United States (Shirley 1991, Avis *et al.* 1996).

As a background to all such considerations it is important to locate students' discussions of work and employment within a framework which examines critically the current taken-for-granted assumptions about society and the economy, and explores a range of alternative positions. Just as the youth training schemes of the 1970s and 1980s dishonestly implied that unskilled school leavers were somehow to blame for Britain's economic crisis, so there is a similar disingenuous and largely unquestioned assumption that only a 'market forces' approach to the economy, education and society can deal with our current problems.

Such an approach is underpinned by the doctrine of 'economic individualism' – which maintains that 'all human behaviour is conditioned by the hedonistic aspirations of each individual wanting to maximise his/her productive capacities' (Shirley 1991: 154). It seeks to inculcate a largely incoherent and ambiguous values system which celebrates naked self-interest under the innocuous and all-purpose 'enterprise' slogan (Heelas and Morris 1992).

By contrast values programmes for VET need to address the concerns of all stakeholders: employers, employees, teachers, trainers, students and the wider community. Indeed, in line with the globalisation of trade and industry, the values associated with social citizenship (Ranson 1994) now need to be interpreted on a global scale which seeks to overcome the parochialism of nationalist prejudices (Esland 1996). Such a reconstructed conception of work and VET would be one which

> acknowledges social and personal aims, values and needs and locates education and training goals in relation to the kind of society we wish to see develop and the qualities in people that are to be fostered and nourished.
>
> (Skilbeck *et al.* 1994: 46)

CONCLUSION

Briefly, then, I hope to have shown that social principles and objectives to do with the development of personal autonomy and social justice have at least as much significance in vocational education and training as in other sectors of education; to have pointed to the impoverished values that underpin the development of 'the new vocationalism' and with this the commodification of education and training in many parts of the world; and to have outlined more honest and richly endowed approaches to vocational education which fit more comfortably with aspirations for personal autonomy and social democracy.

REFERENCES

Ainley, P. (1993) *Class and Skill* London: Cassell.

Allen, R. T. (1982) 'Rational Autonomy: the destruction of freedom', *Journal of Philosophy of Education*, 16 (2), 199–207.

Amis, M. (1985) *Money* Harmondsworth: Penguin.

Armstrong, P., Glyn, A. and Harrison, J. (1984) *Capitalism Since World War II* London: Fontana.

Ashworth, P. (1992) 'Being competent and having competencies', *Journal of Further & Higher Education,* 16 (3), 8–17.

Atkinson, T. (1996) 'Why do Britain's have-nots have less?', *Times Higher Education Supplement*, April 12.

Avis, J., Bloomer, M., Esland, G., Gleeson, D. and Hodkinson, P. (1996) *Knowledge and Nationhood* London: Cassell.

Bennett, R., Glennerster, H. and Nevison, D. (1992) *Learning Should Pay* London: London School of Economics/BP Education.

Brown, P. and Lauder, H. (1995) 'Post-Fordist possibilities: education, training and national development' in Bash L. and Green A. (eds) *Youth, Education and Work* London: Kogan Page.

Callan, E. (1994) 'Autonomy and alienation', *Journal of Philosophy of Education*, 28 (1), 35–53.

CBI (1989) *Towards a Skills Revolution* London: Confederation of British Industry.

Collins, M. (1991) *Adult Education as Vocation* London: Routledge.

Coope, C. M. (1994) 'Justice and jobs: three sceptical thoughts about rights in employment', *Journal of Applied Philosophy*, 11 (1), 71–78.

Corson, D. (ed.) (1991) *Education for Work* Clevedon: Multilingual Matters.

Dearden, R. F. (1972) 'Autonomy and education' in Dearden, R. F., Hirst, P. H. and Peters, R. S. (eds) *Education and the Development of Reason* London: Routledge & Kegan Paul.

Dearden, R. F. (1990) 'Education and training' in Esland, G. (ed.) *Education, Training and Employment* Wokingham: Addison-Wesley/Open University.

Dewey, J. (1966) *Democracy and Education* New York: Free Press.

Edwards, R. (1993) 'The inevitable future? Post-Fordism in work and learning' in Edwards, R., Sieminski, S. and Zeldin, D. (eds) *Adult Learners, Education and Training* London: Routledge/Open University.

EPI (1995) *The Skills Mirage* London: Employment Policy Institute.

Esland, G. (ed.) (1990) *Education, Training and Employment* Wokingham: Addison-Wesley/Open University.

Esland, G. (1996) 'Knowledge and nationhood: The New Right, education and the global market' in Avis, J. *et al.* (eds) *Knowledge and Nationhood* London: Cassell.

FEU (1992) *Flexible Colleges* London: Further Education Unit.

Field, J. (1993) 'Competency and the pedagogy of labour' in Thorpe, M., Edwards, R. and Hanson, A. (eds) *Culture and Processes of Adult Learning* London: Routledge/Open University.

Finn, D. (1990) 'The great debate on education, youth unemployment and the MSC' in Esland (ed.) *Education, Training and Employment* Wokingham: Addison-Wesley/Open University.

Fish, D. (1993) 'Uncertainty in a certain world: values, competency-based training and the reflective practitioner', *Journal of the National Association for Values in Education and Training*, 8 (1), 7–12.

Gonczi, A. (1994) 'Competency based assessment in the professions in Australia', *Assessment in Education*, 1 (1), 27–44.

Green, T.F. (1968) *Work, Leisure and the American School* New York: Random House.

Halliday, J. (1996) 'Values and Further Education', *British Journal of Educational Studies*, 44 (1), 66–81.

Hartley, D. (1995) 'The McDonaldisation of higher education: food for thought?', *Oxford Review of Education*, 21 (4), 409–423.

Heelas, P. and Morris, P. (eds) (1992) *The Values of the Enterprise Culture* London: Routledge.

Herbst, P. (1973) 'Work, labour and university education' in Peters, R. S. (ed.) *The Philosophy of Education* Oxford: Oxford University Press.

Hyland, T. (1991) 'Taking care of business: vocationalism, competence and the enterprise culture', *Educational Studies*, 17 (1), 77–87.

Hyland, T. (1992) 'Moral vocationalism', *Journal of Moral Education*, 21 (2), 139–150.

Hyland, T. (1993) 'Vocational reconstruction and Dewey's instrumentalism', *Oxford Review of Education*, 19 (1), 89–100.

Hyland, T. (1994) *Competence, Education and NVQs: Dissenting Perspectives* London: Cassell.

Jarrett, J. L. (1991) *The Teaching of Values: Caring and Appreciation* London: Routledge.

Jessup, G. (1991) *Outcomes: NVQs and the emerging model of education and training* London: Falmer Press.

Kekes, J. (1995) *Moral Wisdom and Good Lives* New York: Cornell University Press.

Kolb, D. (1993) 'The process of experiential learning' in Thorpe M., Edwards R. and Hanson A. (eds)

Lee, D., Marsden, D., Rickman, P. and Duncombe, J. (1990) *Scheming for Work: A Study of YTS in the Enterprise Culture* Milton Keynes: Open University Press.

Lee Jee-Hun and Wringe, C. (1994) 'Rational autonomy, morality and education', *Journal of Philosophy of Education*, 27 (1), 69–78.

Lyotard, J.-F. (1984) *The Post-Modern Condition: A Report on Knowledge* Minneapolis: University of Minnesota Press.

MacIntyre, A. (1981) *After Virtue* London: Duckworth.

Marshall, T. H. (1950) *Citizenship and Social Class* Cambridge: Cambridge University Press.

McAleavey, M. and McAleer, J. (1991) 'Competence-based training', *British Journal of Inservice Education*, 17 (1), 19–23.

Moon, B. (1990) 'Patterns of reform: school control in Western Europe' in Moon, B. (ed.) *New Curriculum-National Curriculum* Milton Keynes: Open University Press.

NCC (1990) *Education for Citizenship* York: National Curriculum Council.

Neave, G. (1992) 'On instantly consumable knowledge and snake oil', *European Journal of Education*, 28 (1/2), 5–28.

Norman, R. (1994) '"I did it my way": some thoughts on autonomy', *Journal of Philosophy of Education*, 28 (1), 25–34.

Pirsig, R. M. (1974) *Zen and the Art of Motorcycle Maintenance* London: Corgi.

Ranson, S. (1994) *Towards the Learning Society* London: Cassell.

Reuling, J. (1996) *The German Berufsprinzip as a Model for Regulating Training Content and Qualifications Standards* Berlin: Federal Institute for Vocational Training.

Ritzer, G. (1993) *The McDonaldisation of Society* London: Pine Forge Press.

Rustin, M. (1994) 'Unfinished business – from Thatcherite modernisation to incomplete modernity' in Perryman, M. (ed.) *Altered States: Postmodernism, Politics, Culture* London: Lawrence & Wishart.

Shilling, C. (1989) *Schooling for Work in Capitalist Britain* Lewes: Falmer Press.

Shirley, I. (1991) 'State policy and employment' in Corson, D. (ed.) *Education for Work*, Clevedon: Multilingual Matters.

Skilbeck, M., Connell, H., Love, N. and Tait, K. (1994) *The Vocational Quest* London: Routledge.

Smart, B. (1985) 'The right to strike and the right to work', *Journal of Applied Philosophy*, 2 (1), 31–40.

Snelling, J. (1987) *The Buddhist Handbook* London: Rider.

Stone, C. M. (1993) 'Autonomy, emotions and desires', *Journal of Philosophy of Education*, 24 (2), 271–83.

Stronach, I. (1990) 'Education, vocationalism and economic recovery: the case against witchcraft' in Esland G. (ed.) *Education, Training and Employment* Wokingham: Addison-Wesley/Open University.

Taylor, W. (1991) 'School to Work' in Corson, D. (ed.) *Education for Work*, Clevedon: Multilingual Matters.

Thomas, D. (ed.) (1995) *Flexible Learning Strategies in Higher and Further Education* London: Cassell.

Thompson, K. (1992) 'Individual and community in religious critiques of the enterprise culture' in Heelas, P. and Morris, P. (eds) *The Values of Enterprise Culture* London: Routledge.

Walker, J. (1991) 'Building on youth cultures in the secondary curriculum' in Corson, D. (ed.) *Education for Work* Clevedon: Multilingual Matters.

Warnock, M. (1977) *Schools of Thought* London: Faber & Faber.

Watts, A. (1984) *Education, Unemployment and the Future of Work* Milton Keynes: Open University Press.

White, M. (1990) 'Educational policy and economic goals' in Esland, G. (ed.) *Education, Training and Employment* Wokingham: Addison-Wesley/Open University.

Williams, K. (1994) 'Vocationalism and liberal education: exploring the tensions', *Journal of Philosophy of Education*, 28 (1), 89–100.

Willis, P. (1977) *Learning to Labour* London: Saxon House.

Wolf, A. (1995) *Competence-Based Assessment* Buckingham: Open University Press.

Wright, D. (1989) *Moral Competence* London: Further Education Unit.

Wringe, C. (1991) 'Education, schooling and the world of work' in Corson, D. (ed.) *Education for Work* Clevedon: Multilingual Matters.

Part III

AUTONOMY RECONSIDERED

10

IN DEFENCE OF RATIONAL AUTONOMY AS AN EDUCATIONAL GOAL

Colin Wringe

RATIONAL AUTONOMY

Each of us has but one life to live and despite the many differences between us, there is no reason to suppose that one person should use their life to serve the goals, interests and aspirations of another, unless they so choose. It is therefore legitimate, and in each person's interest, to acquire the capacity to choose and sustain the most desirable way of life for themselves, subject only to the requirement to respect the rights of others to do likewise. The precondition of such a capacity is a grasp of the possibilities the world offers and the necessary constraints it imposes. Such has been the justification for education given by a number of philosophers (Peters 1973; Crittenden 1978; White, J. 1982; Jonathan 1983) some of whom, in addition to information about the world and the range of goals worth pursuing have also written of the way in which education enables us to acquire the ability to apply the criteria according to which various categories of claim may be appraised.

In recent years both the moral justification for autonomy suggested above and the epistemological possibility of the kind of rational judgement upon which it is based have been challenged from two directions by groups of writers who, for the sake of convenience and with a degree of regrettable simplification will be referred to as, on the one hand, communitarians and, on the other, postmodernists. It is proposed to examine these two challenges and their educational implications showing that the educational consequences of communitarianism would be morally indefensible and that key propositions of postmodernism are either patently untenable or are less damaging to the educational goal of autonomy than might be supposed.

THE CHALLENGE OF COMMUNITARIANISM

The notion of individuals freely choosing their way of life from a full range of conceivable options and, furthermore, having some kind of a right to do so has been hotly contested, not to say to some extent derided, by a number of writers commonly referred to as communitarians, of whom MacIntyre (1981) and Sandel (1982) may be taken as exemplary.

In a society of individuals deemed equal and capable of choosing their own ways of life, as opposed to one that is hierarchically ruled or oriented towards certain traditional or other values, the fundamental concept of social regulation must be that of rights and furthermore, rights ultimately derived from that very equality and capacity. These delineate what we may legitimately expect from others in the way of abstentions and recipiences. We may expect that others will refrain from harming or interfering with us. Since we obey the law and refrain from taking the possessions of others, we may expect similar protection in our turn, and possibly some provision in circumstances of extreme need (Wringe 1981). The equivalent rights of others are legitimate constraints on the individual's own conduct. Apparent inequalities of rights in particular circumstances may be the justified consequence of trade-offs made by individuals either explicitly in the way of individual transactions such as bargains or contracts, or implicitly when we accept the enforcement of such instructions from institutional superiors or the civil authorities as are strictly necessary for the general well-being, from which we ourselves benefit. The perception of inequalities which cannot be justified in this way may lead to the claim that someone's rights are being infringed.

MacIntyre rejects such an account of the collective life, condemning all such rights claims as nothing but an assertion of an individual's will to power or expression of a desire to obtain something she does not have at the moment, and nothing more. By means of a number of strategically chosen examples, MacIntyre claims to show that such a conception of rights can only inflame conflicts of interest, without doing anything to resolve them.

For MacIntyre, in so far as rights may be spoken of at all, it can only be in the sense of those positive rights which derive from our position in society or in relation to certain others (as a free citizen, counsellor, trader, kinsman, friend, etc.). For him the fundamental guiding concept in our moral life should be that of virtue, namely those dispositions and qualities of character that serve and preserve the way of life of the community to which we belong. These qualities will differ according to the different roles individuals occupy, and from one society to another, for just as there are no universal, ahistorical human rights, so there are no universally valuable qualities, activities or achievements. Those things are valuable in a community which are valued by that community. To speak of rights without reference to the particular community values in which they are rooted would be like the use of isolated scientific or technical terms with no awareness of the web of scientific discourse to which they belong and in relation to which they have meaning.

The main focus of Sandel's contribution to the debate, which is essentially a critique of Rawls' *A Theory of Justice*, is to argue the logical impossibility of an unsocialised and, as Sandel puts it, 'unencumbered' self freely choosing its way of life without reference to the historical and social circumstances in which it chances to find itself. For Sandel, as indeed for MacIntyre, the prior question cannot be 'What should I do?' but 'Who am I?' The self does not choose its ends but is constituted by them. One's ends, therefore, cannot be chosen but are inescapably given.

If accepted at face value, these two arguments would seriously undermine the notion of an individual autonomously choosing her way of life in the light of reason alone, for the good life for her would be predetermined by the beliefs and practices of the society in which she lived. In a non-liberal society the interpretation of these might well be the prerogative of someone else. On such a view, the notion of the self standing back and rejecting the very ends by which it is constituted would be an act of spiritual self-extinction.

THE POSTMODERNIST CRITIQUE

At first sight, the challenge to the notion of rational autonomy posed by post-modernism would appear to be even more devastating than that of communitarianism, for whereas communitarianism simply denies the ability of the individual to choose freely in the light of reason, certain texts commonly referred to as postmodernist – for postmodernism certainly cannot be regarded as a single unified doctrine – deny not only the validity and liberating value of rationality as it has traditionally been understood, but also the possibility of an individual's coming to know and understand her situation in its social and political context, far less make meaningful and reliable value judgements and life choices on the basis of such knowledge and understanding.

The apparently most important postmodernist assertion in our present context, and the one which, if accepted as valid, would be of most devastating consequence to us as educators, is that which rejects truth as a possible characteristic of anything that can be written or said and, by obvious implication, denies the possibility of distinguishing statements which are true from those which are not. This claim would seem to deny the very conditions of both rational autonomy and rationality itself. Expression of this view by post-modernist writers may take a number of forms. All, however, stress the partial, corrupt or contingent nature of whatever happens to pass for knowledge at a particular time and regard as obsolete the so-called Enlightenment schemas of truth, reason, progress, moral obligation and so on (Deleuze 1984; Foucault 1991). What others might describe as true accounts, valid argument or well-tested theories are referred to in postmodernist speak by such value neutral or derogatory terms as discourses (Foucault 1973), rhetorics or phrase regimes (Lyotard 1988).

Correspondence or non-correspondence between what is the case and what is said or written is, on this view, essentially a non-issue. No particular statement or series of statements is allowed to claim 'privileged epistemic status' (Rorty 1991). Distinctions between different intellectual disciplines or categories of enquiry invoking different modes of authentication or tests for truth are necessarily irrelevant, for if there is no truth, there can be no tests for truth. At most there may be differences in styles of writing which are to be appraised and interpreted, if at all, in terms of expressiveness, metaphor and analogy and the absence of gross or conspicuous contradictions between sense and expression.

Thus, for example, Foucault (1973) shows quite convincingly how some forms of knowledge are inextricably linked to power and, far from ensuring the autonomy of individuals, serve to 'normalise' and control deviant individuals such as hospital patients, the insane or criminals. For Lyotard (1979), a cognitive mode of utterance making meaningfully true or false statements about isolated and contingent everyday matters is certainly possible. The quantity, diversity and sheer confusion of these, however, is such that if we wish to speak of more important matters affecting our destiny as a society or as individuals within it we must have recourse to a mode of discourse resembling the aesthetic and exemplified in Kant's discussion of the sublime. This may provide order, insight and perceptiveness to our understanding of the world, but is discontinuous with ordinary everyday cognitive discourse, and depends on metaphor, symbol, hyperbole and other devices of poetic language and, above all, may not be tested against the empirical and rational canons of the everyday cognitive mode. Fish (1989) and Rorty (1991) each give their own reasons for denying the possibility of standing outside the current consensus view on any matter and claim that attempts to do so are of no particular value or significance. Most radical of all, Baudrillard (1989) suggests that we are so bombarded with media stereotypes, political rhetoric and advertising images tuned to the transient moods of mass consumer demand that there would be no possibility of separating truth from falsehood about the world, even supposing such a distinction to be meaningful in principle.

In so far as we are concerned with the practical business of education, we need to adopt a coherent attitude to a body of writing which takes such a disturbing view of both social and institutional life and the conditions of human knowledge and experience.

In order to do this in a meaningful way we are bound to draw for examination from the body of writing concerned a number of explicit propositions, at the price, needless to say, of oversimplifying and to some extent therefore distorting what the texts have to say, and in full consciousness of the contradictions between so doing and the procedures of analysis and interpretation suggested by many of those texts themselves. Surprising as it may seem, such propositions are relatively few, relatively easy to identify and common, either explicitly or by implication, to many or most of the writers referred to as postmodernists. They might be thought to include some of the following:

- Except perhaps at a trivial level, the distinction between statements that are true and those that are not cannot be sustained.

- Methods largely devised at the beginning of the modern era for distinguishing statements that are meaningful and true from those that are not (recourse to evidence, rational argument, application of appropriate methods) are not decisive (notably Deleuze 1984).
- Reasons for believing the two points above include the following: our current bodies of knowledge and the methods by which they are authenticated may be shown to have originated in the particular historical context of certain specific power relations (Foucault 1973); everyday reality is too varied and confused to allow general statements to be made on the basis of them, and such general statements as can be made are untestable against reality (Lyotard 1988); the validity of all statements is limited by the context in which they are made (Fish 1989); our information about the world comes to us through systematically misleading sources (Baudrillard 1989).

EDUCATIONAL IMPLICATIONS OF THE TWO CHALLENGES

It will be seen that both communitarian and postmodernist challenges to our concept of rational autonomy would have certain educational implications. Before going on to assess the validity of those challenges, therefore, it is proposed to consider the educational stakes involved.

Community roles and statuses

It will be recalled that a principal justification for favouring individual autonomy and indeed for democracy itself was that there appears to be no good reason why anyone should, without further justification, be regarded as the subordinate of anyone else or be prevented from seeking the most satisfactory life, consistent with not interfering with the rights of others to do the same. This would appear to have three implications: first, that educational systems should embody the principle of equal educational opportunity irrespective of gender, social or ethnic origin, or whatever and that this should be maintained for as long as possible, even if at the later stages and for whatever reasons, students are allowed to prepare themselves for different occupational and other aspirations; second, that education should, for as long as possible, retain a generalist character making possible changes of career aspiration not only throughout the period of schooling but, indeed, as far as possible throughout life; third, mutual respect for individuals as equals and disregard for social status will be an appropriate goal of moral education.

If, by contrast, we took the view that the principal goal of moral education should be to instil the qualities and virtues appropriate to our predetermined roles as men, as women, as future persons in authority or future subordinates, then one might expect to find a divided educational system calculated to promote not autonomy and social mobility but acceptance of one's ascribed future role, expertise in the performance of that role and the promotion of virtues and attitudes appropriate to it.

Impossibility of the unencumbered self

Sandel's argument is that we cannot choose among a range of possible ways of life in a thoroughly detached way from the outside. Values do not, according to the communitarian position, reside in objects, activities or ways of life as such, but in the communities that value them. If we value some things rather than others it is because they are valued in our community. If this were so, the right to a truly open future would not only be unrealisable but also meaningless. The mere propositional knowledge that ways of life different from that pursued in the local community or restricted cultural sub-class in which the individuals found themselves would do little to raise the aspirations of our pupils. Such an explanation may, indeed be offered for certain of our educational failures (Willis 1977).

If, on the other hand, certain ways of life happened to be valued by the local community even though its older members had no access to it, as when a rural community is impressed by reports or television pictures of city life, the problem might be replaced by another in which the younger generation disvalued the traditional way of life in the village while failing to achieve a lifestyle in the town that corresponded to their expectations. If we were committed to the value and possibility of autonomy our response might be to seek to give pupils actual experience of alternative ways of life either in reality by such devices as boarding education, residential experience or school exchanges, or imaginatively through film, fiction or video. If, on the other hand, we were convinced that values had no other source than the community or if we considered that the moral or religious traditions of the community were of greater account than the right to autonomy in the choice of one's way of life then, far from seeking to widen pupils' experience, we should seek to ensure that our system of education embodied and transmitted those values with little reference to alternatives except as points of negative comparison. We might even wish to discourage or even forbid parents to educate their children according to other community traditions (Taylor 1992).

No truth, no rationality

At first sight, as we suggested, it would appear that the implications of postmodernism for commonly accepted notions of education would be devastating. Certainly it would be difficult to reconcile much of what postmodernists apparently have to say with the traditional view of the teacher's task to promote the autonomy of pupils by teaching them about the physical and social world and the world of values and enabling them to apply appropriate tests of validity to statements about them. If some of the assertions of Baudrillard, Rorty or Fish (in particular) are to be taken literally, then mathematical and scientific truth, judicious understanding of social and historical events and the motives and aspirations of others, a sense of justice and generosity, perceptiveness in aesthetic and speculative judgement and so on must stand on all fours with any kind of superstitious gibberish, fashionable nonsense, social prejudice or beastly ideology, while the task of correcting and guiding students' attempts to get things right – if it were possible at all – would become arbitrary oppression, a transparent exercise of the will of the stronger.

Possibly there are postmodernist texts which solicit precisely this reading. One of the most conspicuous of all aporias, however, is the way in which postmodernist writers, while denying the validity of truth claims, evidence or rationality, attempt to persuade us of their point of view with manifest conviction, reasoned argument with no conspicuous trace of rhetoric and, particularly in the case of Foucault, massive erudition. Clearly, in problematising modernist, i.e. Enlightenment, canons of appraisal, postmodernist writers seek to enhance our critical awareness rather than undermine it. Significantly, in 'What is Enlightenment?' Foucault (1991) no less than three times points to human liberty and autonomy as a goal to be achieved through becoming aware of the spurious and possibly disreputable genealogy of our modern structures of truth.

Being persuaded of the postmodernists' point of view while following their intellectual example would, therefore, not seem to commit us to an educational regime of mindless and stultifying iconoclasm. In this respect postmodernism is quite unlike a brand of aggressive relativism with class-oriented overtones which flourished in some educational circles in the 1970s. Indeed, it would seem likely that much of the content of education would remain somewhat as at present if not actually benefiting from increased critical acuity, breadth and profundity. There seems no reason why basic socialisation and initiation into the everyday courtesies and the conventional skills of reading and writing should be affected. Mathematics, science and technology would retain both their practical utility and their inherent elegance which rival attempts to characterise the material world would lack, as well, perhaps, as being taught with a little more modesty about their academic status as representing 'the' truth than is sometimes the case at present. It is difficult to see how the teaching of foreign languages would be affected for the worse; one might, indeed, expect language teachers of a postmodernist mentality to be more respectful of a range of non-standard idioms than their more traditional counterparts. One might also expect the study of history and the other social science disciplines to be enriched by a postmodernist perspective which questioned common assumptions more rigorously than is sometimes done at present. The postmodernist perspective is already well established in the study of literature and the arts under a variety of names including, in the Anglo-Saxon world, that of Cultural Studies. On whichever side one stands in the controversy over what should constitute the proper canon of such studies (see Martin 1993), one must accept that the controversy itself legitimately forms part of, enriches and extends our understanding of this subject area.

From the above, it might appear that, provided we are prepared to look at what postmodernists actually do in the course of their writing rather than at their more sweeping generalisations, a postmodernist perspective might support rather than threaten the sort of education that favours individual autonomy. It also has the advantage of enabling us, in seeking to promote and encourage the autonomy of others, to give due weight to individual temperament and inclination, as well as purely contingent and temporary elements in one's background, biography and motivation, rather than insisting that goals that can be rationally defended by an unbroken chain of reasoning rooted ultimately in a transcendental argument are always to be preferred (Peters 1966).

BUT ARE THE CHALLENGES VALID?

Common to both our challenges is rejection of the picture of the Enlightenment human being, already socialised into the values of justice and peace and already equipped with the powers of right reason, calmly and objectively surveying an exhaustive menu of human options and choosing among them with the aid of incontrovertible rationality. Clearly there has never been a historical individual whose powers and situation have been thus. But the question is whether this is a plausible ideal towards which, as educators, it is appropriate for us to strive.

In addressing MacIntyre's negative response to this question, we must begin by rejecting his dismissal of the concept of equal rights, given that he provides no reason why anyone should willingly acquiesce in a regime in which their rights were less than equal to those of others, however venerable the tradition by which the regime was hallowed and however unrealistic the individual's chances of actually changing the situation. What might with more justice be asserted is that the qualities, virtues and activities we value may, as a matter of fact, contingently result from the social context in which we find ourselves at a young age. With John White (1990) we might add that it is politic, in so far as this is consistent with the avoidance of indoctrination, to encourage the young to develop qualities and become committed to pursuits and activities from which society as a whole may benefit. But in our global society, our knowledge and possibilities of communication are such that we are no longer limited for our role models to our immediate kinship, or ethnic or local group and no longer limited when envisaging meaningful modes of existence to the acceptance of a range of traditional roles. This is not to say that the range of possibilities is infinite. There will be personal, material and social constraints; we can only live the life that is consistent with the members of some social group somewhere also living the life they wish to live. But to someone in even a moderately affluent group, the actual range of options may be great, and bear little relation to the life led hitherto by any other member of that group.

The above comments will also be relevant to our appraisal of Sandel's criticism of the liberal doctrine of rational autonomy. Of course, we cannot simply choose and develop our way of life in a vacuum. Even the most independent of us must to some extent build on and develop the models we see around us if our fellow human beings are not to be totally nonplussed by our behaviour. Our choices at any point will be partly the results of goals we had embraced before we came to make that choice and which were, as Sandel with some justification maintains, constitutive of our identity. But this identity is not fixed. It has been part of the legacy of Existentialism, but had in any case long been a theme of western and no doubt other literatures, that in the course of our lives, circumstances oblige us to make choices, often painful and sometimes tragic, in which we abandon or betray an existing identity or choose a course of action which will result in our finding a new one.

The challenge posed to the notion of autonomy by postmodernism is, in a sense, the contrary to that of the communitarians. Whereas communitarianism might be construed as suggesting that the individual is or legitimately may be closely constrained in her choices, the views we have centrally attributed to the postmodernists suggest that there is no basis in truth or reason upon which sound choices may be made. From the view that chains of argument are simply alternative discourses to be taken up or rejected according to prevailing fashion or systems of power relations, it may seem but a short step to the conclusion that 'anything goes'.

For traditional philosophers confronting postmodernism the temptation is to make a short way with it by means of some version of the 'self-referring' objection. Since postmodernists cast doubt on the notion of truth, we can scarcely believe what they say. If they claim that rationality is problematic, we must regard their own arguments as suspect, and so on. It may also be said that by denying the validity of such things as truth, evidence and rationality and admitting the existence of only rhetoric and consensual opinion, certain postmodernists provide themselves in advance with knockdown arguments against all contrary opinions. In this they may be accused of resorting to the debating ploys of the psychoanalyst who treats all criticism, however well founded, as simply evidence of repression, or religious fundamentalists who regard all contrary evidence as part of the deceptive work of the devil. Such people may be thought to place themselves beyond the pale of reasoned debate.

A more significant criticism is that many of the apparently more provocative postmodernist assertions, or rather denials, for these are usually rejections of what are taken to be the assumptions of ordinary folk and non-postmodernist thinkers, turn out to be simply a mixture of highly dubious and certainly unsustainable generalisations, and claims that, once stated in sober terms, are perfectly acceptable to traditional philosophers.

Thus, for example, when Baudrillard claims that no valid understanding of social and political processes is possible because our impressions are entirely based on contingent media images, this is clearly false. Many people have access to other sources of information and in any case, it would be quite implausible to suppose that media images were entirely independent of the way things are. The not infrequent suggestion that there is no such thing as 'the way things' are is nonsense. If things are not one way, they must be another, and some attempts to communicate the way they are will be nearer the mark than others. Again it is implausible to suggest that we are never capable of discriminating between competing descriptions, even though we may sometimes fail to do so, and even though no particular description may ultimately be beyond further scrutiny.

On the other hand, the claim that 'the way things are' is necessarily made from a certain perspective and using a certain vocabulary is perfectly true and comes as no great surprise to anyone. When we make such statements, we simply assume that our perspectives and our interpretations of the expressions used are shared by those for whose benefit we are speaking. In this we are sometimes disappointed, and this is how misunderstandings arise. We cannot, of course, be sure that there is ever a direct match between what the speaker or writer intends and what is understood. Nevertheless, what we come to believe as the result of the words of others is often confirmed by our own experience. No one, furthermore, is so foolish as to suppose that this forms part of something called 'THE TRUTH' that will be steadily and progressively revealed to humankind until it is all laid out before us in a form that is immutable, uncontestable and unambiguous.

In the light of the above, we may perhaps feel that we need not take too seriously the apparent threat posed by postmodernism to the project of coming to understand the world and on the basis of that understanding, reaching sensible and independent decisions about how we should live our lives within it. On the contrary, once we have got beyond the discouraging scepticism of what might be called the 'metaphysics of postmodernism' the process and practice of radically questioning many of the fundamental assumptions of the Enlightenment and other more recent progressivist doctrines must prove supportive rather than detrimental to the individual's search for autonomy.

Apart from purely material or physical constraints, the two principal barriers to rational autonomy are not knowing what options are available and the stubborn and persistent belief that certain options are ruled out on either rational or moral grounds. It has been a widely recognised feature of thought in the modern (i.e. post-Enlightenment) era, to encourage speculation and hypothesis, but within relatively rigid frameworks and subject to the test of fairly closely specified categories of evidence. Possibly, something of the kind is the *sine qua non* of rigorous thought and intellectual progress. Conceivably, however, some of our reasoning has been unduly constrained and some of our conclusions regarding what is possible, what is valuable and what is permissible on moral grounds (Foucault 1991) may have been unduly limiting. Undoubtedly, in the past, philosophers, (especially philosophers of education) have, with apparently impeccable logic, overestimated the value of intellectual pursuits and underestimated other modes of achieving a flourishing life (Hirst 1994). Utilitarian goals, long-term prudence, consistency and the avoidance of internal conflict in the conduct of one's life have all figured prominently among the outcomes which educators, from an adult perspective, have recommended to the young for their reasoned acceptance. If acquaintance with certain postmodernist texts can do something to undermine our adult assurance of the undoubted value of these, the cause of youthful autonomy may not have been entirely ill-served.

NOTE

An earlier version of this chapter appeared as 'Two challenges to the notion of rational autonomy and their educational implications', *Educational Philosophy and Theory*, 27, 2, 1995, pp. 49–63.

REFERENCES

Baudrillard, J. (1989) *Selected Writings*, ed. M. Poster, Cambridge: Cambridge University Press.

Crittenden, B. (1978) 'Autonomy as an aim of education' in Strike, K. and Egan, K. (eds) *Ethics and Educational Policy* London: Routledge & Kegan Paul, 105–26.

Dearden, R. (1972) 'Autonomy and education' in Dearden, R., Hirst, P. and Peters, R. S. (eds) *Education and the Development of Reason*, London: Routledge & Kegan Paul, 448–65.

Dearden, R. (1975) 'Autonomy as an educational ideal' in Brown, S. C. (ed.) *Philosophers Discuss Education*, London: Macmillan, 3–18.

Deleuze, G. (1984) *Kant's Critical Philosophy: The Doctrine of the Faculties*, trans. H. Tomlinson and B. Habberjam, London: Athlone Press.

Fish, S. (1989) *Doing what Comes Naturally: Change, Rhetoric and the Practice of Theory in Literary and Legal Studies*, Durham, NC: Duke University Press.

Foucault, M. (1973) *The Birth of the Clinic: An Archaeology of Medical Perceptions*, trans. A. Sheridan, New York: Pantheon.

Foucault, M. (1978) *Discipline and Punish*, trans. A. Sheridan, New York: Pantheon.

Foucault, M. (1991) 'What is Enlightenment?' in Rabinow, P. (ed.) *The Foucault Reader*, Harmondsworth: Penguin, 32–50.

Hirst, P. H. (1994) 'Education, knowledge and practices' in R. Barrow and P. White (eds) *Beyond Liberal Education: Essays in Honour of Paul H. Hirst*, London: Routledge.

Jonathan, R. (1983) 'The manpower services model of education', *Cambridge Journal of Education*, 13, 2, 3–10.

Lyotard, J.-F. (1979) *La condition postmoderne: rapport sur la savoir*, Paris: Editions de Minuit.

Lyotard, J.-F. (1988) *The Differend: Phrases in Dispute*, trans. G. van der Abbeele, Manchester: Manchester University Press.

MacIntyre, A. (1981) *After Virtue*, London: Duckworth.

Martin, J. R. (1993) 'Curriculum and the mirror of knowledge' in Barrow, R. and White, P. (eds) *Beyond Liberal Education: Essays in Honour of Paul H. Hirst*, London: Routledge, 32–48.

Peters, R. S. (1966) *Ethics and Education*, London: George Allen and Unwin.

Peters, R. S. (1973) 'The justification of education' in Peters, R. S. (ed.) *The Philosophy of Education*, London: Oxford University Press, 239–68.

Rorty, R. (1989) *Contingency, Irony and Solidarity*, Cambridge: Cambridge University Press.

Rorty, R. (1991) *Objectivity, Relativism and Truth*, Cambridge: Cambridge University Press.

Sandel, M. (1982) *Liberalism and the Limits of Justice*, Cambridge: Cambridge University Press.

Taylor, C. (1992) 'The politics of recognition' in Taylor, C. (ed.) *Multiculturalism and the Politics of Recognition*, Cambridge: Cambridge University Press, 25–74.

White, J. (1982) *The Aims of Education Restated*, London: Routledge & Kegan Paul.

White, J. (1990) *Education and the Good Life*, London: Kogan Page.

Willis, P. (1977) *Learning to Labour*, Guildford: Saxon House.

Wringe, C. (1981) *Children's Rights: A Philosophical Study*, London: Routledge & Kegan Paul.

11

THE EDUCATION OF AUTONOMOUS CITIZENS

Richard Smith

Education, access to accurate analysis by those better placed than ourselves, and so on, may help to clarify the distal reasons for our proximal experience, and such access therefore becomes in itself a form of power because it gives us a degree of (only potential) control over what happens to us.

(David Smail 1993: 66)

INTRODUCTION

Deep-rooted tendencies in talk of education (western, at any rate) imply an individual, even solitary, learner. An infant teacher ticks boxes to inform next year's teacher that Daniel can 'choose appropriate operations to solve subtraction problems'. This does not allow for the possibility that he may be able to carry out this mathematical task in the company of Chelsey and Peter, who are models of concentration, collegiality and persistence, but not when he shares a table with Paul and Donna, whom maths fills with contagious panic and despair. So too with intelligence in general. We readily forget how much what we take to be our individual intelligence is a function of the group in which we find ourselves: of the respect with which its members treat each other, of the possibilities which the group allows of taking risks, venturing opinions, advancing tentative ideas. I shall have something to say later about other qualities, such as courage and unhappiness, that also tend, perhaps misleadingly, to be seen essentially as functions of individuals.

Many of the well-known problems with autonomy, I shall argue in this chapter, are likewise caused by our deep-rooted tendency to think of persons first and foremost atomistically. Rather we need to regard persons as members of groups from the start, their very being and identity constituted by such membership, and to conceive autonomy in interpersonal rather than intrapersonal terms. To adopt terminology from Seyla Benhabib (1992), autonomy and the rationality to which it is connected must be seen not in 'legislative' terms but in 'interactive' ones, in the same entirely non-mysterious way as intelligence.

I am sceptical about the continuing usefulness of the idea of autonomy. Like all political and philosophical notions, 'autonomy' came into being at a specific historical juncture to do a particular job. Autonomy, to repeat a familiar story, came into its own in Kantian and post-Kantian philosophy to assert the importance of the freedom of the moral will from patriarchy, particularly from the church and modes of political authority. Here we can see, with some clarity, what the problem was that autonomy was intended to solve, what benefits it was intended to bring humankind. More recently, at the time when modern philosophy of education was asserting its academic credentials, emphasis on autonomy was a way of insisting that education, properly so called, is premised on the demands of reason rather than on, say, growth, socialisation, self-expression or creativity. Thus 'autonomy' played a key role in the critique of 'progressivism'. Whatever the general merits of this critique, and although the sovereignty of reason can be questioned, as I have indicated above, it is again clear here what autonomy is *for*, what evils it is meant to preserve us from. It may be that autonomy, torn from its historical setting, is a prominent one of those 'fragments of a conceptual scheme, parts which now lack those contexts from which their significance derived' (MacIntyre 1982: 2).

For in western and westernised societies now 'autonomy' typically works alongside notions of choice and 'the market', separating individual persons from their world and from their fellows, the better to render them subject to control, particularly the control of government, multinational industry and advertising. It threatens, in the name of freedom, to re-shape the emotional lives and identities of young people especially, alienating them from the aesthetic and reflective modes of being in favour of slick versions of evaluation, 'weighing up the alternatives' and 'deciding what I really want' that weigh the odds in favour of the sophisticated forms of colonisation that threaten us. Thus 'autonomy' has become a dangerous ally. Offering, like the goblin in the fairy-tale, to turn the straw of our determined, contingent world into the gold of pure freedom, it threatens in the end to come back and claim the children it promised to save.

Nevertheless, we can hardly do without the idea of autonomy in the end, for this would be to risk abandoning the marginalised and disempowered of our societies. But the variety of autonomy likely to prove useful to them is one which emphasises that our freedom is to be found in what we do with and for each other on the public stage, in reasoning, arguing, supporting, challenging and confronting, as particular occasions require, not the variety that suggests there is a determinate end-point of rationality, the same for all, guaranteeing civilised consensus. Thus towards the end of this chapter I indicate that the kind of autonomy we need requires a particular account of citizenship, of our engagement with each other in the public world.

PROBLEMS WITH AUTONOMY

In the philosophical tradition, of course, autonomy is significantly connected with reason. The connection is as old as Plato, for whom the prisoners in the cave achieve liberation in so far as they exercise their capacity for using their intellects and perceiving reality accurately, and the internal links between freedom and reason are definitively set out by Kant. The oddity of this can be noted first by attending to Isaiah Berlin's now familiar distinction between negative and positive liberty (1969). The former consists in seeing our freedom as freedom from and freedom to: freedom from particular restrictions and freedom to exercise particular rights or choices. The latter by contrast is essentially a matter of putting our destiny into the appropriate hands: those of God, for example, or the state. Recent philosophy has tended to cast freedom and autonomy in the positive way. Our freedom is seen, along Kantian lines, as consisting in the cultivation of reason, our capacity for rationality. It is thus sharply intrapersonal. Within this relatively traditional framework we can identify part of the oddity as the paradox of achieving freedom by giving over control, albeit to a faculty within us. To recent writers all this suggests that something has gone amiss with the notion of the self within which all this is somehow going on, and so there emerges the more radical critique of reason as 'self-transparent and self-grounding', part of the 'illusion of having found an Archimedean standpoint, situated beyond historical and cultural contingency' (Benhabib 1992: 4).

Some defence against these criticisms has been sought in the hierarchical theory of the will. On this view we are the more autonomous in so far as we formulate higher-order desires: desires to have, or to reject, lower-order wants and desires. A teenager addicted to television soap operas, say, may formulate, after critical reflection on his or her interests and habits, the higher-order preference either to embrace whole-heartedly or to abjure the watching of such programmes. Thus the theory seeks to replace the substantively empty picture of reason as 'self-transparent and self-grounding' with a picture of reason as essentially critical reflection. Two important influences on this view of autonomy have been Frankfurt's paper 'Freedom of the will and the concept of a person' (Frankfurt 1971) and Taylor's notion of 'strong evaluation' which offers standards by which desires, inclinations and choices can themselves be judged (Taylor 1985). Dworkin (1988: 20) offers a summary of this conception of autonomy as:

a second-order capacity of persons to reflect critically upon their first-order preferences, desires, wishes, and so forth and the capacity to accept or attempt to change these in light of higher-order preferences and values. By exercising such a capacity, persons define their nature, give meaning and coherence to their lives, and take responsibility for the kind of person they are.

129

Now there seems to be both something very right in this picture of autonomy and something very wrong. The emphasis on the scrutiny of consciousness does justice both to our aspiration not to be controlled by others and to our sense that our occurrent desires are unreliable guides to a life which, viewed as a whole, we would endorse as satisfactory. What is wrong is that our second-order wishes, arrived at by critical reflection, are no more guaranteed to be worthy of that endorsement. The strategies that alcoholics, for example, adopt to avoid recognising their dependency are notorious. Here the second-order desire – not to stop drinking dangerously suddenly, perhaps – is not only no more sound than the first-order craving but appears the product of a particularly sophisticated heteronomy. Or consider how advertisers sell us not a simple product but the idea of a lifestyle in which it prominently figures, and supply us with a set of concepts in which to conduct second- and third-order evaluation favourable to what they are trying to sell. Note here the significance in the United Kingdom, for example, both of chain-stores called 'Choices' and 'Principles' and, again, of government policies emphasising choice and 'the market'. The idea that 'critical reflection' takes us to a level of autonomous evaluation is a nonsense when the tools of such reflection have manifestly been fixed. John Holloway (1983: 22–3) notes that the supermarket permits us to take down all kinds of things from the shelves, so many that we forget 'that there are certain things which we are unable to buy, like silence for the rest of the day, or the chance to do something which we shall think truly worthwhile. Choice is wonderfully free, and so we are free to be our spontaneous selves. But we are less free to be our reflecting selves'.

What, though, if the reflecting self has become subject to manipulation just as much as the self-as-chooser? It may be said, of course, that this is precisely why, fearing the illegitimate influences of others, we look to the self to carry out its own reflection and scrutiny. But there can be no kind of guarantee here. Given a limited or skewed set of terms in which to conduct reflection the individual's reflection will itself be limited or skewed, more so perhaps than the first-order desires which in their very unarticulatedness maintain some defence against external violation and manipulation. (This is why George Orwell, in *Nineteen Eighty-Four*, gives Winston Smith a key to the true past in the taste and smell of chocolate and coffee, where desire and memory do not need the intermediary of words whose meaning can be corrupted.) If, then, as is sometimes said, 'autonomy' tends to be used as a kind of philosophical stop, an indication that no further justification can be given or argument attempted, then 'rationality' and notions of critical reflection operate within the concept of autonomy as an even more desperate back-stop. It will not do to say that people are autonomous to the extent that they give reasons for their actions: as noted above, rationalisations have the same structure as good reasons and can be distinguished from them only by our empirical sense of what is and what is not an evasion, a subterfuge, a piece of self-deception.

Here, it may seem, we reach an *impasse* in the philosophy of autonomy. On the one hand writers in the 'liberal' tradition incline to the view that whatever may be imperfect in the individual's exercise of choice still that is what we have in the end to grant authority to in the kind of society most of us in the west would prefer to live in, and the hierarchical theory does at least acknowledge the importance of scrutinising one's choices. On the other hand choices, needs and wants may be 'superimposed upon the individual by particular social interests in his repression' (Marcuse 1964: 4–5); the prevalence of 'false consciousness' vitiates not just our choices but our evaluation of our choices. There is *prima facie* plausibility in the idea of 'false consciousness' in a world where we learn more and more about the ways in which advertising, the media and those who 'sell' politicians to us operate.

There is both an empirical and a philosophical point to make here about critical reflection. It is, I would say, a matter of empirical fact that we are not well-equipped to penetrate our own subterfuges and rationalisations, those frequent outcomes of second- and third-order reflection. Knowing this well we turn to others for help when we undertake surveys of our first-order commitments, especially at times of crisis. Our increasing sense of the importance of involving others here perhaps accounts for the growth of those 'technologies of the self', as MacIntyre (1982) calls them, such as counselling, whatever theoretical reservations we may hold about them (of which more below). We see the flaws in others' reflections, and they in ours, more easily than we do our own. Few would deny this obvious truth. Yet writers on autonomy often write as if it were not so, fearful that the influence of other people inevitably compromises autonomy. If that is the case, then so much the worse for autonomy. It is not the idea of critical reflection that is at fault here, I emphasise, but the Cartesian model according to which that reflection is essentially done by the solitary individual before and as a basis for venturing out into the public world of subliminal influence, coercive persuasion and other perils. The philosophical point is of course that this Cartesian heritage can be rejected. We can see knowledge as a social and not an individual achievement: the knowing that enters into autonomy can be seen as a function of our shared world rather than as something built up by the solitary self on the foundations of what presents itself as indubitable to the individual consciousness.

Many feminist writers now plausibly claim that talk of autonomy as a goal, in education as in life more widely, seems to presuppose male children and male learners. Women are simply less inclined to conceive their identity in individualistic terms as separate from other people around them. They see their selves as contained in their relationships and may centre their ethics on notions such as 'caring' (cp. the writings of Nel Noddings in particular) rather than the Kantian nexus around 'autonomy'. They may celebrate dependence and interdependence rather than the independence which is the correlate of autonomy (cp. Griffiths and Smith 1989). It is not that they *reject* autonomy, for the right to form their identities by their own lights is as dear to them as to anybody. What they generally reject is the atomistic conception of the individual that is so often implicit in discussions of autonomy. They would perhaps agree with Cuypers (1992: 15) who concludes his critique of personal autonomy as 'the first principle of education' by claiming that in what he describes as the motivational field 'we want our children to become *devoted* and *sociable* people instead of detached observers or cool manipulators'.

While still considering the problems with the notion of autonomy it is worth noticing that the search for a more narrowly specifiable and determinate content to rationality often leads to 'principles': moral autonomy 'represents a particular conception of morality – one that, among other features, places a heavy emphasis on rules and principles rather than virtues and practices' (Dworkin 1988: 47). Principles are supposed to be universalisable and offer the assurance that we are not being moved by self-centred desires. Yet principles are eminently well-suited to register the self-satisfaction of the social isolate. Here, for example, is Dickens describing, in *Hard Times* (Book II, ch. 1), the young man, Bitzer, product of Mr Gradgrind's model school. Not for him the heteronomy of desire:

> His mind was so exactly regulated, that he had no affections or passions. All his proceedings were the result of the nicest and coldest calculation; and it was not without cause that Mrs Sparsit habitually observed of him, that he was a young man of the steadiest principle she had ever known. Having satisfied himself, on his father's death, that his mother had a right of settlement in Coketown, this excellent young economist had asserted that right for her with such a steadfast adherence to the principle of the case, that she had been shut up in the workhouse ever since.

Bitzer's principles are conceived in the loneliness of his own narrow world where feelings have failed to do their normal job of connecting him with other people. They are not the outcome of, nor are they submitted to, interpersonal examination. Still worse, in one of his rare and attenuated personal relationships Mrs Sparsit encourages him in the idea that this makes him a 'man of principle'.

This, then, is where we seem to be situated at present. We need to find some release from the forces that drive us into isolated individualism, the inner sanctuary from which we emerge as lonely individuals to enjoy the benefits of 'the market' and the supermarket. Autonomy as it has usually been conceived does not look to be the key of that release. Where shall we turn?

THE COLLECTIVE TURN

Whether people learn some determinate content or task better on their own or when working in groups will always depend in part on the precise task or content. As I noted at the beginning of this chapter, however, there are aspects of our mental lives that we *must* conceive in more than individualistic terms. Indeed the social or dialogic nature of cognition has been a theme of the influential school of thought known as social constructionism. From work inspired by the psychologist Lev Vygotsky to writing that broadly follows Jurgen Habermas, good grounds have been developed for conceiving rationality in discursive, communicative or dialogic terms, for concluding that 'our ratiocinative capacities are formed by the internalization of communicative interactions we have with others from a very early age' (Burbules 1993: 11–12).

This conception of rationality provides a basis for reconsidering numerous aspects of educational practice. For example, the study of literature arguably reproduces many features of the individualistic, Cartesian tradition, and the rise of the novel is often held to mirror the development of modern ideas of privacy and the self. Reading has become an essentially private activity, and the canonical novels of English literature frequently celebrate the lonely individual defying public opinion. Issues of power are generally ignored in favour of an 'aesthetic' reading, and so literature becomes removed from the public space of history and politics (Knights 1992). Where creative writing is undertaken this is often in the name of the freeing of an inner, repressed or 'secret' self that had been living an underground life, as it were, beneath the social world.

Yet it is possible to read literature in a way that brings group resources to bear on the pathology of reading. Reading a poem or a novel, for instance, may involve tolerating a high degree of ambiguity and deferral of the satisfaction of finding a unitary meaning. A study-group's own relationships of mutual tolerance and patience, or the reverse, determine whether it can let different meanings emerge or must demand immediately to know 'what the author means'. Particular readings may be 'marginalised' along with the members of the group that suggest them, or they may be respected, even if not wholly understood or integrated into the mainstream interpretation current in the classroom. We see here ways in which the dynamics of the group and the teacher's handling of its dynamics has the potential to liberate certain readings and readers and to repress, even oppress, others (cp. Knights 1992: *passim* and especially ch. 2).

To take an example: an adult group appeared reluctant to read Shakespeare's *Henry V* before it had been 'told about' the contemporary historical background and what several members recalled as the 'kingship debate' in Shakespeare. Acceding to such a request can lead to confirmation of the fear that Shakespeare is 'difficult' and not to be confronted without the protection of extensive academic knowledge; and this in turn can confirm the suspicion of less confident students that Shakespeare is not for them. Here it was important to help students to see that the 'kingship debate' is only one level on which the play operates, just as the level of the play's insights into father–son relationships, apparently open to a more instinctive and unacademic reading, is also one level among many. Students may be comfortable with different readings for various reasons, but a group that works well together has the power both to validate each other's approaches and ideas and to open up further approaches for each other.

All this is to insist that modes of education can be developed which offer us back a public space in which we can draw upon the resources of our fellow-learners. We can help each other to penetrate the subterfuges and mystifications of power, as one member of my *Henry V* group, by her unacademic and untutored, but manifestly intelligent, comments on the play helped to free others from their fear that they would somehow be caught out unless they approached literature with notes, interpretive works and detailed knowledge of the author's life and times.

Thus the idea of communicative or interactive rationality, which appears to be of a high level of theoretical generality, can readily be found in application when we take seriously group dynamics in learning. It is possible without difficulty to find examples of the way that our progress towards a quality of consciousness relatively clear of deceptions, self-deceptions and delusions as well as such baggage of the past that we do not, on reflection, want to carry further and so to a kind of autonomy is often best undertaken in the company of others. On this journey the rationality that is co-extensive with autonomy is not a determinate and pre-ordained destination, the same for all; it is a function of the rich and complex activity of giving reasons to each other. Whether a good reason really is a good reason 'depends on how well it "holds its own" in the dialogue between us' (Smith 1985).

Dialogue does not *guarantee* that other people will help us towards autonomy rather than systematically confuse us or use us for their own ends. The only good fellow-dialecticians are those whom we can trust. We can certainly form second-order desires to restrain or give rein to our first-order wants, as the hierarchical theory has it. But we can also choose the company of those whom we know to have our interests at heart, who are capable of distinguishing our needs from their own, and who will even oppose our will when they judge it right. Autonomy is not something we can best achieve on our own.

FRIENDS, COUNSELLORS, CITIZENS

Autonomy, then, should not be thought of in terms of an essentially individualistic journey towards an abstract and determinate rationality, but as a process involving other people in which reasons are demanded and given in dialectic. And if autonomy means having a degree of control over our lives, then we have to help each other understand the ways in which power is taken from us and exercised over us.

This is especially significant when we suffer from the profound lack of autonomy that is psychological distress: depression, anxiety, neurosis and so on are conditions in which to the highest degree we feel ourselves driven, possessed or 'sunk in the depths of', paralysed, our volition immobilised. Sometimes, of course, these are clinical conditions in need of clinical solutions. It is possible, however, that in many cases the problems that people take to doctors, counsellors and therapists are not best seen as functions of their individual pathology but as effects of what has been done to them. In several books David Smail argues powerfully that a good deal of distress which leads people to think there is 'something wrong with them' can be traced rather to changing circumstances of public, professional or institutional life which have seriously undermined the 'patient's' sources of self-esteem and their basis for relating to other people. An accountant, for example, becomes prone to fits of incapacitating anxiety when the altered conditions of his professional world require him to change from being a highly competent and well-qualified accountant who can take pride in his skills and to turn into someone who sells the company's 'image' at business presentations (Smail 1993: 130 ff.). This man, like many of the people Smail describes, is the victim of forces whose origin lies, very distant from him, in the world of international finance, multinational firms and the shifting world of business practice. Remote and baffling forces do us harm that becomes internalised as 'my fault', 'what is wrong with me'. In such cases 'distal power becomes mediated proximally as psychological or emotional distress' (ibid.: 99).

Part of the problem, Smail suggests (following Sennett, *The Fall of Public Man*), is that we have largely lost the 'public space' in which to discuss these things with one another. Actions of politicians may have a huge impact on our lives, but this is difficult to acknowledge and debate in a culture where it is almost indecent to talk politics 'except at carefully prescribed times and places' and in 'those arenas specially constructed to contain it' (Smail 1987: 147). This amounts to a form of repression whose effect is to allow the forces which might otherwise be penetrated and challenged by political awareness to flourish unchecked (ibid.: 56). Meanwhile the therapy or counselling which could contribute to a solution by helping people to perceive the 'distal powers' and their effects often becomes absorbed instead in analysis of its own processes, such as the question of 'transference' between client and therapist (Smail 1993: ch. 3).

Acting morally towards each other, Smail (1987: 161) concludes, that is with a concern for each other's well-being, requires moral space. That can only be created by people acting together on the political and not merely personal level. 'We shall have to force open around ourselves a moral space which gives us room for concerted action, and this can only be done through the re-insertion into that space of a "public dimension"' (ibid.: 161).

This is not in most cases a business for professionals and specialists, for therapists and counsellors. It is for all of us, as friends, colleagues and fellow-citizens, to help each other in unmasking the sources of unhappiness and heteronomy, the 'distal powers' that, to our distress, take control of our lives away from us. Sometimes, simply, this is what friends are for: to help us see ordinary truths about our lives which our own perspective makes obscure to us. Sometimes, however, we do need the experienced counsellor who can help us unravel the complexities of our evasions, or resist the manipulations and bear with the hostility that sometimes seem to go with certain forms of hurt and unhappiness.

As fellow citizens we have the opportunity to create and participate in the kinds of groups and collectives ('political associations, movements, citizens' groups, town meetings and public fora', Benhabib suggests, 1992: 101) which sharpen our awareness both of the sources of power and the nature of its abuses on one hand and of the ways to claim back control of our lives on the other. As Benhabib notes, liberal conceptions of citizenship and 'public space' (ch. 3), with their tendency to focus on the limits and justifications of state power, are not well designed to remind us of the importance of these more local forms of association. Perhaps, as she suggests, we need something more like a 'discursive model' in which public space is 'viewed democratically as the creation of procedures whereby those affected by general social norms and by collective political decisions can have a say in their formation' (ibid.: 105), a notion of participation which goes beyond the 'narrowly defined political realm' to those areas which we sometimes think of as social and cultural. (And so, incidentally, as more private. It is 'his choice' whether or not to drive a fast car or eat meat.)

A participationist model of citizenship would be opposed to 'integrationist' models which look for consensus and emphasise the revival and regeneration of values at the expense of institutional solutions (Benhabib 1992: 77). This contrast makes much sense of recent trends in the UK where, famously, Prime Minister John Major has painted a cosy picture of 'a nation at ease with itself', watching cricket and drinking warm beer, and ministers have attempted to confer pariah status on those such as single mothers. Such visions of consensus are linked to the ideal of a shared, substantive rationality of the sort that I have argued is a fatal flaw in prevailing versions of autonomy. We need to move to a simpler idea of autonomy as comprising an understanding of where power over us is held and how it is maintained and exercised, together with a degree of ability to act in concert with each other to take back that power and control our own lives; a sense that 'we have a say in the economic, political and civic arrangements which define our lives together, and that what one does makes a difference' (ibid.: 81).

A reconstituted notion of autonomy might do more to underpin education which foregrounds ideas of citizenship and co-operation than all the current ideology of the market, despite its origins in notions of public space (the *agora*) and exchange. That is a striking irony. If it is not the product of one more confusion inflicted on us, it is certainly one that we shall have to go on helping each other to sort out.

ACKNOWLEDGEMENT

I am grateful to the School of Education and the Staff Travel Fund of the University of Durham for support in the preparation of this paper.

REFERENCES

Benhabib, S. (1992) *Situating the Self*, Cambridge: Polity Press.

Berlin, I. (1969) *Four Essays on Liberty*, Oxford: Oxford University Press.

Burbules, N. (1993) *Dialogue in Teaching*, New York: Teachers College Press.

Cuypers, S. (1992) 'Is personal autonomy the first principle of education?', *Journal of Philosophy of Education,* 26.1.

Dworkin, G. (1988) *The Theory and Practice of Autonomy*, Cambridge: Cambridge University Press.

Frankfurt, H. (1971) 'Freedom of the will and the concept of a person', *Journal of Philosophy*, LXVIII. 1.

Griffiths, M. and Smith, R. (1989) 'Standing alone: dependence, independence and interdependence in the practice of education', *Journal of Philosophy of Education*, 23.2.

Holloway, J. (1983) *The Slumber of Apollo*, Cambridge: Cambridge University Press.

Knights, B. (1992) *From Reader to Reader: Theory, Text and Practice in the Study Group*, London: Harvester.

MacIntyre, A. (1982) *After Virtue*, London: Duckworth.

Marcuse, H. (1964) *One Dimensional Man*, London: Routledge.

Sennett, R. (1980) *Authority*, London: Secker & Warburg.

Smail, D. (1987) *Taking Care: An Alternative to Therapy*, London: J.M. Dent & Sons.

Smail, D. (1993) *The Origins of Unhappiness*, London: HarperCollins.

Smith, R. (1985) *Freedom and Discipline*, London: Allen & Unwin.

Taylor, C. (1985) *Human Agency and Language*, Cambridge: Cambridge University Press.

12

POST-TOTALITARIAN
LIBERALISM AND EDIFICATION

James S. Kaminsky

INTRODUCTION

In the 1990s we exist in a unique time. It is a time when both tolerance and intolerance are in cultural ascendancy. Both freedom and oppression are at home in the world. The origin of today's contentious cultural politics are tightly tied to two events: 1) the re-emergence of a nationalistic religious and political fundamentalism; and 2) the intellectual collapse of the Hegelian Marxist epic. The signature theme of the present, then, is the appearance of a contentious cultural politics in which tolerance and intolerance prowl around each other in an unsettling and puzzling dance.

The resurgence of a nationalistic intolerant and oppressive religious fundamentalism in the United States and the medieval politics of the Christian Right has been marked by the licensing of the Christian Broadcasting Network by Pat Robertson in 1972 and the success of tele-evangelists like Jimmy Swaggert, Jim and Tammy Baker, Robert Schuller, and the popularity of Pat Buchannan's paternalistic, oppressive and exclusionary politics in the 1996 Republican primary elections. Its reactionary nationalism has been distinguished by the atavistic politics of the Montana Freemen and various survivalist militia groups. From an international perspective a similar phenomenon is evident in the presence of neo-Nazism in Europe, ethnic cleansing in Bosnia, and the ascent of culturally and politically aggressive Islamic fundamentalism in the Middle East.

Conversely, liberalism and religious tolerance seem to be on the ascent at the same moment in history. The restoration of liberalism in contemporary philosophical discourse has been marked by the decline of Hegelian Marxist epic, the destruction of the Berlin Wall in 1989, the politics of Mikhail Gorbachev and Boris Yeltsin and the Tiananmen Square insurrection. Its politics and thought is also witnessed by the popularity of post-totalitarian thinkers such as Václav Havel and Milan Kundera, and 'out-of-the mainstream' intellectuals, playwrights, poets, journalists who are committed to the fluorescence of countercultural feminism, multiculturalism, civil rights movements of all descriptions, gay rights, and free speech in the arts.

The politics of the Left and Right has had confusing cultural implications. Within the umbra of this contentious cultural politics ordinary people, as well as lawmakers, intellectuals, journalists, and educators alike, seem unable to distinguish between piety and bibliolatry, science and fancy, news and tabloid journalism, patriotism and political oppression, and so on. Moreover, contemporary politics seem unable to choose between tolerance and intolerance – although it is inclined to commend intolerance and fret over tolerance. Intolerance in this contentious politics is presented by the Right as a fundamental condition of cultural solidarity in a world filled with ethnic conflicts that threaten the peace of every state and the security of every person (cf. Rawls 1993: xxiv–xxv). Left proponents of intolerance justify it in terms of a renunciation of oppression and subordination in all natural cultures (cf. Isaac 1992). That is, they both feel more at home with intolerance and oppression than tolerance and freedom. The latter seems to be too risky for both.

Right proponents of this new twentieth-century medievalism, Christian and Islamic alike, question the plural and diverse texture of modern life – often playing upon the fears and anxieties of modern life's cultural, social and economic uncertainties. Left proponents of a new twentieth-century postmodern renaissance question the plural and diverse texture of modern life pointing out the oppressive and exclusionary features of all natural cultures – often playing upon the same fears and anxieties.

Predictably enough, the politics of both groups are at odds with the bourgeois values and creature comforts that have been generated by political and economic détente and science and technology in a more cosmopolitan and internationally aware world, just as they are at odds with many modern and egalitarian discussions of tutelage (cf. Jacoby 1994). That is, both are opposed to, or at least wary of, giving individuals the opportunity and means to assert their own definition and thereby choose their own lives. The Right objects in the name of a reformational and paradisaical past and the Left in the name of a utopian and paradisaical future.

Be that as it may, a new and robust post-totalitarian liberalism is growing in response to the intolerance of the age. It presumes that the idea of democracy may be the last conceptual political revolution that the modern state requires (Havel 1987; cf. Rorty 1989: 63). It also presupposes a new discussion of tutelage ('edification') (see Rorty 1980: 360). It eschews the Right's assertion of a monolithic cultural politics and old-fashioned and elitist view of education just as it eschews the Left's claim of an epistemologically privileged politics and its related claims as to education's conservative if not oppressive and exclusionary cultural role. Post-totalitarian liberalism assumes that a free and tolerant democratic politics and a worldly and cosmopolitan version of edification are key factors in development and maintenance of a harmonious, stable, pluralist and modern state.

One example of this robust post-totalitarian liberalism can be found in the contemporary Central European literary renaissance that rejects all forms of cultural life whose maintenance and extension is dependent upon oppressive state power. In support of this robust liberalism Kundera writes:

> The unification of the planet's history, that humanist dream which God has spitefully allowed to come true, has been accompanied by a process of dizzying reduction. True, the termites of reduction have always gnawed away at life: even the greatest love ends up as a skeleton of feeble memories. But the character of modern society hideously exacerbates this curse: it reduces man's life to its social function; the history of a people to a small set of events that are themselves reduced to a tendentious interpretation; social life is reduced to political struggle, and that in turn to the confrontation of just two great global powers. Man is caught in a veritable whirlpool of reduction where Husserl's 'world of life' is fatally obscured and being is forgotten.
>
> (1988: 17)

That is, post-totalitarians argue that their version of Liberalism must ensure that the life of each individual is not reduced to the requirements of some antecedent need. It must ensure that in a very real sense everyone has, at least, the possibility of 'having their own life'.

The post-totalitarian intellectuals Václav Havel (1987) and Milan Kundera (1991) submit that the recent history of the 1989 revolutions in Central Europe are evidence of the failure of the Hegelian Marxist epic, its postmodern offspring, and all other attempts to 'live out' a social order that is dependent upon the oppressive power of the state, just as it is evidence of the inability of the Catholic Church to reduce Central Europe to its antecedent requirements (cf. Rawls 1993: 37). The latter is just cultural and political kitsch. Cultural and political kitsch is a matter of reducing civil society to a formula. Kundera notes:

> Since the days of the French Revolution, one half of Europe has been referred to as the left, the other half as the right. Yet to define one or the other by means of the theoretical principles it professes is all but impossible. And no wonder: political movements rest not so much on rational attitudes as on the fantasies, images, words, and archetypes that come together to make up this or that political kitsch.
>
> (1991: 257)

It is, political kitsch, recipe politics of ends known *a priori* – American, Russian, Chinese, Catholic and so on – that post-totalitarian liberals disdain. What post-totalitarians offer is a simple story of tentative politics, heroes and fools, false starts, and journeys and grails, in a confusing but open world.

In opposition to various Left authoritarian and monolithic politics, their post-totalitarian liberalism drops the rhetoric of conspiracy and oppression, unmasking and emancipation, just as it abandons the rhetoric of the New

Right's atavistic and reactionary cultural order. Unlike New Right politics, it adopts a reformist rhetoric that maintains the possibility of a good and just society within the terms of, or at least beginning within the terms of, existing democratic institutions (Kundera 1991, Havel 1987). It refuses to assert final cultural ends or a politically correct social order (Kundera 1991: 254).

Post-totalitarianism is quite at home with political liberalism (e.g. Rawls 1993: 40–3, Rorty 1989: 63). The post-totalitarian liberalism of Kundera and Havel has adapted classical elements of liberalism and anarchism to the new world of organised international pluralism and technological modernity. The former requires political participation and a democratic government to assure a system of fair co-operation. It requires universal, state-financed edification as a prerequisite for personal liberty and cultural efficacy – classical requirements of liberalism (cf. Goldfarb 1989: 222, Kloppenberg 1986: 162, Rawls 1993: 41, and Rorty 1989: 63). Like John Dewey (see 1954) and to a lesser extend like John Stuart Mill (see [1848] 1891) they believe that experience not rationality is the only basis for knowledge. They argue that history not ideology is the best guide for action, gentle persuasion is preferable to and more enduring than revolutionary violence, and democracy is preferable to any form of paternalism (Kloppenberg 1986: 199; cf. Kundera 1991, Havel 1987). All of this, of course, is very comfortable with the elements of classical liberalism and just as comfortable with Rorty's neo-liberal pragmatism.

Post-totalitarian liberalism recognises modern society's capacity for murderous intolerance and domestic oppression (Kundera 1991: 176). Ortega y Gasset noted, correctly, that society had to await the beginning of the twentieth century to see how brutal, evil and ignorant humanity can be (1944: 61). Be that as it may, post-totalitarian thought presupposes a politically supportive bourgeois society that at least aspires to a cultural order beyond brutality, evil and ignorance. This presupposition is

> based on nothing more profound than the historical facts which suggest that without the protection of something like the institutions of bourgeois society, people will be less able to work out their private salvations, create their private self-images, reweave their webs of belief and desire in the light of whatever new people and books they happen to encounter.
> (Rorty 1991b: 84–5)

Despite the fact bourgeois societies of every kind have a well-documented record of being racist, sexist, Eurocentric and imperialist one might note that their civil rights record is at least as good, or better, than any civilisation of which we have records (see Harris 1969). Therefore, bourgeois societies are recommended by the fact that they are very worried about being racist, sexist and so on and they have demonstrated a willingness to mend their ways in the attempt to achieve, hopefully, a system of fair co-operation, fraternity and autonomy for all (Kloppenberg 1986, Rorty 1991b: 81).

TECHNOLOGY AND POST-TOTALITARIAN EDIFICATION

What follows is a discussion of the possibility of edification as suggested by various literary elements of the Central European political renaissance. This work talks about 'edification' as suggested by Richard Rorty in another context because as he suggested: education has come to sound a bit flat. It has, Rorty maintains, lost its power as a metaphor in contemporary discourse. That is, it has forfeited its ability to lead discussions of tutelage to a point beyond traditional interpretations that end in 'education'. Therefore, this chapter suggests backing away from discussions of education while moving on to other terms in the hope of finding more allegorical power in them.

This work discusses, among other things, edification as a device to focus the measure of tutelage against individual human needs, not paradisaical social agendas. In other words, it focuses the measure of edification upon the requirements of personal authenticity – 'living within the truth' – as a means to suggest a denotation for edification beyond political kitsch.[1] This chapter presents edification as a useful metaphor, a metaphor more equal to the allegorical requirements that modernity places upon the tasks of teaching and learning.

In the modern world writers such as Michel Foucault ([1975] 1979) despair of discovering or creating any form of tutelage that is not corrupted by the oppressive and exclusionary power of the state (cf. Marshall 1990, Wain 1996). Unlike Foucault's work this chapter is more hopeful. It assumes that edification in a personally authentic and peaceful world is possible. It also suggests the possibility of a definition for edification and the world that is beyond political kitsch – American, Russian, Chinese, Catholic and so on. The assumptions and suggestions of this chapter turn away from the idea that education should be measured in social terms and suggests a more personal and, if you will, anarcho/libertarian measure. This turning implies a movement away from politics during highly notable moments in private lives. It is a turning away from politics during studying, working, raising a family, finding a home and so on. This movement, it is argued here, lies at the core of the ability of each individual to propose and endorse their own self-description and, of course, their own edification. Thus, the proper measure of edification is its ability to produce human comfort and diminish pain in the short and long term.

The idea of edification presented here relies upon the liberalisms of Kant and Mill. I believe the work of Kant and Mill leads to requirements for edification that are designed to foster the values of autonomy, individuality and, counterintuitively, fraternity. That is, it counsels both individuality and fraternity, although it is dubious about the necessity of community (Rawls 1993: xvi). Consequently:

> It will ask that children's education include such things as knowledge of their constitution and civic rights so that, for example, they know that liberty of conscience exists in their society and that apostasy is not a

legal crime, all this to insure that their continued membership when they come of age is not based simply on ignorance of their basic rights or fear of punishment for offenses that do not exist.

(Rawls 1993: 199)

To all our children it also makes available the various incompatible yet reasonable comprehensive versions of reality that are important aspects of our fellowship. It does not assert an official version of reality. It has little to do with advocating this or that life world as preferable to this or that life world or remembering this or that history in preference to this or that history. In other words, the issue of preference is left to vicissitudes of time and history.

The post-totalitarian task of edification then is to provide each individual with the opportunity to acquire the tools necessary to assert a description of themselves and their life projects within the context of the various comprehensive versions of reality that stand as reasonable elements of their association. That is, edification must provide each individual with the means to confirm or escape from the life that the accidents of time and history present to each individual. Edification in this view must be such that it allows each individual to live within the truth and within the company of others (cf. Havel 1987: 57).

Post-totalitarian liberalism offers a theory of action that allows individuals to accomplish a society in which both autonomy and fraternity can exist in harmony as co-requisites. Edification is, therefore, committed to a balancing act in which it guarantees people the possibility of their own lives and reasonable support for the background institutions of democracy that makes pluralism possible in large populations. Post-totalitarian edification (transformation through the power of strangeness and remembering), in support of autonomy, presents individuals with an opportunity and mechanism to regard themselves in a manner that otherwise they, most likely, would never be able to entertain. In support of fraternity, edification presents a theory of politics in which different and even antagonistic conceptions of the good can be affirmed and pursued in a modern pluralism that recognises incompatible yet reasonable comprehensive cultural doctrines and world views – it assumes a method that only requires certain democratic procedural allegiances. (cf. Rawls 1993: xvi, 71, 199). 'These principles give priority to those basic freedoms and opportunities [edification among them] in civil society's background institutions that enable us to become free and equal citizens in the first place, and to understand our role as persons with that status' (Rawls 1993: 41). It supports an instructional philosophy that replaces force, violence, and oppression with discourse, persuasion and justice (cf. Rorty 1989: 60).

Post-totalitarian liberalism assumes more than pluralism (autonomy and tolerance); it equiprimordially assumes technics (action and efficacy). The assumption of action and efficacy provides post-totalitarian liberal theory with a contextual theory of work. As Hanna Arendt notes, work is one of the most important expressions of human agency (1958). It provides stability and order in the world. It also provides the social and political institutions that are prior to the possibility of a meaningful life in any mass society (see Isaac 1992: 110–18). It is a prerequiste of autonomy and fraternity.

To the minds of post-totalitarians a political or social philosophy that is impotent – unable to provide food, comfort and the means to respond to contemporary problems – is empty and pointless. Thus, for them the realm of philosophical discourse or politics has to do with the goals of real people, not the human project in the abstract. The realm of autonomy has to do with the goals of each individual, not individuals in the abstract. Fraternity in post-totalitarian society means a system of fair co-operation, the benefits and costs of which – in terms of goods and services – are fairly distributed across all members of the community. Human action requires that both fraternity and autonomy are connected to a theory of action and a potent means. Post-totalitarians maintain that a politics based on discourse, a politics divorced or indifferent to the immediate and long-term well-being of community and all of its members is irrelevant if not dangerous to the entire commonwealth.

Post-totalitarians know that edification must be potent as well as wise. Their theories of action depend upon engagement, the effective connection of ends and material means. Goals of individuals and their projects cannot be accomplished without technics, the attitudes and procedures of technology. Technology demonstrates that utopian means (not empirical or instrumental means) to ultimate ends are silly if not hazardous to the prospects of their projects. In the world in which people actually live and inhabit, things happen through the intermediary of organised procedures, i.e. technology not ideology. Given the power of technology's potent engagement, optimising the balance between realising joy and minimising suffering while assuring basic freedoms and opportunities in civil society's background institutions is, pretty much, the last word that needs to be spoken about the assessment of various human projects (cf. Rawls 1993: 41, Rorty 1989: 63). That is, the measure of any post-totalitarian society is its ability to assist people in making their way in the world.

Notwithstanding the former, the idea of 'civil society' and its background institutions deserves a few more words. A short aside to a couple of concerns of Dewey and Heidegger will be useful at this point to extend the post-totalitarian concern for efficacy (technology) in the establishment and maintenance of freedom and fraternity in a democratic society.

Thomas Hobbes knew and so did John Dewey that unrestricted competition for the 'goods' of life meant that life would be 'solitary, poor, nasty, brutish, and short' (Hobbes 1958: 107). To Dewey's mind it was obvious that human experience and human labour could assure not only individual survival, the survival of the species and the possibility of a good life; it could just as well assure poverty, famine, disease and the end of human life as we know it. His answer to the dark chill of alienated existence was to nestle together with others in the 'great community' in order to identify with society and uphold co-operation – not war – as the sole path to the future and the possibility of plenty (cf. Diggins 1993: 51).

Dewey, the social democrat, outlined the centrality of technology to community (Hickman 1990). What Dewey captured is the contingency and fragility and risky business that is implied by the human project (Rorty 1991b: 34). What he captured is the deep historicity of life in general and the deep historicity of each life in particular. In addition he also understood a sense of the dependency of each life upon others for its own possibility. Dewey knew that the life-world of each individual was profoundly conditioned by the technological efficacy of the community in which the individual found himself or herself. He was aware, as Rorty points out, that the real threat to both autonomy and fraternity was scarcity of food and the secret police (see Rorty 1980: 389).

The interest of Dewey in technology was tied to its potential for social engineering and its impact upon the structures of society (Hickman 1990: 198–9). It was a matter of determining technology's role in the creation of the urban industrialism's social pain and its potential for participating in a coherent programme of social amelioration. If technology was responsible for privation it could also be responsible for plenty. Dewey realised that both fraternity and democracy depended upon the fact that society was not engaged in that unrestricted competition for the 'goods' – a war for sheer existence. He also realised that autonomy assumed goods in excess of subsistence. Thus, for Dewey, procuring food, proper housing, clothing for children, medicine and so on is prerequisite to both fraternity and autonomy (Dewey 1989). The concern of post-totalitarians is very similar to Dewey's. In the shadow of the collapse of the Soviet empire they understand the importance of efficacy as a prerequisite for the life-world of each individual and each society.

Heidegger's interest in technology, on the other hand, calls attention to the centrality of the individual in each human project and each individual's determination to pursue a life that is their own – a life that is defined by their own unique voice. Each life for Heidegger is a project that is personally realised, a project that should not be limited or determined by history, politics, ideology or the metaphors of others. He was mostly concerned with solving technology as part of a general assertion of self-definition (see Heidegger 1962). The same can be said for post-totalitarians.

Heidegger's concern for technology was tied to his obsessive concern for the apparent potency of technology to resolve everything in its terms, the self included. Heidegger's answer to the 'dark chill of alienated existence' was to assert the right of each individual to define themselves in their own uniquely individual vocabulary. His answer to the 'dark chill of alienated existence' was to damn the darkness in a voice that only he could claim. For Heidegger it was not a matter of 'huddling together against the darkness'; it was a matter

145

of each individual raging against the night. Like Kundera, Heidegger reminds of the danger of being reduced to a cipher. As Kundera noted in the voice of Sabina, 'My enemy is kitsch' (1991: 254).

If one face of edification has to do with the attainment of self-assertion through the power of strangeness, the other face has to do with achieving the possibility of fraternity through efficacy. Post-totalitarian theory recognises that it must pay attention to both perspectives (Kundera 1988: 17, Havel 1987: 57). In other words, post-totalitarian theories of culture are Janus-faced, one face addressing autonomy and the other addressing fraternity. Neither autonomy nor fraternity occur spontaneously or as a matter of will alone. If edification is to accomplish autonomy it must not be afraid of presenting the power of strangeness and remembering to technology while finding some reconciliation of the demands of both if it is to accomplish fraternity.

The power of strangeness and remembering as it is present in the exotic elements of literature, plays, science and so on must be available to everyone if edification is to accomplish successfully autonomy. On the other hand, if it is to accomplish fraternity, edification, in the post-totalitarian scheme of things, must be potent. Edification's potency must be measured against problems of literacy just as it must be measured against the everyday problems of procuring food, proper housing, clothing for children and so forth. Fraternity's assumption of engagement forces an active (efficacious) orientation to edification – the orientation of manipulation not supplication.

Technology, post-totalitarians recognise, is part of the human determination to institute erudition in place of a fearful ignorance and fatalism (Havel 1987). The possibility of technology is a matter of *embracing* courage, and adventure, and *taking* responsibility for the quality of existence (cf. Nietzsche 1960: 414). By focusing upon engagement, post-totalitarianism takes courage toward its ultimate orientation, individuality (autonomy) and technology (power), therein it abandons fatalism (material impotence) and nihilism (moral impotence). Potent engagement is a requirement, of course, for getting along in the world as it is – a partially defined game of social life, played with a nominal cast of referees, and an ill-defined set of rules from which there is no escape. Engagement, they note, is part of the human attempt to make life less vicious and more secure by the creation of an arena in which both autonomy and fraternity can be realised and rewarded within the requirements of dangers and potentials of the world's expanding populations.

Under the influence of the ideology of the Age of Reason and its experience of life within the realities of the Hegelian Marxist epic, post-totalitarianism abandoned the possibility of revealed omniscience. It radically limited the reach of knowledge to the domain of the natural world, tied knowing to experience, and extended the role of enquiry in the architecture of experience. Post-totalitarians have bonded edification to 'usefulness' not 'truth'. They then accepted warranted or reasonable understandings of 'what's what' as important only if said understandings were or could be shown to have promise for being transformationally powerful in the world.

They assumed a version of technology that *enframed* reality. Technology as *enframing* marks a different human stance toward existence. Technology's *enframing* defines reality and *modifies* humanity's relationship to itself and everything else (cf. Heidegger 1977: 27). Technology in this context is the satisfaction of the pre-linguistic urge to reconstruct 'what's what' – the 'present-to-hand' – in human terms and in terms of human ends. On the other hand they also noticed that technology was a device that, while it was efficacious, fashioned a predatory world which primarily obeys only its own technological laws and translates all other traditions of the world's natural cultures into its own terms (cf. Ellul 1965: 14). It one sense it is systematically at odds with post-totalitarianism's other major orientation, autonomy. Thus one of the major tasks of edification is to keep up with the tension between these two major orientations.

Technology represents the resolution to abandon fear and bewilderment as the primeval and primitive emotion of humanity and embraces erudition in the face of ignorance, heroism and an absurd existence (cf. Heidegger 1962: 389–96). A mastery of technology is, consequently, a means for both autonomy and fraternity. Phrased in a different way, technology is the appropriation of and commitment to material manipulation and symbolic expression of reality as the most effective fashion in which to apprehend and dominate the realms of metaphysics, physics and existence. Thus the first task of edification is to convince the individual to abandon the impotence of supplication and accept their manipulative role in the architecture of experience and then to instruct each individual in the obligations and responsibilities of their own self-assertion.

Technology presents and establishes a new courageous moral equilibrium with the 'whos' and 'whats' of reality. It is the manipulative and instrumental elaboration of technique and, thereby, the definition of – in so far as we can describe – 'what is' and 'what can be.' Technology expresses morality in the instrumental realisation of self-esteem and expectation. It is distinguished by a determination to reject fatalism and define the world in human terms, not supernatural entreaty (cf. Malinowski 1942: 634–40). In other words, it looks toward the technical potential of its time and history for the commendation and delimitation of human conduct, as referenced to each individual as an invaluable member of the 'kingdom of ends'. It requires that individuals and communities surrender the Byronic quest for ultimate political utopias or moral codes, while being willing to adopt a warrantable political conduct and moral codes that can, and do, direct human activity with charity, good will and beneficence among real publics. Edification, it might be added, is held to similar standards.

147

MORAL EDIFICATION

The reality of the Gulag, extant in every Central European state since the close of the Second World War, confirmed the insight of all post-totalitarians thinkers that the central problem of ethics was not insight into the good, but rather the recognition and extension of moral rights to all members of the nation. It was the partition and differential distribution of ethical standing that was the corruption of public morality. It was the partition and differential distribution of ethical standing that explained why only serious Gulag questions about the Gulag institution were raised by the 'plebs' who were its victims. Post-totalitarians therefore argue that it is the partition and differential distribution of ethical standing that leads to the corrupt difference that can exist between the meaning and intent of moral discourse and the realities of its practice (Klíma 1991).

Therefore, the basic task of moral edification is not insight into the good – assuming that post-totalitarians can come to at least core agreements as to what is and what causes pain, comfort and human joy, something they would argue experience provides at every opportunity – but a matter of convincing everyone that *all* members of the group are entitled to *all* extant moral rights, obligations and responsibilities. Morality is, as Rorty argues, 'a matter of the sort of thing "we do" and the sort of thing *we* don't do' when we are at our best (cf. Rorty 1989: 59). These 'we intentions' are a summation of what we understand as 'the right things to do', in ordinary as well as difficult and complex situations. The basic task of moral edification, then, is to show the population the 'unfamiliar country' in which all individuals would have equally legitimate and culturally acknowledged claims to *all* extant rights, obligations and responsibilities and then convince them to accept and extend such a state of affairs, in fact, to all residents of the commonwealth. Moral life within fraternity and autonomy is a matter of extension not knowledge. As Hannah Arendt notes,

> The realm of human affairs, strictly speaking, consists of the web of human relationships which exists wherever men live together. The disclosure of the 'who' through speech, and the setting of a new beginning through action, always fall into an already existing web where their immediate consequences can be felt. Together they start a new process which eventually emerges as the unique life story of the newcomer, affecting uniquely the life stories of all those with whom he comes into contact.
>
> (1958: 183–4)

Morally engaged individuals bound together by a common situation and a common fate can hope for no more and, of course, no less than to be free and equal inhabitants of a just community in which they, at least partially, define the rules of the game, individual, social and cultural. The choice of autonomy and fraternity is a matter of finding the connection between identity and human solidarity and asserting its extension to all, thereby declaring moral engagement as a primary focus of human conduct.

Thus, the work of moral edification is judged like that of engineers, novelists, accountants, police and so on (Rorty 1991b: 97). It is measured against its usefulness for resolving real human difficulties – intellectual, social, political, economic and so on – relieving human suffering and oppression and achieving human freedom and delight (cf. Rorty 1991b: 25). In this description there is no one big thing to be known, there is no eternal thing to be found out, and there is no truth that is detached or behind all the little patterned and sequential discoveries of culture. Among the members of the autonomous 'kingdom of ends', edification is a procedural routine for maximising the 'pool of all possibilities' in a just society. Edification's first moral questions pertain to procedures for and the possibility of the extension of a moral relationship between all members of the community within the requirements of autonomy and fraternity. Edification's other moral questions are those that pertain to human suffering, torment and persecution just as they pertain to human joy, kindness and benevolence.

EDIFICATION

Edification is obligated to realise two great human engagements, one personal and individual and the other fraternal and social. Consequently, edification's instructional obligation is tied to the general proximal effort of every person to create him or herself through engagement, just as edification is reciprocally tied to the task of achieving the plurality of life worlds that make up the fraternal order in the modern state. The binary task of edification then is the creation of wisdom, comfort, security and autonomy on the one hand, and justice, order, solidarity and fraternity on the other.

The reweaving of the human community from generation to generation is not something that happens in the abstract when the great truths behind appearance are somehow revealed. 'It is a matter of scratching where it itches, and only where it itches' (Rorty 1991a: 18). Edification is a matter of liberating culture from obsolete vocabularies, re-emphasising, developing and extending vital cultural vocabularies as they are related to autonomy and fraternity within the projects of various human cultures.

The problem of modernity for edification is a matter of keeping up with and introducing the new and innocent members of the state's various life worlds to the unusually ambivalent content of twentieth-century life. Edification is not a matter of passing on a Victorian comedy of manners or the cultural solutions of the sixteenth century as somehow commensurate with the questions of today's world. Nor is it merely a matter of commending the bohemian singularities of an 'Isadora Duncan' version of modern life and all of its possible indulgences. Edification is a matter of providing individuals with the

149

qualities that are equivalent to and capable of dealing with the ambivalent content of twentieth-century life.

In keeping up with the modern world, edification must notice and make provision for the price extracted and dividend paid to the community and the vast majority of individuals for physical and individual labour, the loss of family and the extension of association, the expansion and extended consequences of choice, the growth of law and the simultaneous loss of security, the extension of suffrage and the loss of political sovereignty, the radical production of material wealth and mass poverty, otherwise the potency of engagement will be lost. This concomitant task of edification is to assist both fraternity and autonomy in meeting the demands of the age while continuing the attempt to define ourselves and establish a cultural order in which all individuals are free and equal citizens of a just community, a community which is, quite probably, democratic.

Post-totalitarians argue that the Enlightenment was overly optimistic and so was one of the Enlightenment's major institutions, the school. Philosophy, technology and science, it would appear, cannot create a time or historical situation that is free of stupidity and ignorance. Collaterally, the school cannot stifle wisdom (a blessing) nor banish ignorance (a curse). Every period of history is blessed with its own wisdoms and its own stupidities. Both wisdom and stupidity are mutual properties of time and history (Rorty 1991a: 76–7).

The first assumption of post-totalitarianism is this: It is impossible to argue about guarding against the stupidity and ignorance of the age in a world that is hungry, insecure and besieged within and without by those who are dedicated only to nihilism. The second assumption is this: Edification is always incomplete and always in some state of construction, reconstruction, renovation or development. The third assumption is this: Democracy requires that the process of edification explain the fundamental grails and journeys of our history that have contributed to 'the essential aspect of our conception of ourselves as moral persons and of our relation to society as free and equal citizens' in the same way that it gives an intimate view of technology in the 'forms of life' that make up the various life worlds of humanity (Rawls 1980: 520; cf. Taylor 1994: 57). The fourth and last assumption is that: Autonomy and fraternity as cultural orientations require background institutions that will support fair co-operation among a multiplicity of conflicting and irreconcilable world views (see Dewey 1954: 147–8, Rawls 1993). It is in this last assumption – the creation of democracy – that autonomy, fraternity and edification come together.

CONCLUSION

In a post-totalitarian world, democracy and edification are co-dependent cultural events. Democracy is responsible for making sure that governments devote themselves to encouraging all members of the community to honour terms of fair co-operation within the public as a whole while ensuring the safety of all from threats from without and degradation from within. The role of edification is responsible for accomplishing a non-custodial version of 'living within the truth' for ourselves and all our children after us. Here curriculum is *histoire morale*. Edification begins in enculturation and ends in acculturation. It begins in dramatic stories about who we were and ends in stories about our most profound hopes for who we might one day become as individuals and compatriots. Fraternity and autonomy as addressed by edification are connected to a theory of action and potent means. That is, edification divorced or indifferent to the immediate and long-term well-being of community and all of its members is irrelevant if not dangerous to the entire commonwealth. Edification's success, then, is measured against its role in helping create justice, order, solidarity and fraternity just as it is measured against the satisfaction of ordinary human needs, security, health, food, comfort, shelter and so on.

NOTE

1 Obviously, the idea of political kitsch and many other elements of this chapter have been suggested by the writings of Central European post-totalitarian writers such as Milan Kundera and Václav Havel.

REFERENCES

Arendt, Hannah (1958) *The Human Condition*, Chicago: University of Chicago Press.

Aronowitz, Stanley and Giroux, Henry A. (1991) *Postmodern Education*. Minneapolis: University of Minnesota Press.

Burnheim, John (1985) *Is Democracy Possible?*, Berkeley: University of California Press.

Dewey, John (1954) *The Public and its Problems*, Denver, CO: Alan Swallow.

—— (1989) *Freedom and Culture*, Buffalo, NY: Prometheum Books.

Diggins, John Patrick (1993) *The Promise of Pragmatism*, Chicago: University of Chicago Press.

Ellul, Jacques (1965) *The Technological Society*, New York: Alfred A. Knopf.

Foucault, Michel ([1975] 1979) *Discipline and Punish*, New York: Random House.

Goldfarb, Jeffrey C. (1989) *Beyond Glasnost: The Post-totalitarian Mind*, Chicago: University of Chicago Press.

Harris, Marvin (1969) *The Rise of Anthropological Theory*, London: Routledge & Kegan Paul.

Havel, Václav (1987) *Living in Truth*, London: Faber & Faber.

Heidegger, Martin (1962) *Being and Time*, New York: Harper & Row.

—— (1977) 'The Question Concerning Technology', *The Question Concerning Technology and Other Essays*, New York: Harper & Row Publishers.

Hickman, Larry A. (1990) *John Dewey's Pragmatic Technology*, Bloomington, IN: Indiana University Press.

Hobbes, Thomas (1958) *Leviathan*, ed. Herbert W. Schneider, New York: Bobbs-Merrill Reprints.

Isaac, Jeffrey C. (1992) *Arendt, Camus, and Modern Rebellion*, New Haven, CN: Yale University Press.

Jacoby, Russell (1994) *Dogmatic Wisdom*, New York: Doubleday.

Klíma, Ivan (1991) *Judge on Trial*, New York: Random House.

Kloppenberg, James T. (1986) *Uncertain Victory*, New York: Oxford University Press.

Kundera, Milan (1988) *The Art of the Novel*, New York: Grove Press.

—— (1991) *The Unbearable Lightness of Being*, New York: Harper & Row.

Malinowski, Bronislaw (1942) 'Culture' in E. R. A. Seligman and A. Johnson (eds) *Encyclopaedia of the Social Sciences* vol. 3, New York: Macmillan.

Marshall, J. D. (1990) 'Asking Philosophical Questions about Education: Foucault on Punishment', *Educational Philosophy and Theory* (22) 2.

Mill, John Stuart ([1848] 1891) *Principles of Political Economy*, New York: D. Appleton and Company.

—— (1985) 'Inaugural Address at St. Andrews University' in John M. Robson (ed.) *John Stuart Mill: A Selection of his Works*, New York: Macmillan.

Nietzsche, Friedrich (1960) 'Thus Spake Zarathustra', *The Portable Nietzsche*, New York: The Viking Press.

Ortega y Gasset, José (1944) *Mission of the University*, Princeton: Princeton University Press.

Rawls, John (1980) 'Kantian Constructivism in Moral Theory', *The Journal of Philosophy* (LXXVII) 9: 515–72.

—— (1993) *Political Liberalism*, New York: Columbia University Press.

Rorty, Richard (1980) *Philosophy and the Mirror of Nature*, Oxford: Basil Blackwell.

—— (1989) *Contingency, Irony, and Solidarity*, Cambridge: Cambridge University Press.

—— (1991a) *Objectivity, Relativism, and Truth* vol. 1, Cambridge: Cambridge University Press.

—— (1991b) *Essays on Heidegger and Others* vol. 2, Cambridge: Cambridge University Press.

Taylor, Charles (1994) 'The Politics of Recognition', in Amy Gutmann (ed.) *Multiculturalism*, New Jersey: Princeton University Press.

Wain, Kenneth (1996) 'Foucault, Education, the Self and Modernity', *Journal of Philosophy of Educaton* (30) 3: 345–60.

13

PERSONAL AUTONOMY AND PRACTICAL COMPETENCE

Developing politically effective citizens

David Bridges

INTRODUCTION

The language of personal autonomy occupies a central position in the discourse of liberal democracy and indeed in western thought the two concepts are integrally related. Democratic governments presuppose and depend on, to some extent, an autonomous citizenry capable of exercising independent and informed political choices; and it is a feature of democratic states that they are governed by laws and constitutions designed to prevent them from overweening interference in the exercise of such individual autonomy. More strongly, 'developmental' arguments in support of, in particular, participatory democracy suggest that democratic procedures provide the conditions under which personal autonomy will be cultivated and developed (cf. Mill 1971; Parry 1972).

The notion of autonomy, therefore, attracts a great deal of attention and being, apparently, such an unqualified good thing is made the vehicle for a whole package of what are held within the liberal democratic ideology to be the necessary or desirable features of its citizens. As Dworkin suggests, the concept is made to do a lot of work:

> It is used sometimes as an equivalent of liberty . . . sometimes as equivalent to self-rule or sovereignty, sometimes identical with the freedom of the will. It is equated with dignity, integrity, individuality, independence, responsibility and self knowledge. It is identified with qualities of self-assertion, with critical reflection, with freedom from obligation, with absence of external causation, with knowledge of one's own interests. . . . It relates to actions, to beliefs, to reasons for action, to rules, to the will of other persons, to thoughts and to principles. About the only features held constant from one author to another are that autonomy is a feature of persons and that it is a desirable quality to have.
>
> (Dworkin 1988: 6)

In this chapter I want to review briefly something of the range of the qualities which have featured in particular in educational discourse about

153

autonomy and then to discuss one of the ingredients of personal autonomy which, in spite of the considerable attention which the concept has received, seems to me to have been neglected. For these purposes I shall refer to this ingredient as personal *competence*. This is a choice of language which will have particular and perhaps controversial resonances in the context of educational discussion in the United Kingdom, because the language of competence has been used by among others the Department of Employment (as distinct from what was until recently the separate Department for Education) in the context of its promotion of learning which is more directly related to the needs of the workplace or, more widely, adult life in the community and in the context of its particular responsibilities for vocationally-orientated training as distinct from (though is it in fact so distinct from?) general education. In the UK, therefore, there is a tendency for the language of competence to be seen as having rather illiberal overtones disassociated from the language of personal autonomy. In this chapter I want to explore this relationship a little more carefully and to suggest some more positive connections.

However, first, let us at least note something of the wider range of personal qualities which have been attached to the notion of autonomy, in particular in the literature in philosophy of education which has been concerned with the development of personal autonomy as an educational aim within a liberal democratic society.

INGREDIENTS OF PERSONAL AUTONOMY

Contemporary literature in philosophy of education has tended to address the issue of personal autonomy (expressed too in the language of individual freedom) as a question partly about teaching and learning styles and partly about curriculum. In the 1960s the debate about the kind of teaching and learning which was conducive to or respectful of individual autonomy was partly framed by Green's 'topology of the teaching concept' (Green 1964), but got somewhat bogged down in argument about the concept of indoctrination in which substantive moral questions about how we ought to teach became rather submerged in linguistic debate about the meaning of the word 'indoctrination' (cf. Snook 1972). In the 1970s these issues were revived, in what to my mind was one of the most provocative and important debates of the period, by the work of the Humanities Curriculum Project and the associated hypothesis that in handling controversial social issues in the classroom teachers would better contribute to students' understanding and, by extension, their autonomous judgement by adopting a stance of procedural neutrality. Central to a multi-faceted debate here was the argument that, if students were to be able to make up their own minds on these matters, then they needed to understand the controversy, which itself entailed understanding different points of view on the controversy, which was itself best served by adopting particular teaching strategies. In the 1980s, a period dominated by the development of the national *curriculum*, Bailey was among the relatively few in philosophy of education who continued to write about the *teaching methods* conducive to the development of personal autonomy (Bailey 1984).

On the whole, however, the dominant body of literature in philosophy of education has addressed the issue of personal autonomy as an issue of curriculum content (in so far as this can ever properly be separated from the manner of teaching and learning). It has asked, in particular, what are the ingredients of personal autonomy, what knowledge and understanding does one need to acquire in order to be able to exercise personal autonomy and then argued directly or by implication that these ought to provide the core of a properly liberal education. Indeed, the argument that the acquisition of certain knowledge and understanding is a condition of exercising personal autonomy, has been seen (in White 1973, for example) as a central justification for a level of compulsion in respect to schooling or curriculum which might otherwise be seen in liberal terms as an unwarranted intrusion in individual liberty. So how have the components of personal autonomy been identified?

Philosophy of education in the United Kingdom has tended to focus on the cognitive conditions of personal autonomy. Dearden's definition of autonomy, indeed, expresses it exclusively in cognitive terms:

> A person is autonomous to the degree that what he thinks and does, at least in important areas of his life, are determined by himself. That is to say, it cannot be explained why these are his beliefs and actions without referring to his own activity of mind. This determination of what one is to think and do is made possible by the bringing to bear of relevant considerations in such activities of mind as those of choosing, deciding, deliberating, reflecting, planning and judging.
>
> (Dearden 1972: 461)

Hirst's much referenced paper on 'Liberal education and the nature of knowledge' (Hirst 1965) and much of his subsequent writing made the connection between being a free person, having a developed mind and having acquired in some measure an understanding of the central concepts and tests for truth which mark the different 'forms of knowledge' or ways we have developed of making sense of our world. Passmore's parallel work in the United States articulated these forms of knowledge in the even more apposite language of 'the great human traditions of critico-creative thought' (Passmore 1967: 200) – an identity which expresses even more directly the notion that critical and creative (and hence presumably autonomous) responses to our world have to be rooted in some kind of familiarity with the evolved traditions of, for example, science, philosophy or history which embody both the historically received knowledge and understanding necessary to critico-creative responses and the procedures necessary for the critical examination and development of this knowledge and understanding. Thus, if we are to be able to develop some independence of thought (an ingredient, at least, of autonomy) we need some kind of mastery both of relevant bodies of knowledge and understanding and of relevant ways of subjecting this to critical scrutiny and (not entirely the same thing) to creative development.

But the autonomous individual needs to make choices not just about what beliefs to accept or reject within the framework of traditional forms of knowledge, but also about what kind of life to lead. This is a central feature of White's argument in 'Towards a compulsory curriculum': 'He [sic] knows about as many activities or ways of life as possible which he may want to choose for their own sake' (White 1973: 22).

The exercise of freedom or autonomy (and I am not going to dwell here on some of the finer distinctions) requires at least some basic understanding of the options between which one may be choosing. Such autonomy is restricted both by total ignorance of the possibilities (one is not free to choose what one simply remains ignorant of) and by inadequate understanding of the possibilities of which one is vaguely aware. Autonomous choice or 'real' choice on this argument is an informed choice. White uses this approach to develop a view of a curriculum whose compulsory nature is justified by the service it provides to the development of individuals' capacities to choose activities which they may wish to engage in for their own sake and (more interestingly to my mind) ways of life (for example a life of political engagement, a life of domesticity, a religious life, a life of commerce) into which these activities might be fitted. Again, a certain body of knowledge and understanding is presented as a condition of the exercise of (autonomous) choice about in this case the kind of life which is to be led.

Autonomy, in the sense of self-regulation, is usually contrasted with heteronomy, or regulation by others. A crucial condition of autonomy therefore is the ability of individuals to separate in their minds the self and the other, to distinguish the sources of motivation, the 'voices' which speak to us and urge this thought or that action, and by extension to act on those ideas or principles which we have originated or independently validated for ourselves rather than those which are uncritically or unconsciously received from elsewhere. For Bonnett, for example:

> underlying the whole notion of autonomy is an idea of being true to oneself, that one's thoughts and actions are in some sense an expression of one's true self. That is to say that autonomous thought and action are at least authentic thought and action in some sense.
>
> (Bonnett 1978: 55)

Bonnett follows Heidegger (1973) in suggesting that this requires that:

> Man [sic] is self-aware, meaning by this not merely that man differentiates self from other – becomes an object for himself – but that he is self-knowing, self caring and thus has a sense of personal place.
>
> (Bonnett 1978: 55)

Other accounts of autonomy draw attention to this element of self-knowledge and with it an ability or inclination to choose and act out of what is in some sense the chosen or self-originated self rather than the self which is unreflectively the product of outside influences. Dearden argues, for example, that: 'without self-knowledge much in our choices, and especially in our reactions to others, is not determined by us in any relevant sense at all' (Dearden 1972: 463).

On other accounts what is required for the achievement of personal autonomy is some really quite sophisticated 'self-awareness', 'self examination' (Kleinig 1982) or 'reflective self evaluation' (Frankfurt 1971) – tasks which call for both the honesty and rigours of the confessional (it is not surprising that the roots of existentialism are to be found in Kierkegaard's confessional preparation, 'Purity of Heart') *and* for the kind of social and political 'conscientisation' presented by Freire (1985) as a condition of individual freedom and empowerment. In other words we have to reflect both on the character of our inner motives and impulses and on the ways in which these may have been shaped and formed by external influences and power structures, which work most insidiously when they lead us to take certain assumptions for granted and conceal the contingency of the social structures in which they are located. For Poole (1975):

> I am autonomous just to the extent that I have played a part . . . in the development of my present conative, cognitive and emotional structure. Where aspects of this, and as a result, patterns of my present behaviour, were fixed in some very early experiences (say, socialisation) in which I had no power of participation or intervention, then to that extent I am not my own person, i.e. I am not autonomous. Under these circumstances I can work towards autonomy and, through a process of self examination, perhaps discover the extent to which what I now am expresses what has been external to me. In order to do this, I must be able to distance myself, and treat it as if it were external. Only by thus identifying myself independently of that aspect which is under examination will I be able to assess it as answering or not answering to my present wants, beliefs, principles, and so on. That the I who undertakes such an examination is, pro tem, an unexamined I is inevitable, but it need not remain unexamined. That we must . . . reconstruct our personal boat while sailing on it, does not mean that there is some part of it which must remain forever unreconstructed.
>
> (Poole 1975: 13)

In this section I have reviewed some of what have been put forward as the ingredients of personal autonomy and hence ingredients for liberal educational programmes dedicated to the development of personal autonomy. These have included:

- a grasp of the knowledge, understanding, central concepts, tests for truth and critico-creative processes constitutive of the fundamental 'forms of knowledge' or ways of knowing which have evolved historically;
- knowledge and understanding of the kinds of activities which we might choose to engage in for their own sake;
- knowledge and understanding of ways of life which we might choose for ourselves;
- reflective knowledge of ourselves and of the sources of our understanding and motivation.

Now any and all of these claims invite (and indeed many of them have received) detailed examination and discussion. For the purposes of this chapter, however, I do not wish to embark on this process. Rather my concern here is with what is missing even if all of them are put together.

THE EXERCISE OF PERSONAL AUTONOMY: FROM KNOWING ABOUT TO CARRYING OUT

What worries me about the picture of the autonomous person presented by these approaches individually and even collectively is that they seem to present a very partial or incomplete description of what is required if someone is to be able to act autonomously in a social context. There is an almost exclusive concern with the capacity to judge for oneself, to think critically and independently, to be aware of the range of choices and to choose, to be aware of one's own motives and to determine what kind of choice would be an authentic one – all of these, perhaps, necessary (if rather exclusive) conditions for personal autonomy, but are they sufficient? There seems to me to be a real risk that an education or curriculum founded on these perspectives on personal autonomy would produce a superbly reflective, analytic, critical individual who might nevertheless be totally incapable of performing the minimal acts necessary for basic survival let alone acting in or upon the hectic dance of a bustling economic, social and political world.

There is an interesting and morally important sense in which a person might still be personally autonomous while also being cold and hungry (because they cannot find employment and are too overwhelmed by the bureaucracy to claim benefit), out of communication with other people (because they have neither the know-how nor the confidence to make contact with potential friends, support groups or people with shared interests), berated in newspapers and political platforms as being part of an idle, parasitic and potentially criminal underclass (accusations which they have to tolerate in silence because they have no practical capacity to organise themselves so as to represent their position more effectively). The kind of knowledge and understanding collected in the versions of personal autonomy which I have outlined above would enable such individuals to reflect critically upon their situation; it would enable them to entertain a wide range of theoretically possible choices of life-styles or activities that they might like to engage in; it would enable them to consider their own identity and motives; but it would not in itself do anything much to get them out of a situation in which the actual practical pursuit of most of the choices they might like to contemplate is denied them.

White (1990) argued that: 'one cannot talk about individuals exercising their autonomy unless they become autonomous in the first place' (p. 23). It is equally true that if being autonomous means no more than is contained in the accounts which I have reviewed so far, then it is difficult to see that it is suf-ficient for people to be able to *exercise* autonomy, which in turn makes it look a pretty impoverished representation of what it is to *be* autonomous in the first place. In particular in any context in which the notion of personal autonomy is associated with the conditions demanded for the realisation of democratic citizenship, it is an odd and limited notion of personal autonomy which sees it as describing a set of intellectual conditions which are, however, insufficient for enabling individuals to pursue their chosen courses practically in a social world inhabited by other people engaged (sometimes competitively, sometimes even combatively) in the same pursuit.

So what do we need to add to the account provided of personal autonomy so far – either as an extension of the notion of personal autonomy itself or as a supplement to it – to meet these requirements? And what, more particularly, are their implications for the curriculum? I think we can draw interesting insight from some rather discrepant sources.

In 1974 Robin Richardson drew together what at the time were a rather diverse assortment of educational campaigners for peace, for environmental protection, for social justice and against racism in the World Studies Project. Its ambition was to place these issues more firmly and coherently in the school curriculum either as a new subject in its own right or as a set of themes and perspectives integrated with other subjects. The World Studies Project shared with, for example, the Humanities Curriculum Project (Schools Council/Nuffield Humanities Project 1970) concern to develop stu-dents' *understanding* of these issues and their capacity to make their minds up about where they themselves stood in relation to them, and this was an important part of the project. However, the World Studies Project did not stop there. It took the view that students needed not only to take a view on these matters, but also *to act politically and socially* in support of the position they had adopted using the repertoire of practice acceptable to a democratic polity (World Studies Project 1976). Thus it proposed that: 'Students can be attached temporarily to political parties or pressure groups, or to charities or churches with political or semi-political concerns, and share in their routine activities' (World Studies Project 1976: 93). Furthermore, students should be prepared for, be involved in and practise a variety of forms of political activity, including:

organising meetings
writing, printing and distributing leaflets
fund-raising
writing to, or lobbying, politicians, both local and national
writing to the press
taking part in radio phone-in programmes
trying to place news releases in the media
organising marches, boycotts, sit-ins, fasts etc.
canvassing for votes . . .

(World Studies Project 1976: 93)

These proposals were controversial at the time and remain so. Few schools had the stomach to pursue them seriously and one or two that did found themselves in conflict with, for example, their local Member of Parliament (Aucott *et al*. 1979). Some were happy to incorporate games and simulations which gave insight into forms of political activity, but were unwilling or unable to tackle this in a way which was closer to the real thing. The rights and wrongs of the issue merit fuller consideration. For the moment however I simply want to observe that the approach proposed by the World Studies Project illustrates the point that teaching for political practice is a necessary adjunct to political understanding if people are really to be equipped to play their part as autonomous citizens in a democracy, if they are to engage in democratic practice and not merely be interested and even reflective observers of the political scene. Further, while part of what is being learned in that practice is more knowledge and understanding (e.g. about voting procedures or lobbying techniques), another part is a mixture of skilled behaviour and self-confidence (informed by the understanding) which requires rehearsal and practice in progressively demanding social settings, i.e. the kind of treatment which we sometimes associate with training.

In the last five to ten years in the UK a number of groups have been trying to articulate demands for a re-orientation of the school and indeed higher education curriculum with a view to giving more substantial emphasis to what might be broadly described as the *doing* side of human experience and which is variously expressed in the language of 'capability', 'competence' and, in a particular context, 'enterprise'. The Education for Capability project, for example, articulates 'a new concept of education' which develops 'people who "can do" as well as who "know about"' (Stephenson and Weil 1992: xii). The general argument is well expressed in the manifesto of the Education for Capability group:

There is a serious imbalance in Britain today in the full process which is described by the two words 'education' and 'training'. The idea of the 'educated' person is that of a scholarly individual who has been neither educated nor trained to exercise useful skills; who is able to understand but not to act. Young people in secondary or higher education increas-

160

ingly specialise, and do so too often in ways which mean that they are taught to practise only the skills of scholarship and science. They acquire knowledge of particular subjects, but are not equipped to use knowledge in ways which are relevant to the world outside the education system.

This imbalance is harmful to individuals, to industry and to society. A well-balanced education should of course embrace analysis and the acquisition of knowledge. But it must also include the exercise of creative skills, the competence to undertake and complete tasks and the ability to cope with everyday life; and also doing all these things in co-operation with others.

(Royal Society for the Arts 1991: 5)

Klemp (1977) made a similar observation in relation to what he saw as the limitations of the higher education curriculum in the United States:

The experience of higher education, it is commonly held, better prepares one to take on the mantle of career and life. . . . And yet, soon after embarking on their new careers and lives . . . new graduates discover that the knowledge and ability acquired in school are not enough, that something is missing in their preparation that prevents them from translating what they have learned into effective performance.

(Klemp 1977: 1)

The RSA manifesto urges the development of practical competence and the application of knowledge in a broad context of 'the world outside the education system' and 'everyday life'. Many other initiatives share this broader (liberal?) objective but have a particular case to make in relation to the world of work. The Training Agency/Employment Department Enterprise in Higher Education initiative has addressed curriculum change in higher education with a view to developing more 'enterprising' students, which one of its projects defined as: 'creative, adventurous and ready to take initiative . . . responsible, forward looking, pro-active, dynamic and effective communicators of ideas and achievements' (ERTEC 1990). The Training Agency/Employment Department outlined its objectives for the project as being to:

- secure curriculum development and change so as to enhance personal effectiveness and achievement at work;
- offer students the opportunity to develop and apply skills including those of communication, team work, leadership, decision-making, problem solving, task management and risk taking;
- develop students' initiative.

(Training Agency 1990: Appendix 2)

What these last initiatives have in common is a frustration with forms of education which, it is held, provide a certain level of knowledge, understanding and even, let us suppose, analytic and critical capacity, but which fail to

161

equip students to apply this in everyday life, including working life, fail to provide them with the kinds of skills, competence or capability which will make them effective, achieving individuals. They develop the 'know about' capacities but neglect the 'can do' capacities.

One outcome of these concerns in the context of vocational and professional training has been the development in the UK (as previously in the United States) of competence based approaches to assessment and curriculum. If you want to be assured that, for example, teacher training courses or police training programmes really are producing people who are capable of effective practical performance in the workplace, then you assess them, not on the basis of paper examinations sat in a university or college hall, but on the basis of agreed criteria of practical competence displayed in an appropriate variety of settings in the workplace. Interestingly, new competence based training and assessment procedures for higher level professional work have raised the issue I have been addressing in reverse: not so much 'does knowledge and understanding need to be supplemented with practical competence?', but 'is a description of practical competence incomplete without an account of what is sometimes referred to as "underpinning knowledge and understanding"?'

What has all this got to do with personal autonomy?

My argument is that personal autonomy is seriously incomplete unless the kind of knowledge and understanding which is widely recognised as supporting it is also joined with certain kinds of practical competence. It is one thing, and an important thing, to be able to make independent and authentic choices; but to be autonomous surely implies additionally some capacity to pursue these choices effectively. The sources I have been quoting are not all equally concerned with the development of whatever forms of practical competence are needed to support individual's self-chosen goals, but they are wrestling in various ways with the problem of how necessary practical competence is identified (e.g. through functional analysis as the UK National Council for Vocational Qualifications prefers or through critical incident research as the McBer corporation has proceeded in the USA); how it is described and assessed; how it relates to reflection, knowledge and understanding.

It is presumably difficult to determine in advance which are the 'certain kinds of practical competence' which the exercise of personal autonomy in general or one person's autonomy in particular may require, since the competence required will depend upon the kind of choices made. We might nevertheless be able fairly readily to begin to identify some fairly basic areas of competence which are fundamental to the central domains in which we see personal autonomy being exercised. The kinds of political practice which the World Studies Project identified, for example, seem to me to be fairly central to the exercise of one's political rights in a democratic setting. The exercise of moral autonomy (i.e. acting morally in one's own lights and not merely coming autonomously to one's own opinions) would in most forms of moral practice require the capacity to as it were pick up messages about other people's feelings and concerns and to convey successfully one's own intentions. Both of these are complex skills which can however benefit from intelligent reflective practice. To take a different sphere, it is arguable that the capacity to secure and maintain employment and/or to secure and manage an income of some kind will be an important condition for the pursuit of many of the things which an individual may wish to pursue for their own sake in life, so training in the capacities which are likely to secure these conditions will better enable that individual to live the life he or she has chosen.

If even this seems too specific, then it might be worth giving closer attention to the analysis of what are variously referred to as 'core', 'generic' or 'transferable' skills, to those forms of skilled or competent behaviour which seem to have the most generalisable or fundamental application in enabling one to turn intentions and projects into practice, or to what I have called 'transferring skills' (Bridges 1994), which are those capacities which we engage in transferring knowledge and skill derived from or practised in one situation to another situation which is materially different.

Precisely what is involved in translating autonomously derived purposes and projects into successful practice I shall leave conveniently for the moment as 'a further question'. What I hope to have shown in this chapter is that a notion of personal autonomy which fails to include some such competence is an incomplete one, and hence that a curriculum which is intended to contribute to the development of personal autonomy must also contribute to the development of these capacities. Education for personal autonomy must also include training in those competences which are necessary to the exercise of that autonomy in a social world.

REFERENCES

Aucott J., Cox H., Dodds A. and Selby D. (1979) 'World studies on the runway: one year's progress towards a core curriculum', *New Era* 60, 60: 212–29.
Bailey, C. H. (1984) *Beyond the Immediate and the Particular: Towards a Theory of a Liberal Education*, London: Routledge & Kegan Paul.
Bonnett, M. (1978) 'Authenticity and education', *Journal of Philosophy of Education* 12: 51–62.
Bridges, D. (1992) 'Enterprise and liberal education', *Journal of Philosophy of Education* 26, 1: 91–7.
Bridges, D. (1994) 'Transferable skills: a philosophical perspective', in Bridges, D. (ed.) *Transferable Skills in Higher Education*, Norwich: ERTEC/UEA.
Dearden, R. F. (1972) 'Autonomy and education' in Dearden, R. F., Hirst, P. H. and Peters, R. S. (eds) *Education and the Development of Reason*, London: Routledge & Kegan Paul.
Dworkin, G. (1988) *The Theory and Practice of Autonomy*, Cambridge: Cambridge University Press.
Eastern Region Teacher Education Consortium (1990) *ERTEC: The Eastern Region Teacher Education Consortium*, Norwich: ERTEC.
Frankfurt, H. (1971) 'Freedom of the will and the concept of a person', *Journal of Philosophy* 68, 1: 5–21.

Freire, P. (1985) *The Politics of Education: Culture, Power and Liberation* trans. Macedo, D., London: Macmillan.

Green, T. F. (1964) 'The topology of the teaching concept', *Studies in Philosophy and Education* 3, 4.

Heidegger, M. (1973) *Being and Time*, trans. Macquarrie, J. and Robinson, E., Oxford: Basil Blackwell.

Hirst, P. H. (1965) 'Liberal education and the nature of knowledge' in Archambault, R. D. (ed.) *Philosophical Analysis and Education*, London: Routledge & Kegan Paul.

Kierkegaard, S. (1846, 1948 edn) *Purity of Heart*, trans. Steere, D. V., New York: Harper Row.

Kleinig, J. (1982) *Philosophical Issues in Education*, London: Croom Helm.

Klemp, G. O. (1977) *Three Factors of Success in the World of Work: Implications for Curriculum in Higher Education*, paper presented to the 32nd national Conference on Higher Education of the American Association for Higher Education, Chicago, March.

Mill, J. S. (1971) *Representative Government*, London: Oxford University Press.

Parry, G. (ed.) (1972) *Participation in Politics*, Manchester: Manchester University Press.

Passmore, J. (1967) 'On teaching to be critical' in Peters, R. S. (ed.) *The Concept of Education*, London: Routledge and Kegan Paul.

Poole, R. (1975) 'Freedom and alienation', *Radical Philosophy* 12: 3–15.

Royal Society for the Arts (1991) *Education for Capability*, London: RSA.

Schools Council/Nuffield Humanities Project (1970) *The Humanities Project: An Introduction*, London: Heinemann.

Snook, I. (1972) *Indoctrination and Education*, London: Routledge & Kegan Paul.

Stephenson, J. and Weil, S. (1992) *Quality in Learning: A Capability Approach to Higher Education*, London: Kogan Page.

Training Agency (1990) *Enterprise in Higher Education: Key Features of the Enterprise in Higher Education Proposals*, Sheffield: The Training Agency.

White, J. P. (1973) *Towards a Compulsory Curriculum*, London: Routledge & Kegan Paul.

White, J. P. (1990) *Education and the Good Life*, London: Kogan Page.

World Studies Project (1976) *Learning for Change in World Society*, London: World Studies Project.

14

DEVELOPING PERSONAL AUTONOMY IN CONTINUING PROFESSIONAL DEVELOPMENT

Gaye Heathcote

INTRODUCTION

This chapter outlines, as a case-study from which generalisations are tentatively drawn, a validated curriculum designed with the explicit purpose of developing personal autonomy in teachers, their students and their colleagues. The curriculum, predicated on a national (UK) research and development project into teachers' in-service needs in personal, social and health education, has been piloted, evaluated and disseminated nationally as an example of excellence. More recently, its underlying philosophical principles and defining methodologies have been adopted by several countries undergoing transitional ideological, political and economic changes in pursuit of democracy and market. There is reason to believe, therefore, that the distinctive features of this programme for personal autonomy have validity and applicability beyond current ethnocentric considerations.

The chapter initially identifies 'empowerment' as a central organising concept for personal autonomy. It explores the theoretical relationship between empowerment, power, oppression and authenticity and illustrates ways in which these concepts may be operationalised to offer a rationale for a curricular framework, a set of criteria for content selection and, importantly, a range of enabling methodologies. The emphasis on a process-led programme that promotes the enhancement of self, self-confidence and self-knowledge, within a 'frame' of reciprocal valuing, sharing and discovering, highlights a range of skills and a set of relationships (personal and structural) which education for personal autonomy will seek to address. The chapter considers methodological, linguistic and political aspects of empowering in this context, seeking, for example, to identify the extent to which individuals and groups can negotiate roles and relationships to achieve authenticity and, where necessary, challenge cultural and historical norms/political conventions.

Finally, the potential of a process-led, skills-based approach to education for personal autonomy is evaluated as a model of working in societies experiencing periods of rapid structural change and seeking to strengthen democratic citizenship. Its strength in achieving a range of educational objectives in a variety of different contexts is also discussed, particularly in those areas of human endeavour that are contested, involve relations of power and require the skills and insight of empowered individuals and groups.

The chapter is in two parts. The first is a theoretical exploration of the nature and interrelationships of the key concepts associated with autonomy; the second part describes, evaluates and comments on an extended illustration, drawn from education for health, of personal autonomy in practice.

REFLECTIONS ON THE NATURE AND INTERRELATIONSHIPS OF AUTONOMY, EMPOWERMENT AND ASSOCIATED CONCEPTS

Notwithstanding relativist positions on the issue of societal and personal values, it is taken as axiomatic that certain values must be adopted, accepted or encouraged to develop in any continuing society. Consensus values are therefore identified as at least a partial solution to the problematics of human nature and its predicament. This is not to argue that values are deduced from the facts of the human condition or from its environments, but to assert that certain social principles emerge as common-sense responses that enable us to live more harmoniously and co-operatively than we otherwise would in the absence of such principles. The most basic of these may be expressed as:

1 Not harming others physically or psychologically (non-maleficence).
2 Giving positive help to people wherever necessary (benevolence or bene- ficence, and compassion).
3 Treating people fairly or equally before the law, in the ownership and trans- fer of goods and services, rewarding labour and, in general, in determining social conditions (justice).
4 Striving to produce the best possible consequences (or the greatest happi- ness) for the majority (utility).

(Downie *et al.* 1990)

Correspondingly, certain individual and personal values may be identified as essential both as contributors to the necessarily harmonious and co-operative functioning of a continuing society and as an aspiration for a good, in the sense of a flourishing, individual human life. Once again, empirical inquiry is best replaced by an analysis of the components of a life which is flourishing in the sense of well being. Here, consensus might focus around some con- ception of having some measure of control over one's life, of being able to choose what one wants to do or be, and of being able to develop one's talents. Specifically, there is likely to be agreement that important personal values are embedded in and inform activities that achieve certain desirable skills and qualities, for example:

1 The ability to be self-determining, to be able to choose for oneself and execute one's own plans and policies.
2 The ability to be self-governing, to be sufficiently detached to stand back from one's own self-interest and be able to take account of others' needs as well as one's own.
3 The ability to exercise a sense of responsibility in relation to one's own thoughts and actions, particularly as they relate to others (empathetic understanding).
4 The ability to undertake self-development and to achieve self-realisation in ways which engender a sense of coherence in one's life, and feelings of self-esteem.

(Downie *et al*. 1990)

These four values – self-determination, self-government, a sense of responsibility and self-development – are clearly linked, conceptually by reference to the 'self' and operationally in the sense that actions undertaken in pursuit of, say, self-determination, inevitably contribute to the achievement of another or others. It is therefore useful to accept the view that these stated values are different, but dynamically interrelated facets of a single concept – autonomy. Such a conclusion, however, implicates two further assumptions: that, as a unifying value of individual personality, autonomy has, in common with all values, cognitive, affective and conative aspects and, second, that references to an autonomous individual who is self-determined, self-governing, exercises responsibility and has an interest in self-development is also inextricably linked to *alter's* needs, feelings, plans and understandings. The ingredients of autonomy all carry an essential reference to society and indicate that autonomy can only be understood in the context of the social. This conceptualisation of autonomy is essentially problematic for those who equate 'autonomous' with the notion of a 'real', 'essential' or 'authentic' and essentially pre-social state.

Symbolic interactionists, cultural relativists and role theorists may, in their varying ways, promote alarm in those who seek contact with a self that has an enduring 'core' identity, capable of withstanding challenge from the turbulent environments of historical development, ideology, creed or socialisation. Narratives that portray modern social life as enactments in 'small life worlds' that lack overarching meaning systems (Luckman 1978) or as prisons that offer 'life scripts' or destructive games which people play together (Berne 1969) can only be 'written away' through person-centred counselling and psychotherapy aimed at liberating the 'originally autonomous' individual. The social, thus, is unfailingly brutalising and false and is the antithesis of authenticity.

It has been said that to be truly oneself is a high ideal in modern western societies (Strawbridge 1993) and that this is contrasted in everyday language with 'play-acting' and 'putting on a show'. Paradoxically, our most valued relationships are those that are intrinsically satisfying, those in which we can be our 'real selves', valuing each other for ourselves and yet, inescapably, rooted in a social and cultural context. Marxists have argued that the very idea of an 'essential self' is a 'bourgeois', 'individualist' notion, whilst other commentators, influenced by structuralist theories of language, have differentiated between 'subject' (socially produced in relationships through systems of meaning of language and culture, and responsible for 'decentering' personal identity) and 'self' (a personal identity that is separate from and often in opposition to the social). It is suggested that a solution to the paradox is found in G. H. Mead's concepts of 'I' and 'Me' (Mead 1962). The pre-social 'I' in its development towards an awareness of others and in its growth of a socially-acquired identity ('Me') acquires a reflexivity, a consciousness which includes, at least implicitly, reference to an 'I'. This self-consciousness is fundamentally social: it develops out of relationships with others. The 'I' is therefore not an essence or an entity but a capacity for reflection and reflexivity. The relationship between autonomy and authenticity is thus dependent upon a fundamentally social capacity for self-consciousness, self-awareness and self-analysis. This is an essential prerequisite for engaging, with Kant, a perception of individual and social values as being two aspects of a single principle, expressed as 'Respect the autonomous nature of human beings whether in your own person or in that of another' (Kant 1949).

It is helpful to consider autonomy not so much as a quality or characteristic which human beings possess, but as a value, an ideal or, according to Kant, an obligation, the qualities of which we need to develop so as to make ourselves distinctly social. Our personality lays claims on us to 'be all we can be' through the exercise of the personal values of self-determination, self-government, a sense of responsibility and self-development, framed by social values of non-maleficence, benevolence, compassion, justice and utility.

Such values provide the inspiration and source of empowerment which constitute societal and individual well being. It has to be recognised, however, that many people are hindered or barred from achieving autonomy through their interpersonal and structural relations in the social, material, ideological, emotional and political domains. Poverty, inadequate housing, unemployment, low self-esteem, blocked access to educational opportunity, alienating personal relationships, traditions of behaviours such as sexism, racism, ageism and political disenfranchisement are examples of empirical situations which act to disempower. Other expressions of this phenomenon are Foucault's study of the historical development of 'expert' knowledge which constructs everyday understandings of normality and deviance ('normal sex', 'a healthy body', 'a stable personality') (see Rabinow 1986) and Althusser's notion of the 'authorless theatre' in which ideology seeps insidiously into the subjective consciousness of individuals, delimiting personal space and individual identity (Althusser 1971). To understand how autonomy can be developed, one needs to understand how individuals can be empowered to take control of their lives as opposed to being buffeted by external forces outside their sphere of influence. This involves the analysis of the nature and scope of empowerment and its relationship to relations of power inherent in the society in which one lives.

'Empowerment' is a fashionable concept in Britain and the western world, coined by practitioners in the health education, welfare and caring services to describe a situation in which 'lay people', working collaboratively with well-intentioned 'experts' (usually professionals), identify and articulate need, and participate actively in the delivery of services. The underlying assumption is that some people have more power than others and that they should be encouraged to share this power with those who have less. In this context, Gomm (1993) identifies four expressions of a power relationship, viz.,

1 an 'oppressive/liberating relationship' in which the victims (e.g. women, blacks, gays) of oppression (patriarchy, racism, heterosexism) are liberated through 'conscientisation', 'consciousness raising', and 'demystification' and group solidarity to challenge and contest the power of capital.
2 a 'helping relationship' in which professionals (e.g. teachers) identify (pupils') needs and satisfy them, or assist them to satisfy themselves – a relationship which relies on a 'deficit' model where empowerment is the acquisition of important skills and qualities to bring deficient individuals up to some 'norm' or standard.
3 a 'disabling relationship' where professional expertise is either demystified through the introduction of mechanisms of consumer responsiveness and accountability (thus further empowering central government) or is abolished altogether, ostensibly to encourage the self-reliance of individuals or the development of self-help groups (but in practice providing an opportunity for cost-cutting).
4 'brokerage relationship' in which less competitive groups are enabled and compete for scarce resources in a pluralist, market-oriented society through professional-led advocacy and self-advocacy systems.

Gomm's relationships draw attention to the range of meanings currently given to 'empowerment' and to empirically valid enactments of power relations. His statement that 'to empower someone else implies something which is granted by someone more powerful to someone who is less powerful' and his conclusion that 'those people who say they are in the business of empowering rarely seem to be giving up their own power: they are usually giving up someone else's and they may actually be increasing their own' (Gomm 1993: 137) are predicated on the false assumption that power has to be a finite quality that can be successfully re-allocated and equitably distributed. Power and oppression, as we have seen, are capacities for imposing control, for constructing the life experiences and life chances of others, and processes for maintenance and reformulation over time. Critics of the term 'empowerment' have argued that the term 'lacks specificity and glosses over significant differences, acting as a 'social aerosol', covering up the disturbing smell of conflict and conceptual division' (Ward and Mullender 1991: 147). Empowerment, it is asserted, must be linked to a commitment to challenging and combating injustice and oppression. To be empowered therefore means to be enabled politically; to empower necessarily means to educate for political literacy and to understand that empowerment/disempowerment works not only in the behaviours, values and attitudes of individuals and groups, but in institutions, structures and common-sense assumptions (Mitchell 1989).

In exploring the relationship between autonomy, authenticity, power, empowerment and oppression, it has either been explicitly argued or strongly implied that empowerment can offer analyses of control, can enable the challenge of oppression, can involve the articulation of rights and facilitate participation in democratic processes. Self-empowerment, a reflective variant of empowerment, offers explanations of 'consciousness raising', 'autonomy', 'demystification', 'challenge' and 'positive self-image', offers skills of interpersonal communication, self-advocacy, assertiveness and facilitation, and cultivates qualities such as 'respect for others', 'sensitivity towards social and cultural difference' and 'self-confidence'. In short, empowerment as the essential foundations of autonomy holds the promise of a liberating relationship with ourselves and others in which power relations, now understood (if not equalised), are harnessed to the achievement of a good and beneficent society, a society in which individuals and groups maximise their potential for well being and in which previously powerless groups can secure improved life chances. These principles already suggest the framework of a curriculum, the explicit goal of which is to educate for autonomy. The following section describes and evaluates the operationalisation of the key concepts discussed above (as either components or outcomes of 'autonomy') by reference to a curriculum in personal, social and health education.

EDUCATION FOR AUTONOMY: A CASE STUDY FROM HEALTH EDUCATION/PROMOTION

The nature, content and methods of 'education for health', or health education as it is known, are not well understood by those operating outside the field, to the extent that surprise is expressed when it becomes clear that health education is only partially concerned with medical facts about the causes of disease or with advice about how to be healthy. It also comes as a surprise to some that health education is the practice of an extremely wide range of professionals in the health, welfare, caring and education services in both statutory and voluntary spheres, and that its agencies in the UK include government departments, the national health service, the national body for health education (the Health Education Authority), community health councils, local government, the mass media, commercial organisations, retail pharmacists, occupational health services, education authorities, social services departments, environmental health, trade unions, local voluntary and community groups – to name but some. Finally, and importantly here, health education has, for at least two decades, been engaged in an in-depth exploration of the meaning and content of 'education for autonomy' using the operationalisation of the concept of 'empowerment' to inform curricular decision-making.

At this point, some clarification of the terms 'health', 'health promotion' and 'health education' is apposite. The much-quoted and universally criticised World Health Organisation definition is, nevertheless, powerful in its ability to map out a territory of shared understanding of this concept among the many agents and agencies identified above – as well as lay people.

> Health is a state of complete physical, mental and social well-being, and not merely the absence of disease or infirmity.
>
> (WHO 1946)

This indicates that health, and therefore health education, is concerned with the whole person, and encompasses physical, mental, social, emotional, spiritual and societal aspects. It also indicates that a positive and negative dimension may be identified: positive health which tends to be linked to well-being and fitness, and negative health which covers subjective aspects such as illness and discomfort and objective aspects expressed in concepts of disease, injury, handicap or deformity. 'These strands are linked via the idea of abnormal, unwanted or incapacitating states of a biological system, which in turn presupposes the idea of a good or flourishing human life' (Downie *et al.* 1990).

Health education is seen as a component of the broader concept of health promotion, and overlaps with prevention and health protection. Its role is to seek, through educational means, to enhance positive health and prevent or diminish ill-health, influencing beliefs, attitudes and behaviour. The stimulation of a healthy environment – social and political as well as physical – is an important objective and thus involves the education of power-holders in society as well as empowering individuals, groups and communities through clarifying values, developing life-skills, fostering self-esteem and employing participating methods. An understanding of the constraints to freedom of choice in health-related decision-making is acknowledged and the effects of socio-political factors on health are recognised, thus:

> Views concerning health and illness in society are always related to the distribution of power and authority within it. . . . Health education is, and must be, a political and ethical activity. The choice of a health education strategy will both reflect and influence social and political organisations.
>
> (Tucket 1979: 3)

The curriculum in personal, social and health education described here is a postgraduate in-service training programme for teachers which sets out to explore the essentially problematic nature of health education through the development of autonomy and empowerment in practice. The programme has been funded over a ten-year period by the Health Education Authority in London and has involved research, development, pilot, implementation, evaluation, modification and dissemination phases. Initially, data was collected in 1988 from teachers working across the full range of educational provision, from their employers, managers, from education authorities and from health services. The analysis of this data provided clear, unambiguous messages:

1 The health education/promotion role of schools and colleges in terms of enhancing the health of individuals, groups and environments is a central and crucial one. Teachers have a moral responsibility to set out the spectrum of health-related choices for their pupils/students, and to provide the necessary knowledge base and skills that enable these students to take decisions about their lifestyles and health-related behaviour.

2 Teachers recognised substantial benefit in multi-disciplinary training. Health education training taken in isolation from the many professionals in health, social, community and caring settings deprived them of valuable opportunities for extending their own health knowledge and skills, and from participating in dialogues which promoted the cross-fertilisation of ideas.

3 Health education/promotion is informed by the dialectic of social science and medical theorising on the one hand, and practice-related communicative and educational competence on the other. Models of directed learning are therefore inappropriate. Teachers should experience those ideas and methodologies which they, in turn, offer to their students. Thus, in keeping with the orientation of current orthodoxy about the nature and approach of health education/promotion programmes in the UK, a student-centred approach was adopted.

In 1990, the pilot course was launched, incorporating a set of principles implicated in the data: these remain distinctive features of this programme. They are:

● A curricular framework, conceived as a 'framework of experience', as opposed to a highly prescribed curriculum. Participating teachers (who have now, in 1996, been joined by a range of other professionals from medicine, health, community and social work settings), their employers and the course providers (in this case the Manchester Metropolitan University) actively negotiate the detail of the curricular content so as to respond to the personal, professional and organisational aspirations and objectives which participants bring to the course and to capitalise on the resources (in terms of existing knowledge and expertise) which they also bring with them. Thus curricular content is re-negotiated each time, and participants develop a personalised pathway through the programme.

● The main aim of the programme is to identify and develop/enhance the skills of empowerment and self-empowerment. This involves provision

172

of (health-related) knowledge, the practice of skills – decision-making, communication, interpersonal, conflict management, group work, prioritising, coping with sensitive issues, developing trust, providing feedback, facilitating, etc. – and the development of qualities such as respect for persons, valuing, self-image, self-esteem, assertiveness, empathy, compassion.

- A process-led curriculum, incorporating non-directive and non-authoritarian methodologies. These feature facilitation, empowerment strategies, self-help, sharing, peer-led learning, mutual exchange of knowledge and other resources, role interchange, multidisciplinary team-work, negotiated work-based activity, in- and post-course networking, attention to the use of language, opportunities for reflection, reflexivity, trust-development and self-disclosure, and a multicultural and international dimension.

The programme seeks to integrate two different strategies currently used to promote health – 'personal counselling for health' and 'community development for health' (Beattie 1991). Personal counselling for health involves interventions at individual and group level in which participants are invited to engage in active reflection and review of their own personal lifestyle and their individual scope for change. Pedagogy focuses on individual biography, reflection on the scope for personal choice and change, and emphasis on skills which effect change (confidence-building, self-assertion, decision-making, action-planning and contract-making). Here the individual is assisted in these processes by a facilitator who acts on a one-to-one basis or in the context of a supportive peer group (Heathcote 1994). Community development for health ('self-help health', 'community health action' or 'health out-reach'), with a similar pedigree and ideological underpinning to 'personal counselling for health', is concerned with mobilising groups which face common problems or share perceptions of disadvantage and purpose (e.g. local residents' groups, black and minority groups, women's groups, etc.). This approach is a 'way of helping groups of people who are otherwise alienated or depowered in matters of health – the most deprived or oppressed groups – to 'find a voice' for themselves' (Rosenthal 1980, quoted in Beattie 1991). The role of the health educator here may involve identifying and working with potential groups, acting as a facilitator to ensure free debate, distributing group resources and undertaking advocacy (see Gomm 1993, discussed earlier).

The course delivery incorporates a number of processes which are intended to maximise personal autonomy on the part of the participants. The five modules which comprise the programme are offered through the integrated use of workshops (in which participants work together, with a facilitator, in pairs, groups or individually), open learning materials (incorporating interactive exercises, short assignments and self-assessed questions), telephone tutorials, paired learning, self-help groups (based in the localities where participants live or work) and networking (both during and after the completion of the course). These particular approaches to teaching/learning afford the maximum 'space' to participants to map their own study routes to maximise group interaction and resource-sharing, increase personal control over the direction, nature and pace of personal and professional development, and offer the necessary flexibility to accommodate pressures and concerns in their personal lives. They also offer potential for developing life-skills and for practising facilitation and the empowerment of self and others. The post-course networking activities ensure that the skills, values and knowledge acquired in the programme can continue to flourish, with the support of colleagues, once the course is over.

The framework of experience offered to participants involves the creation of opportunities for reflection and reflexivity. The introductory module, for example, involves participants identifying targets for personal and profes-sional growth in the light of their consolidated experience to date and in plan-ning activities which they, supported by others (colleagues, family, friends), can take to achieve these goals. Against a backcloth of understanding of the contested and often problematic nature of health education, a broad menu of possible curricular content and in-course experiences are presented for discus-sion, negotiation and 'fine-tuning' within the group. A consensus is attempted concerning worthwhile and relevant content and experience to be offered within the course, and individuals are invited to volunteer to facilitate par-ticular sessions/topics. This encourages role interchange between tutors and course participants and offers opportunities for individuals to share their interests and talents with others. In selecting particular topics for study by the group, participants 'dovetail' their existing experience and personal resources to group and individual aspirations. The central focus of this module therefore is to enable each participant to 'map' the territory and boundaries of their conceptual and practice-related understanding of the field, and to undertake practical measures to widen the scope and nature of this understanding. One focus of this endeavour is undertaking novel experi-ences outside the immediate ambit of their routine professional work. Thus, a family doctor may spend time 'shadowing' an environmental health officer or a teacher may accompany a district nurse on her visits to patients in their home. This type of activity also offers opportunities for paired learning, team-building, the celebration of 'difference' and a re-appraisal of taken-for-granted assumptions (some of which may act to inhibit or disempower).

Further values clarification and the extension of experience, combined with the practice of a range of enabling skills, occurs in the second module. Here the emphasis is on providing theoretical frameworks and opportunities for reflection so as to 'order' and review professional and personal experiences. The 'space' in which to experiment, explore and discuss ideas in a non-threatening and supportive environment is also central to this module. The heterogeneity of the group in terms of culture, religion, professional and social background promotes the cross-fertilisation of ideas and the analysis of structural opportunities and constraints. These themes are continued in the following two modules which are located in course participants' workplace and which explore the possibilities for personal autonomy at work. Here the issue of power relations in professional practice is addressed through carrying out a set of innovatory activities with fellow workers, facilitated by the moral and resource-related support of the employer/line-manager. Skills acquired in the previous modules are implemented to effect work-based change, promoting the health of workers and their work environment. The precise focus of this change is negotiated and endorsed by the organisation's resource-holders. The next stage, dissemination, involves work-based colleagues becoming agents of continuing change through being empowered by the course participant who works co-operatively with them and the managers. In this way, the skills acquired from the programme are shared and worked with in the larger work-based community. In the case of teachers, this activity is designed to involve students, other teachers and the community beyond the school (parents, governors, neighbours). An advantage of this 'cascading' process is that course participants, on their return to their employing agency, are seen as valued and valuable resources.

From these brief illustrations it will be noted that the programme embodies certain assumptions:

1 the centrality of the concept of autonomy, and its interrelationships with 'empowerment', 'authenticity' (through reflective self-consciousness) and power (and therefore oppression);
2 the operational qualities of 'empowerment' in relation to the act of negotiating curricular content and valid experience, identifying appropriate teaching/learning methodologies, and developing a process-led curriculum;
3 the potential of a person-centred, experiential and process-led model for achieving not only personal development but also empowerment of groups and communities with regard to possible contradiction between individual and collective goals;
4 the recognition of the role of knowledge/understanding, values clarification, skills and interpersonal relationships in the pursuit of personal autonomy.

CONCLUDING REMARKS

This chapter has suggested that the development of autonomy and the use of empowering processes, relationships and language are particularly appropriate in areas of human endeavour that are contested, involve power relations and require skills in decision-taking in areas of central importance to one's life and to those in one's community. The programme described here has been adapted in culturally sympathetic ways to meet the needs of a number of countries undergoing socio-economic and political transition, notably in

Eastern Europe, and has been seen as assisting the development of political democracy. It is hoped and believed that this illustration of autonomy in practice has relevance and applicability in curricula for a wide range of other educational purposes and contexts.

REFERENCES

Althusser, L. (1971) 'Ideology and ideological state apparatuses', *Lenin and Philosophy and Other Essays*, London: New Left Books.

Beattie, A. (1991) 'Knowledge and control in health promotion: a test case for social policy and social theory' in Gabe, J., Calman, M. and Bury, M. (eds) *The Sociology of the Health Service*, London: Routledge.

Berne, E. (1969) *Games People Play*, Harmondsworth: Penguin.

Downie, R. S., Fife, C. and Tannahill, A. (1990) *Health Promotion: Models and Values*, Oxford: Oxford University Press.

Gomm, R. (1993) 'Issues of power in health and welfare' in Walmsley, J., Reynolds, J., Shakespeare, P. and Woolfe, R. (eds) *Health, Welfare and Practice*, London: Sage/ Open University Press.

Heathcote, G. (1994) 'Postgraduate training in health education and health promotion in the United Kingdom' in Benkö, Z. (ed.) *From Health Education to Health Promotion*, Szeged: Juhász Tanárkepzö Föiskola.

Heathcote, G. (1996) 'Health in the community: contradictions posed by an "empowerment" model of health promotion', *Journal of Community Studies* 3(i): 4–14.

Heathcote, G. and Issitt, M. (1994) 'Integrating theory and practice in health promotion through accredited work-based experience', in Vitró, A. and Benkö, Z. (eds) *Employers and Health Promotion Training*, Szeged: Juhász Gyula Tanárkepzö Föiskola.

Kant, I. (1949) [1782] *Groundwork of the Metaphysics of Morals*, 1st edn, ed. Paton, H. J., London: Hutchinson.

Luckmann, B. (1978) 'The small life-worlds of modern man' in Luckmann, T. (ed.) *Phenomenology and Sociology*, Harmondsworth: Penguin.

Mead, G. H. (1962) *Mind, Self and Society from the Standpoint of a Social Behaviourist*, ed. Morrisk, C. W., Chicago: University of Chicago.

Mitchell, G. (1989) 'Empowerment and opportunity', *Social Work Today*, 16 March: 14.

Rabinow, P. (ed.) (1986) *The Foucault Reader*, Harmondsworth: Penguin.

Strawbridge, S. (1993) 'Rules, roles and relationships' in Walmsley, J., Reynolds, J., Shakespeare, P. and Woolfe, R. (eds) *Health Welfare and Practice*, London: Sage/ Open University.

Tuckett, D. (1979) 'Choices for health education: a sociological view' in Sutherland, I. (ed.) *Health Education: Perspectives and Choices*, London: Allen & Unwin.

Ward, D. and Mullender, A. (1991) 'Empowerment and oppression: an indissoluble pairing for contemporary social work', *Critical Social Policy* 32: 21–30.

World Health Organisation (1946) *Constitution*, New York: WHO.

15

EMPOWERMENT: EMANCIPATION OR ENERVATION?

Michael Fielding

Empowerment is a notion which is centrally important in debates about identity, autonomy and citizenship which are at the heart of social and political dilemmas many countries and regions are facing at the present time. However, for some time now it has been possible to argue that empowerment has reached a critical stage in its development, particularly within the arena of educational discourse. Simultaneously championed on the one hand by proponents of market-led reforms and on the other hand by those whose concerns have more to do with the development of an emancipated citizenry than with the proliferation of free-wheeling consumers, its semantic fabric is inclined to fall apart at the touch. However, whilst it is true the burgeoning use of 'empowerment' has gone hand in hand with its increasingly elusive meaning, paradoxically, its significance has become more rather than less compelling.

In the face of the kind of conceptual enervation to which writers like Vincent (1993: 374) rightly draw our attention, together with evidence from the United States that 'the concept of empowerment has come to be regarded by many teachers as yet another cynical and reformist panacea' (LeCompte and de Marrais 1992: 22), the temptation is to write empowerment off as a reliably and unremittingly vacuous notion suggesting we would be as well to just get on with our lives by ignoring it, making grudging allowances for it, and/or regarding the speaker with appropriate suspicion. None of these responses is appropriate. However fatuous or pretentious its utterance, empowerment is neither trivial nor trite in its ambitions or consequences. To ignore or marginalise its use is to misunderstand the seriousness and power of language even if, or especially when, it is used carelessly or crudely. The social and political threads which comprise the various linguistic cloths that then become the garments of conversation and debate have in their weave the texture and colour of different ideals of human flourishing. The intention of this chapter is to render problematic the notion of empowerment in educational discourse, to examine with appropriate care and attentiveness the assumptions that inform its use, to map the conceptual frameworks which support and enrich those assumptions, and, finally, to make a number of suggestions with regard to its future development.

EMPOWERMENT AS PROCESS

The dominant account of empowerment, both in education and in industry, is what I shall call the 'process' or 'neutral' view. On this account empowerment is about those with power giving those whom they decide are appropriate recipients greater capacity to make decisions about the nature of their work or greater involvement in their legitimate sphere of interest.

The general presuppositions of the word empowerment within 'process' discourses are that: (a) there is an agent of empowerment, i.e. someone or something is doing the empowering; (b) power is akin to property which is transferred from one agent to another whether it be teachers, parents or students/pupils; (c) those who have been empowered are given the opportunity to exert greater control over matters which are thought to be important to them. It is the exercising of that control, often through processes involving others, that is at the heart of empowerment. On this account it is not *what* is decided that is important; rather it is the double fact that the empowered, first, are now able to make decisions without reference to others in senior position and, second, in cases where wider institutional matters are at stake they have an entitlement to be involved in processes of negotiation and discussion; hence my umbrella term – the 'process' view of empowerment.

My initial critique of the process account of empowerment has two broad aspects. The first is to do with the extent to which those doing the empowering retain control, often in covert rather than open ways. The second concerns a range of more strictly philosophical issues which have partly to do with the nature of power and partly to do with the process of empowerment itself. Some of my other concerns, to do with what is left out as opposed to what is mistakenly included and more fundamentally to do with the philosophical inadequacy of its individualist foundations, are addressed in the sections below on the emancipatory and postmodern approaches to empowerment.

My first concern about the process view of empowerment is that there is frequently a substantial limitation on the extent to which power is unambiguously and publicly devolved or retained. The word empowerment carries with it a promise of autonomy and the capacity to shape work in ways which not only reflect but develop the skills, expertise and aspirations of the person who is empowered. The reality is more likely to be one in which the arena of empowerment is relatively small and the boundaries firmly fixed, though often indistinctly drawn.

Even more important than this managerial point is the issue of curriculum. The key argument here is that empowerment is too grand and too misleading a banner to wave if the most important area of life in schools remains outside the ambit of teachers' professional influence. The ironies and contradictions of affirming an enhanced professionalism whilst at the same time removing the possibility of curriculum dialogue are picked up by a number of writers such as Aimee Howley (1990: 30), Andy Hargreaves (1994: 68) and Wayne

178

Ross (1990). Reflecting on the historical context of the current push to empowerment, Ross wryly observes of the USA context that 'It's paradoxical that a situation which has led to the slow erosion of teachers' control over their jobs has been combined with the rhetoric of increased professionalism' (Ross 1990: 11). Whilst acknowledging that 'Professionalism and increased responsibility go hand in hand', he observes that 'in this case teachers find themselves making more technical/management decisions, working longer hours, and *having less control over the curriculum they teach*' (Ross 1990: 11; emphasis mine).

Whilst empowerment is often advocated as a liberating process for those involved, it is just as possible to experience it as the reverse. This is not only to do with the degree of control which teachers have over their work; it is also to do with the nature of the work in which their empowerment now invites or requires them to be involved. Many 'empowered' teachers become demoralised and deskilled: demoralised because their particular expertise and experience in helping their pupils to learn joyfully as well as effectively seem decreasingly important and increasingly difficult to sustain; deskilled because the freedom they are given focuses on concerns and processes with which they are unfamiliar or out of sympathy or both.

An additional substantial concern of critics of the process view of empowerment is that its ascendancy has gone hand in hand with an equivalent increase in centralisation. In the UK, for example, processes of centralised control through the agency of a heavily conditioned and distinctly relative local autonomy are discernible in the self-absorption of the self-managing school. It is not just that schools are involved in what amounts to professional self-mutilation; they are active agents in a process over which they seem to have little or no control. As Stephen Ball argues, 'Within the microtechnologies of control (like self-management) those who exercise power are just as much captured as those over whom power is wielded' (Ball 1993: 78).

Furthermore, that process of control is additionally enhanced by the language of empowerment itself. The work of Smyth (1987: 18) in Australia and Fielding (1994: 29–31) in the UK point firmly to the dissembling character of much empowerment discourse where the vocabulary of liberation is deliberately used to entice and dupe.

The points considered thus far in my critique of the process view of empowerment are to varying degrees amenable to change and are contingent on the values and purposes of those who are in dominant positions of power. The following four are of a different order since they come closer to a more fundamental consideration of the nature of power and its relation to empowerment.

The first argues that too often the stubborn reality of power as a zero-sum notion is ignored or resisted. Thus, in a recent critique of empowerment in community education, Bob O'Hagan argues that power is not a thing but a relationship and that power must involve at least two people. 'In other words an individual or group has power only to the extent, indeed the identical extent that another individual or group is deprived of power' (O'Hagan 1991: 18). Refusal to grasp this, perhaps uncomfortable, feature of power invariably compounds unrealistic expectations of those being empowered and overcomfortable perceptions of those who are doing the empowering. Whilst not all writers within the process tradition would subscribe to power as a zero-sum notion, for those who do there is a necessity, but often a reluctance, to acknowledge that if X is the person doing the empowering and Y is the person being empowered then X (or someone else whom X has previously invested with power) has, as a direct consequence of that act, less power.

A second point concerns empowerment and the legacy of dependency. Peters and Marshall (1991) remind us that, whilst the recent past has seen the term colonised by both the Left and the Right, the linguistic origins of 'empowerment' lie in a quasi-legal nexus of relationships in which one person transferred power to another. Whilst semantic genealogy is not always pertinent it seems to me that there is a double point here which helps to bring into sharper relief the nature of the power relations involved and the susurrus of dependency which lies beneath the surface. First, the transfer of power from one person to another (viz. the Latin prefix 'en' or 'em' meaning 'to give') underscores the dependency relationship between the person being empowered and the person doing the empowering. Empowerment is dependent upon the goodwill or self-interest of the person with the power who, for whatever reason, decides not just that power will be transferred, but how much power and what sort of power. Second, in establishing the boundaries, intersections and common terrain of power the relationship between the two must not only, by definition, be unequal, the internal logic of empowerment implies, at least initially, a passivity on the part of the person being empowered. That person is in the position of receiving whatever power the other decides it is appropriate to give.

A rather odd manifestation of these essentially unequal relations is now increasingly relevant in the form of mandated empowerment, i.e. 'You will be empowered whether you like it or not. Empowerment is good for you!' Given that much of the rhetoric of empowerment within the process tradition aspires to the creation of professional circumstances in which teachers have greater satisfaction through greater professional scope and control there is, initially at least, an apparent inconsistency or puzzlement about empowerment as something which is required or mandated. Mandated empowerment slips too readily from an enlightened expansion of professionalism and the proper acceptance of responsibilities to the desperate or cynical dumping of unwanted and unwarranted tasks and requirements on staff who are already stretched to the limit.

A final point of concern often raised by critics of the process view concerns the adequacy or otherwise of the response to the question 'Empowerment for what?' The insistence, not just on the importance of this question, but also on its location at the start of any discussions about empowerment bring into sharp relief those who regard processes as good in themselves and those for whom processes cannot be separated from the ends which they seek to serve. These issues are particularly pertinent in times where some schools clearly regard the 'empowerment' of the marketplace as the legitimation of predatory behaviour towards neighbouring schools, whilst others change their admission policy for reasons they are reluctant to acknowledge.

EMPOWERMENT AND EMANCIPATION

An emancipatory account of empowerment argues that to characterise the notion purely in terms of process and without reference to particular values which form part of its texture is to miss the point. It is these values and purposes that give empowerment its attraction and its capacity to change things for the better for those who have previously been excluded from power. To make the question of values and purposes extrinsic to the notion of empowerment is to run a much greater risk of empowerment being used as a buzz word whilst enabling those who do the 'empowering' to get on covertly with the real business of ensuring the world remains much the same as it is or only moves in the direction in which their interests lie.

There are four main points which seem to me to characterise the emancipatory view of empowerment and set it apart from its process counterpart. One of the most striking concerns the unremitting insistence on adopting the standpoint of the powerless and the underscoring of the differences between the two parties. Thus, Roger Simon argues that in an educational context empowerment is most appropriately used in the spirit of critique and that 'Its referent is the identification of oppressive and unjust relations within which there is an unwarranted limitation placed on human action, feeling, and thought' (Simon 1987: 374).

Empowerment, then, is not just a set of processes; it is a struggle in difficult and often hostile contexts. What sustains those involved in that struggle is also a key area of difference between the process and emancipatory accounts. The point of the struggle is to realise a view of social justice and the development of the democratic way of life. As Colin Fletcher has it, 'Empowerment is the direction and achievement of a critical democracy' (Fletcher 1989: 59). Within the semantic enclosure of empowerment lie social and political ramparts which are part of the geography of its meaning. The context of individual growth cannot be separated from the kind of flourishing that is thought worthwhile.

Fletcher's emphasis on critical democracy points to another recurring feature of the emancipatory account of empowerment – the obligation to challenge, critique and question in ways which push the powerful back onto the ethical and political haunches of the current distribution of power. In arguing that empowerment is centrally about 'the ability to think and act critically' (Giroux 1993:11), Henry Giroux goes on to articulate the importance of that thinking and acting having the tenacity and courage to challenge at a fundamental level. Empowerment is thus not about giving power or allowing freedom of thought and action within a clearly defined sphere; it is about rupturing that sphere and shaping it anew.

The differences between the emancipatory and the process accounts with regard to the intensity and scope of challenge is also reflected in distinctions some commentators seek to draw between 'enabling' and 'empowering'. In her critique of a consumerist approach to education, Carol Vincent argues that the accompanying model of empowerment which sees itself as concerned with an individual's capacity to manipulate the system to their own ends is more appropriately described as 'enabling' (Vincent 1993: 375). In an emancipatory account empowerment is transformational in a collective and communal sense.

A further debate within the emancipatory tradition centres round the notion of 'voice'. One view is that empowerment is crucially about enabling those who are oppressed to speak and to be heard. However, writers like Giroux and McLaren (1986) and Simon (1987) argue that, whilst it is true that part of what is meant by empowerment is to 'counter the power of some people or groups to make others "mute" . . . to enable those who have been silenced to speak' (Simon 1987: 374), this is not enough. There needs to be a recognition of and an appropriate strategy for transforming the structural context in which those voices speak to each other.

POSTMODERN APPROACHES TO EMPOWERMENT

It seems to me that the emancipatory account of empowerment is very much more compelling that its proceduralist counterpart; it is less likely to be hijacked by those whose motives have more to do with retaining rather than releasing power over fundamental areas of human interaction; it is transparent about its commitment to certain values and is therefore open to explicit challenge or agreement which itself enriches the quality of public life; and its view of human being and becoming has within it a creative tension between optimism and vulnerability which releases tremendous energy, transformational learning and the desire for a better future. However, it has recently come under sustained attack from writers like Ellsworth (1989), Gore (1989, 1990, 1993), Lather (1991) and Peters and Marshall (1991) writing from, largely Foucauldian, postmodern standpoints.

As with the emancipatory critique of the process view of empowerment, postmodern antipathies to many aspects of the emancipatory accounts can be broadly divided into two areas of concern. First, those that have to do with what are seen as flaws at the heart of the humanist, Enlightenment project; second, those that focus more intently on the underlying notions of power.

Interestingly enough, a number of the postmodern criticisms of emancipatory accounts echo emancipatory objections to process views. Thus the apparent refusal of many process advocates to take the issue of context seriously is, albeit in a different form, also seen as true of some emancipatory writing. Writers like Jennifer Gore argue that much emancipatory advocacy is too general, too broad a brush and pitched at a level of abstraction which, despite its best intentions and the strength of its purposes and commitments, is debilitating rather than empowering. The magnitude and urgency of the commitments find expression in language which dwarfs and immobilises the very agency it intends to encourage.

The paradoxically immobilising passion and ambition of much emancipatory exhortation is also seen as, not just psychologically paralysing, but seriously wide of the mark with regard to what is actually achievable in the daily reality that teachers face. Thus Gore argues that '(T)hese claims to empowerment attribute extraordinary abilities to the teacher, and hold a view of agency which risks ignoring the context of teachers' work. . . . Overly optimistic views of the agent of empowerment also set up serious shortcomings in the use of empowerment rhetoric' (Gore 1989: 9; see also Peters and Marshall 1991: 127). The cause of emancipatory empowerment is not well served by transforming the teacher into a revolutionary icon.

The breadth of the canvas on which many emancipatory writers paint their pictures of preferred futures is also seen as one of the major theoretical weaknesses typical of the humanist tradition with which so many postmoderns take deep exception. Because critical and feminist theorists are concerned for 'context at the broad level of societal relations and institutions and ideologies (be they capitalist and/or patriarchal) [this] leads to totalising or universalising tendencies which imply their concern is for "all teachers" or "all students" or "all women"' (Gore 1990: 11). Too many advocates of empowerment move too quickly to the presumption that their visions and values have general significance rather than local, transitory reference. Many writers such as Peters and Marshall also argue that errors of this sort are not primarily to do with the excesses of intellectual over-excitement, but rather with a fundamental flaw in the Enlightenment notion of the human subject (Peters and Marshall 1991: 128).

Too often the totalising tendency of writers within the emancipatory tradition is accompanied by the hint of what is perceived as barely concealed arrogance and prescriptiveness which sits uncomfortably alongside a commitment to empowering others to free themselves from oppression. The persistent difficulty here is giving an adequate answer to the question 'Who decides what is socially just or responsible?' As Gore reminds us, 'If we claim moral superiority or emancipatory authority we risk the arrogance of assuming that we can say for others what they need' (Gore 1989: 12).

Charges of arrogance and prescriptiveness are often accompanied by the companion point that any advocacy from whatever standpoint is inevitably biased or partial. Utilising Foucault's notion of 'regimes of truth' in which the seamless interweaving of power and knowledge provide the backcloth against which discourse is legitimately conducted, those in the emancipatory vanguard are attacked for a seeming reluctance to acknowledge that they too are necessarily susceptible to the distortions, limitations and partiality of their newly-imposed regimes of truth.

A related concern of Gore's is not just that any position is inevitably partial, inevitably flawed, but that these necessary limitations are exacerbated by the kind of misperceptions and distortions that accrue with the sheer distance between the reality and the experience of oppression and the comfortable positions held by those intellectuals arguing for its elimination (see Gore 1989: 13).

The last of the postmodern objections clustering around their opposition to the totalising tendency of emancipatory writers parallels the earlier critique of the process view. Here the suggestion is that in the reality of today's schools and other educational institutions empowerment cannot achieve what emancipatory advocates want of it. If it is true that the process view overreaches itself, how much more true is this of the emancipatory view which aspires to a transformation which is even more fundamental? The very attractiveness of the emancipatory account of empowerment thus turns out to be a major obstacle to its actual realisation in practice.

Gore's further criticisms of many emancipatory accounts of empowerment coalesce more closely round the nature of power. One of her worries is that there seems little willingness to face up to the perhaps necessarily oppressive aspects of an emancipatory account. Gore argues that, if empowerment is linked to emancipation and emancipation often involves coercing those who are not being emancipated, are there not tensions here that need to be addressed more explicitly and more often?

A further concern, again linked to possibly oppressive paradoxes within the interstices of empowerment, turns its attention inward and asks, 'How do we help others to feel empowered when we have to rely on our authority and privilege to do so, and which sets us in a specifically contradictory position?' (Gore 1989: 15).

The most important of Gore's objections to emancipatory accounts of empowerment arises from her advocacy of a Foucauldian view of power. On this view, it is a mistake to regard power as a commodity or as a zero-sum notion. Foucault's account of power suggests it is circulating, exercised, and exists only in action. For him

Power is employed and exercised through a net-like organisation. And not only do individuals circulate through its threads; they are always in the position of simultaneously undergoing and exercising this power. They are not only its inert or consenting target. They are always also the elements of its articulation. In other words, individuals are vehicles of power, not its point of application.

(Foucault 1980: 89)

If this is true, then much of the writing in the emancipatory tradition is seriously flawed since it is predicated on too crude and too restricting an understanding of power.

Given their wish to acknowledge and celebrate the constantly shifting, contradictory nature of human subjectivity, given their mistrust of the tendency of emancipatory projects to speak too stridently, too arrogantly, and too impenetrably on behalf of those they seek to empower, given the perceived propensity of writers within the emancipatory tradition to pay too little attention to the specific, concrete nature of the contexts of struggle, it is not surprising that the positive recommendations of postmodern writers are frequently sparing and tentative. In seeking to construct a postmodern account of empowerment which attempts to avoid the totalising pitfalls of their humanist predecessors four suggestions emerge which stress the necessity of humility, realism and reciprocity.

First, given the sensitivity to the constantly shifting, layered nature of human identity, many postmodern writers are impatient with binary oppositions like dominant/subordinate, power/powerless and, like Gore, insist on '(t)he multiplicity and contradictions of power relations' (Gore 1989: 16). Second, the very complexity and situated nature of circumstances and relationships leads unsurprisingly to the advocacy of a persistent and pervasive provisionality. Realism, humility and reflexivity should be writ large in our work. Third, the tentative, hesitant tenor of these orientations towards empowerment initially led Gore to argue that its multiple, complex nature suggests that 'rather than embrace a notion of empowerment which assumes an imbalance of power between social actors, it may be more helpful to think of negotiating actions within particular contexts' (Gore 1989: 16). Writing a year later she developed her position to offer a reconstruction of empowerment as 'the exercise of power in an attempt to help others to exercise power' (Gore 1990: 21) and argued that scholars within the critical and feminist traditions might consider redirecting their emancipatory gaze inwards 'at seeking ways to exercise power toward the fulfilment of our espoused aims, ways that include humility, scepticism and self-criticism' (Gore 1990: 21). Fourth, in contrast to Gore, Peters and Marshall, while equally adamant about many of the failings of the humanist project, resist her apparently inward turn and retain the traditional emancipatory commitment to the communal nature of human being and becoming. For them, empowerment is essentially bound up with a notion of 'community-in-process' which 'openly and critically appraises difference and heterogeneity as a basis for collective self-consciousness and community action' (Peters and Marshall 1991: 128).

BEYOND EMPOWERMENT: THE CASE FOR CONCEPTUAL COURAGE

The postmodern critiques of empowerment have some important cautionary reminders which those within the emancipatory tradition would do well to take heed of. However, it is unsatisfactory for at least two sorts of reasons. First, their insistence on valuing the layered and dynamic nature of difference and identity pays too little attention to their increasingly tenuous link with the deeply transformative aspirations of the emancipatory project with which they clearly remain in broad sympathy. Second, despite its fierce reputation as a demolisher of the old certainties the postmodern accounts of empowerment remain timidly rooted in the soil of an unadventurous present.

Gore's empowerment-as-negotiation is helpful in the sense that it moves us away from too crude a view of social and political reality which paints the particularities and practicalities of specific circumstances in too narrow a range of starkly contrasting colours. However, in the desire to acknowledge the dangers of emancipatory arrogance and encourage the empowered to pursue their own agenda, empowerment-as-negotiation seems to lose its urgency and loosen its grip on justice. A postmodern notion of empowerment which privileges the possibility of negotiation over the brute reality of oppression weakens its engagement with the reality it is trying so hard to transform. The fact is that a fundamental imbalance of power remains a recalcitrant reality for huge numbers of people in many aspects of their lives. The technical possibility of 'negotiating actions within particular contexts' may be formally true, but, in a lived sense, persistently and painfully false.

Gore's subsequent empowerment-as-the-exercise-of-power-in-an-attempt-to-help-others-to-exercise-power is an imaginative and ingenious attempt to incorporate Foucault's notion of power into a postmodern account of empowerment. However, as an account of empowerment it remains unsatisfactory. It is unclear on this account whether the help is conditional and for how long it is to be offered. In other words, there are likely to be limits to the nature and longevity of the help, but neither are acknowledged or seen as problematic.

What is of particular concern is that postmodern sensitivities to the integrity of those who are to be empowered seem to result in an unwillingness to raise the question so central to the emancipatory tradition, namely, 'Empowerment for What?' It is unclear from Gore's work how she is to avoid the slide back to empowerment-as-process. Whilst her proposals are more challenging of old certainties than one normally associates with the process view, there seems to me to be a residual difficulty for her empowerer in distinguishing between what is trivial or iniquitous and what is worthwhile.

In the end, the notion of empowerment won't do what is being asked of it by any of its advocates, whether they be in the emancipatory or transformative postmodern traditions. Empowerment remains recalcitrantly a victim of its internal logic; it has within it the inescapable dependency of someone who 'receives' at the discretion of another who 'gives'. This remains as true for a Foucauldian account as for any other.

This will be persistently true for as long as those who have been empowered regard empowerment as an appropriate term to describe the context as well as the scope and manner in which they act. There will, however, come a point when it ceases to be appropriate. If empowerment leads to the empowered being able to rupture the boundaries that circumscribe their work in ways which are permanent then they are no longer 'empowered' to take certain sorts of decision – they 'make' the decision without reference to the original source of power. Just as empowerment takes a huge step forward from delegation so another notion is needed to help us take, not just a large step, but a quantum leap from empowerment to arrangements in which individuals, groups, even organisations themselves act in ways which are significantly different. Empowerment is best seen as a useful stepping stone from dependency and domination to a social and political circumstance in which interdependence and the importance of human agency are paramount; to develop that agency in ways which are liberating and exploratory we need a language which opens up possibilities in ways which existing discourse discourages or disallows.

One possibility would be to acknowledge both the interminability and the inevitability of disputes surrounding the notion of empowerment in much the same way as Steven Lukes (1974) and others have in suggesting that power is an essentially contested concept. That is certainly an option, but not one that addresses the issue at the heart of this chapter, namely, that there is too much about the notion of empowerment that too often looks too willingly and too warily over its shoulder. What is needed is a notion which is at once exploratory and courageous in its disposition, communal and reflexive in its approach, historical and concrete in its awareness, and democratic and transforming in its aspirations.

Given the growing importance of issues of power and identity in the world today, the pursuit of conceptual exploration in these areas is an undertaking worth trying, even if the substantive journeys are not as revealing or groundbreaking as one would wish. There are three related points which together provide justification for a project of this nature. First, the language we use to talk about our work and our aspirations opens up and closes down possibilities for us. Second, there are substantive historical examples of creative conceptual mapping (see Fielding 1996: 414), which not only helped to mark out distinctions between different political and social viewpoints, but also provided a cartography of human aspiration which sustained and developed the understanding of those who spoke its language and inhabited its, then only partially charted, terrain. Third, in certain circumstances there is a case for trying to develop a language which matches and extends our sense of possibility.

Empowerment honestly understood within the process tradition may not require a severing of ties with those who sanction its development. Those ties may be seen as both enabling and necessary in a number of respects. Many teachers undoubtedly feel more comfortable with empowerment arrangements that involve a greater degree of relative autonomy to do the job in ways which enable them to exercise their professional judgement and responsibility, but which nonetheless retain the familiar, potentially supportive sources of both power and authority. For other teachers such a view espouses a perhaps benevolent, but nonetheless unacceptably limiting dependency that is too often prone to deference, none of which is in any genuine sense transformational, inspiring or democratically fitting. Those within the emancipatory tradition and its postmodern, or, as some would have it, 'neomodern' (Alexander 1995) counterpart cannot with integrity or conviction countenance a central place accorded to any notion which retains the conceptual and practical birthmarks of a dependant and intrusively conditional freedom.

Those of us who wish to shape the world more closely to the intent and the integrity of our aspirations must match them with language that affirms what we wish to become, rather than remind us of what others wish us to remain. Empowerment has run it course; it is time to move on.

ACKNOWLEDGEMENT

Earlier versions of this chapter were read as papers at the Cambridge Branch of the Philosophy of Education Society; at the International Conference on Educational Reform, National Taiwan Normal University, Taipei, Taiwan 14–16 March, 1995; and at the Philosophy of Education Society Annual Conference at New College, Oxford 31 March–2 April, 1995. My thanks and acknowledgements to the Philosophy of Education Society of Great Britain for financial assistance with regard to the Taiwan conference. My thanks, too, to participants at both conferences for their observations and criticisms. Special thanks for the support of friends and colleagues who commented on the various drafts of these papers, in particular David Hargreaves, Fred Inglis, Richard Smith, Harry Torrance and Patricia White. Finally, thanks to David Bridges and Wilf Carr for patience and encouragement well beyond what could reasonably be expected, to the comments and encouragement from the *Journal of Education Policy* reviewer, to the editor of that journal, Stephen Ball, and to Taylor & Francis for permission to draw substantially on the extended version of this chapter.

REFERENCES

Alexander, J.C. (1995) 'Modern, Anti, Post, Neo', *New Left Review* 210, March/April: 63–101.

Ball, S.J. (1993) 'Culture, Cost and Control: Self-Management and Entrepreneurial Schooling in England and Wales' in J. Smyth (ed.) *A Socially Critical View of 'The Self-Managing School'*, London: Falmer Press.

Ellsworth, E. (1989) 'Why Doesn't This Feel Empowering? Working Through the Repressive Myths of Critical Pedagogy', *Harvard Educational Review* 59, 3: 297–324.

Fielding, M. (1994) 'Delivery, Packages and the Denial of Learning: Reversing the Language and Practice of Contemporary INSET' in H. Bradley, C. Conner and G. Southworth (eds) *Developing Teachers Developing Schools*, London: Fulton.

Fielding, M. (1996) 'Empowerment: Emancipation or Enervation?', *Journal of Education Policy* 11, 3: 399–417.

Fletcher, C. (1989) 'Towards Empowerment in Community Education' in C. Harber and R. Meighan (eds) *The Democratic School*, Ticknall: Education Now.

Foucault, M. (1980) 'Two lectures' in C. Gordon (ed.) *Power/Knowledge: Selected Interviews and Other Writings 1972–1977*, London: Harvester Wheatsheaf.

Giroux, H. (1993) *Border Crossings*, London: Routledge.

Giroux, H. and McLaren, P. (1986) 'Teacher Education and the Politics of Engagement: The Case for Democratic Schooling', *Harvard Educational Review* 56, 3: 213–38.

Gore, J.M. (1989) 'Agency, Structure and the Rhetoric of Teacher Empowerment', paper presented to the Annual Meeting of the American Educational Research Association, San Francisco, CA, 27–31 March, 26 pp.

Gore, J.M. (1990) 'What Can We Do For You! What *Can* "We" Do For "You"?: Struggling over Empowerment in Critical and Feminist Pedagogy', *Educational Foundations*, 4, 3: 5–26.

Gore, J. M (1993) *The Struggle for Pedagogies*, London: Routledge.

Hargreaves, A. (1994) *Changing Teachers, Changing Times*, London: Cassell.

Howley, A. (1990) 'Teacher Empowerment: Three Perspectives', paper presented at the Southern Regional Council on Educational Administration, Atlanta, GA, 11–13 November, 39 pp.

Lather, P. (1991) *Getting Smart: Feminist Research and Pedagogy With/in the Postmodern*, London: Routledge.

LeCompte, M.D. and de Marrais, K.B. (1992) 'The Disempowering of Empowerment: Out of the Revolution and into the Classroom', *Educational Foundations* 6, 3: 5–31.

Lukes, S. (1974) *Power: A Radical View*, London: Macmillan.

O'Hagan, B (1991) 'Empowerment: A Fallacy?', *Community Education Network* 11, 4: 18–19.

Peters, M. and Marshall, J. D. (1991) 'Education and Empowerment: Postmodernism and the Critique of Humanism', *Education and Society* 8, 2: 123–34.

Ross, E.W. (1990) 'Teacher Empowerment and the Ideology of Professionalism', paper presented at the Annual Convention of the New York State Council for the Social Studies, Buffalo, New York, 6 April, 13 pp.

Simon, R. (1987) 'Empowerment as a Pedagogy of Possibility', *Language Arts* 64, 4: 370–82.

Smyth, J. (1987) 'Teachers-as-intellectuals in a critical pedagogy of schooling', *Education and Society* 5, 1&2: 11–28.

Vincent, C. (1993) 'Education For The Community?', *British Journal of Educational Studies* 41, 4: 366–80.

16

PUPILS' AUTONOMY, CULTURAL HEGEMONY AND EDUCATION FOR DEMOCRACY IN AN AFRICAN SOCIETY

Akilu Sani Indabawa

INTRODUCTION

Although there are certain universal demands on the educational structure in any time and place, any aim of education is essentially specific to *society* and *time*. Aims of education are designed so that education helps to bring about some state of affairs that the power hierarchy in a society has defined as desirable. The definition of worthwhile aims of education and the selection of appropriate curricula contents to match these is to a large extent subject to the dictates of (for example) what is taken to be in the national interests as these are conceived by those in authority. That is one reason why most aims of education are contentious.

One contentious aim of education is the development of pupils' capacities to become autonomous (Dworkin 1976, Young 1980, Fleming 1981, Callan 1988, Macedo 1990, White 1990, Norman 1994). Discourse on individual or personal autonomy as an educational aim largely focuses on the conditions that are necessary and sufficient for pupils to become autonomous. Whether or not the development of personal autonomy *should be* a universal aim of education is, however, also an issue for continuous debate. While some societies and cultures may accept the development of pupils' personal autonomy as an educational aim at specific times in their history, others may and do take a very different position. There is an issue which arises here, which is how the development of personal autonomy as an aim of education should be discussed and understood in the contexts of cultural pluralities and emerging liberal democracies. This chapter examines the place of autonomy as an educational aim in relation to the apparent tensions between cultural pluralism and relativism on one hand, and the demands of an emergent democratic dispensation on the other. Examples will be drawn from Nigeria – one of the most culturally complex societies of twentieth-century Africa.

190

CONCEPTIONS OF AUTONOMY

Although there is an apparent general endorsement of the basic ideas (of some forms of freedom) entailed by autonomy, the concept is clearly a contested one which encompasses a variety of different principles. Lee and Wringe (1993), for example, identified three conceptions of autonomy which feature in the debate: voluntarist, existential, and rationalist. There are also other competing conceptions of personal autonomy, but much of the debate on autonomy as an educational ideal is centred around these three conceptions.

A voluntarist conception of autonomy is centred on the idea of respecting the autonomy of others in such a way as 'to see them as ends, not solely as means, for to respect the autonomy of others is to voluntarily relinquish control over their actions' (Lee and Wringe 1993: 69). Individuals are treated not as means to any defined ends, but as ends in themselves. They have desires, feelings, etc., as well as capacities to reason and independently define their distinctive courses of action, feelings or thoughts. The voluntarist view seems to have been premised on Hume's ideas that desires are given, 'the functions of reason being simply to identify the means by which they may best be achieved' (Lee and Wringe 1993: 70). The voluntarist conception of autonomy may be challenged on the ground that it gives little or no regard to the individual's right to 'autonomous choice of goals itself' (Lee and Wringe 1993: 70).

The existential conception lays stress on the individual's image of independently creating his or her own destiny – one being his or her own person. The existential conception does not make a distinction between one being his or her person, and self-origination of one's own decisions and choices. It also does not seem to take the context for making choices into consideration.

The rationalist view of autonomy is rested on Kant's theory of autonomy as the ability by a person freely and independently to make rational choices in a non-coercive atmosphere. The rationalist theory of autonomy is at one with Mill's view of personal autonomy as self-determination. This conception has been criticised by many philosophers, among them Bonnet (1986) and Wringe (1988). Reasons and rationality are not to be detached from specific social, political, historical and economic contexts. Reasoning structure is not strictly a neutral affair, it is also rooted in the contexts which are referred to. Indeed it can even be claimed that the reasoning structure employed in making rational choices and decisions is itself defined by the larger structure of thoughts and actions in place at any time in any society.

Autonomy may be conceived in the *positive* – following Mill's tradition – as the capacity for an individual to make independent and rational choices and decisions. The liberal tradition within which context autonomy is discussed sums up this conception of personal autonomy as one's capacity for 'self-determination' and 'self-origination'. But both self-determination and self-origination have been variously challenged as being insufficient for autonomy. Mill's conception – autonomy as self-determination – (*On Liberty*) centres around the ideas of independent and rational choice made by the person. But self-determination alone is not sufficient for autonomy unless its proper meaning is articulated and its conditions spelt out. One may determine causes of action for himself or herself, but only within a range of possibilities *known* to him or her, or *available* to him or her, at any particular time. The knowledge of these possibilities changes with changes in the conditions which make them possible. Being predicated on these, personal autonomy as self-determination and self-origination also changes so constantly and frequently that it is not possible to say categorically when exactly a person is indeed autonomous.

Similarly self-origination appears as a weak characterisation of personal autonomy. An idea, a cause of action, for example X, may originate from a person although conditions have been laid for him or her to have little or no alternative to X. One may also have a limitation in making ill-informed, mistaken or outright wrong choices which are not consistent with his or her interests. So while an autonomous person requires some capacities for *independent choice* and *rationality* in his or her thoughts, feelings, emotions, actions, etc., the two operative terms are nonetheless heavily loaded with possibilities for historical, social and ideological underpinnings. An autonomous person can only live within the contexts of *a specific time and space*, within which dynamics, cultures and ideologies also feature. These are then some essential factors which are necessary for any conception of an autonomous person. The cultures or ideologies define whether or not any form of personal autonomy is required by the society as one of its educational ideals.

Given the holistic and explanatory elements involved in the debate on autonomy (for example, cultures, ideologies, history) the conception of an autonomous person needs to transcend conceptual analysis. Social factors are thus to be taken as central to understanding and explaining the development of 'personal autonomy' as an aim of education, since education itself is a society-and-time-specific project of socialisation. The relationship between 'community' or 'socialisation' and the development of personal autonomy (Feinberg 1973, Young 1980, Bernstein 1983) is to be considered in the debate on whether or not the development of personal autonomy should be an educational aim. This is one of the arguments from the perspective of education as socialisation.

The socialisation arguments state, in similar ways as hard determinist arguments, that 'we do not choose our convictions, desires and so forth in anything like the way required by talk of autonomy' (Young 1980: 571). Socialisation exerts tremendous influence on the development of our self-concept and self-awareness, both of which are crucial to the development of personal autonomy in us as individuals. The social context in which autonomy is developed and exercised needs therefore to be understood – and with this the process of socialisation itself – if we are to understand personal autonomy itself. Hence, too, the relationship between *cultural pluralism* and *relativism*, and the development of autonomy as an aim of education needs to be explored.

CONTEXTS AND AUTONOMY

A person is either autonomous or heteronomous only in relation to other people, customs, institutions, cultures, etc. Autonomy has to be treated as a 'social concept' (cf. Kleinig 1982). It is a *socially relational* concept. It does not make sense for any one to be described as autonomous or otherwise except within a given social context. This eliminates a Robinson Crusoe kind of person from being termed autonomous.

Personal autonomy is a particular characteristic of a particular form of society, i.e. of a liberal-democratic society and more specifically of a western model of such a society. Talk about autonomy as an aim of education has essentially rested on the demands of a liberal-democratic order. Where other forms of society different from, or even contradictory to, liberal democracy exist, the demand for autonomy as a goal of any educational encounter is less obvious, perhaps even out of the question.

Although there is a shift towards liberal democracy at the global level, there are many societies whose *form* and *orientation* are still emerging within this global political trend. Autonomy can only sensibly be listed as a goal of education in a politically and culturally appropriate context – it cannot be discussed in a cultural vacuum (cf. Whitty and Young 1976, Harris 1980, White 1983, etc.). The pursuit of pupils' autonomy does not even arise in contexts where supportive liberal-democratic structures are not in place or are not being put in place.

AUTONOMY AND DEMOCRACY

An autonomous person has a place within the context of a liberal-democratic order. To recognise and allow for pupils' autonomy is, first, to provide for the right of pupils in the schooling system to have their talents, potentials and capacities exposed and developed for the good of the individual pupil and of the democratic society. Second, recognising and allowing pupils' autonomy within the context of the school is one particular way of promoting democratic values in both the school and the society. Not only is the production of autonomous pupils an ideal which is fully consistent with a liberal-democratic society, but failure to grant pupils' autonomy in that context stands as a negation of democracy and democratic values.

The development of personal autonomy has the potential of promoting the values of tolerance and mutual respect for each other, by citizens living in the same state. Autonomy, being in the main consistent with the free personality required for the exercise of democratic rights and the defence of democratic ideals, may be considered a fundamental requirement of liberal democracy. There cannot be democracy without some well-defined rights, obligations and freedoms. A free society exemplified by a democratic setting entails an association of free citizens. But they are individually and collectively free only in relative terms, i.e. each citizen or group of citizens in a democracy enjoys its freedoms in relation to the collectivity and the individual persons comprising the collectivity. Freedom and free persons in a democracy do not make any sense if these are not considered within the social whole. So the autonomous individual required by a democratic society exercises his or her freedom within the context of the social, economic, cultural and political relationships with other people in the same society at the same material time. To talk of freedoms and exercise of personal autonomy in isolation from other members of the community or the society is to make no sense of autonomy as a goal of any educational enterprise. (See on this chapters 10, 11 and 12 in this volume.)

IDEOLOGICAL DYNAMICS AND AUTONOMY AS AN EDUCATIONAL AIM

All societies or cultures make normative judgements on the basis of which they go ahead to make such ideological choices as are appropriate to their perceived interests. The dominant interest in each society at any time in history determines what 'national interests' are, or are supposed to be. The dominant interests in the society therefore function in this regard within contexts that are more ideological than crudely objective or rational. What is taken as objective and rational in making the choice of the form of society which is desired in any particular timeframe is subject therefore to the structure of interests which is controlling that society at that time. Issues of cultural relativism then arise in an attempt to decide whether or not the development of personal autonomy should be an educational aim for any particular society. This is important because one perceives and evaluates the world in the lenses of one's own culture.

While autonomy may be valued in western cultural paradigms, other cultures do not so value it as an educational ideal. It may also serve as a negation of some cultural frameworks. As Mazrui observed, 'an Ayatollah in Iran views the world qualitatively differently from how Henry Kissinger has viewed it' (1990: 7). Similarly what one may value as goals towards which one's society may be oriented depends to a large extent on the dominant culture in the particular society and time in question. Also motives for one's behaviour have a lot to do with one's cultural paradigms. It is the interplay between these ideological variables – *dominant interests, cultural relativism, standards of rationality*, etc. – that at the end of the day justifies or refutes the choice of autonomy as an educational aim within any educational system.

The power of culture and ideology in the acceptance or rejection of the development of pupils' personal autonomy as an aim of education is tremendous. The debate on personal autonomy as an educational aim cannot proceed without a consideration of the cultural dynamics across societies and at different periods of their history. It is even more crucial to the debate because cultures may sometimes serve as a protective shield for freedom. Autonomy then cannot be taken as granted as being a universal, culture-free value which all societies must pursue through their respective educational systems. In societies that are less inclined towards the values of western civilisation within which the idea of personal autonomy is encased, autonomy as an aim of education is merely an interesting theoretical proposition. One such society where the interplay between traditional, religious and modern cultural frameworks bears particularly strongly on the debate on autonomy as an educational ideal is contemporary Africa. I write of course with a particular perspective drawn from life in contemporary Nigeria.

African society is in a state of transition from the traditional to the modern. The social, economic and political structures in Africa have been, since at least the nineteenth century, undergoing transformation in response to the demands of the global political economy and its cultural superstructure. Contemporary Africa rests ideologically on three contrasting cultural pillars: traditional pre-capitalist values still very much adhered to; religious commitments (from the three main sources of traditional religious practices, Islam and Christianity); and modernity – represented by, for example, liberal politics and economy. This last cultural pillar of contemporary African society resulted from the influences of colonialism and centuries of contacts with western civilisation. Each of these three ideological pillars has its own response to the ideas of, and demands for personal autonomy as an aim of education.

Traditional values and autonomy as an aim of education

African cultural traditions are still strongly upheld, especially among the majority of the rural peoples. Traditional practices in social organisation, social relations, to some extent power relations, etc., are very much respected among most African unlettered peoples. So are traditional medical practices, superstitions, even magic and traditional religious beliefs. Relations among members of many communities in Africa are governed by traditional definitions of roles as provided for by each community's cultural codes. Inter-community relations too are conducted within these bounds. There is therefore a predominance in the cultural sphere of pre-capitalist traditional values in an increasingly capitalist (liberal-democratic) Africa. The main issue is now an attempt to locate the place of autonomy as an educational aim from the perspective of the African traditional values and value systems. An example is here given of the Hausa ethnic group.

Most African cultures may, from the perspectives of western cultural paradigms, fail the test of democracy. Some of these cultures are more authoritarian than liberal, more closed, less open. The Hausas in Northern Nigeria, for example, have a strictly disciplinarian culture. The notion of pupils' autonomy is almost an abomination. The young Hausa child may exercise or enjoy some degree of autonomy but this is always subject to the veto of his or her elders, especially parents. The child's choices are heavily restricted and constrained by the veto power exercised on the child by the parents. This continues throughout one's life so long as his or her parents are alive. In other words, the Hausa culture does not recognise individual autonomy as a phenomenon isolated from the rights of the parents to boss around their son or daughter, no matter how old they may be. This appears like an autocratic dispensation. Be that as it may, the point is that the Hausa cultural standards do not recognise and allow for pupils' personal autonomy in the way in which western civilisation does. To do so would be to negate Hausa standards of disciplined social relations to the extent that the Hausa would fear that if a child was allowed autonomy, then a breakdown of authority and respect for parents and elders in the community would follow.

The Hausas are in a very good company of other African cultures. The traditional society in Africa is one that is centred around hierarchy and status. There is found in all African cultures, a chain of authority at various levels of the society. Each member of the society is placed appropriately on a given social position, and his or her roles in the scheme of things are relatively but appropriately defined. He or she is indeed expected to conform by way of discharging his or her cultural obligations like obeying commands and instructions even if this is against his or her wishes and choices. The person is expected to respect such an arrangement so long as his or her elders are in command. Talk of developing pupils' autonomy is almost excluded from such a cultural context, since the achievement of personal autonomy challenges the cultural and traditional authority of elders over their subjects, and parents over their wards – no matter how old they might be.

In some cases the Hausa culture is claimed to be legitimated by religious considerations. But what is the response of religion to the issues of autonomy as an educational aim?

Religion and the place of autonomy as an educational ideal

Religion is a second and protected ideological pillar in contemporary African society and social systems. Even though modernisation trends witnessed by Africa as a direct result of colonial and post-colonial global contacts have brought a relative decline in adherence to religious values among African peoples (Mazrui 1990: 5–6), religion is still a very strong cultural factor among the vast majority of African people. The rise of Islamic fundamentalism in the Middle East has, for example, spread to all parts of the Muslim world. As a reaction to this, Catholicism has also been registering new forms of zeal among its adherents in Africa. Africa is a cultural space where those who adhere to their religious beliefs do so extremely.

For Islam in particular – a political religion (with its own political, economic and social systems) – sovereignty belongs to Allah. A Muslim submits himself or herself to the will of Allah who prescribes for him or her a *shari'ah* – i.e. a fundamental code of laws. The shari'ah makes provisions for the Muslim's overall conduct in life, and covers every imaginable aspect of human life. It is to this extent that Islam transcends the level of a religion per se; it is also an ideology in contest with other ideologies such as capitalism and its socio-political expression: liberal-democracy (Yahya 1980).

Within the confines of the shari'ah, human choices are as such limited by the will of Allah. Development of personal autonomy as an aim of education within such a context is allowed only in so far as one's range of autonomous practices do not violate or come into conflict with the Islamic shari'ah. Freedoms and autonomy for humanity are, to that extent, delineated by the bounds of the shari'ah. This sharply contrasts with the liberal-democratic dispensation.

Liberal democracy and the demand for autonomy

Liberal democracy sets out to demand autonomy for individuals as socio-political actors and economic agents. Democracy cannot thrive where freedoms are not granted and guaranteed. The demand for autonomy as an aim of education is a manifestation of the requirements for a liberal-democratic society. In addition to the two ideological pillars of tradition and religion which define the African socio-political space, liberal political and economic systems are also high on the agenda in contemporary Africa.

Democracy now dominates the agenda of world politics. Pressures for democratisation in the former Eastern bloc, and a culmination of other factors (the discussion of which is beyond the scope of the present chapter) took a dramatic turn in Africa. African societies have been under intense (local and international) pressures to democratise. There have been clamours for change from totalitarian rule (of different varieties) to democracy (even if narrowly conceived). National conferences with this goal mainly in view were held in many countries in Africa, from Togo to Niger, Ghana, Zaire, Mali and Cameroon, for example.

A democratic dispensation has a number of implications for education. For example, I argued earlier that democracy requires, within the schooling system, 'some' autonomy for pupils. It is perfectly acceptable and indeed defensible for a democratic education system to have, as one of its aims, the development of the pupils' personal autonomy for this aids the development and defence of democracy. Education for democracy requires at least the cultivation of autonomy in its young.

Cultural pluralism and its relativist implications in an African society such as Nigeria compound, however, the problem of allowing for the development of pupils' autonomy as a foundation for a democratic society. By contrast to liberal democracy the other two of Africa's triple ideological pillars do not necessarily make a space for autonomy as an aim of education. It is questionable whether, given the triple ideological pillars on which contemporary African societies stand, they can have it both ways. That is, can they promote democracy without making provisions for freedoms in their schools including developing personal autonomy as an aim of their educational systems?

CONCLUSION

There is an interesting paradox which African societies face in the definition of the aims of their educational systems: as an integral part of the global political economy and cultural order they are also clamouring for political and economic reforms as is the case in all other parts of the globe. But they also jealously guard their strong religious and traditional affinities. Is this a case of difficulties for the dynamic forces of change or a self-imposed barrier to Africa's progress? Both propositions may be true. But on a closer look, the issue of having or not having autonomy as an aim of education in any society at any particular time depends to a large extent on the expressed or perceived interests of the society as expressed or defined by the dominant power structure (cultural, political and economic) that enjoys a position of hegemony at any given time in the history of that society. So the acceptance of the development of personal autonomy as an aim of education is in the end a matter of cultural and ideological interests. The decision is ideological just as the conception of autonomy itself has to be understood in relation to a particular societal setting at a particular point in history.

REFERENCES

Aviram, A. (1994) 'Autonomy and Commitment: Compatible Ideals', paper for the Annual Conference of the Philosophy of Education Society of Great Britain, New College, Oxford, 8–10 April.

Bernstein, M. (1983) 'Socialisation and Autonomy', *Mind* XCII, 365: 120–3.

Bonnet, M. (1986) 'Personal Authenticity and Public Standards', in Cooper, D. (ed.) *Values and Education: Essays for R. S. Peters*, London: Routledge & Kegan Paul.

Callan, E. (1988) *Autonomy and Schooling*, Montreal: McGill Queen's University Press.

Cuypers, S. (1992) 'Is Personal Autonomy the First Principle of Education?', *Journal of Philosophy of Education* 26, 1: 93–113.

Dworkin, G. (1976) *Autonomy and Behaviour Control*, Hasings Centre Report, 6.

Dworkin, G. (1988) *The Theory and Practice of Autonomy*, Cambridge: Cambridge University Press.

Feinberg, J. (1973) *Social Philosophy*, Englewood Cliffs, NJ: Prentice-Hall Inc.

Fleming, N. (1981) 'Autonomy of the Will', *Mind* XC, 358: 201–23.

Gewirth, A. (1975) 'Morality and Autonomy in Education', in Doyle, J. F. (ed.) *Educational Judgements: Papers in the Philosophy of Education*, London: Routledge & Kegan Paul.

Gutkind, P. C. W. and Waterman, P. (eds) (1977) *African Social Studies: A Radical Reader*, London: Heinemann Educational Books.

Harris, K. (1980) *Education and Knowledge*, London: Routledge & Kegan Paul.

Kleinig, J. (1982) *Philosophical Issues in Education*, London: Croom Helm.

Lee, J. and Wringe, C. (1993) 'Rational Autonomy, Morality and Education', *Journal of Philosophy of Education* 27, 1: 69–78.

Macedo, S. (1990) *Liberal Virtues*, Oxford: Clarendon Press.

Mazrui, A. A. (1990) *Cultural Forces in World Politics*, London: James Curry.

Mill, J. S. (1956) *On Liberty*, edited by C. V. Shield, Indianapolis: The Bobbs-Merrill Company.

Norman, R. (1994) 'I Did it My Way: Some Thoughts on Autonomy', *Journal of Philosophy of Education* 28, 1: 25–34.

Wen, S. M. (1994) 'Taiwan's Modernisation: A Case of Lack of Autonomy in Education', paper for the Annual Conference of the Philosophy of Education Society of Great Britain, New College, Oxford, 8–10 April.

White, J. (1982) *The Aims of Education*, London: Routledge & Kegan Paul.

White, J. (1990) *Education and the Good Life*, London: Kogan Page.

White, F. C. (1983) *Knowledge and Relativism: An Essay in the Philosophy of Education*, The Netherlands: Van Gorum, Assen.

Whitty, G. and Young, M. F. D. (eds) (1976) *Explorations in the Politics of School Knowledge*, England: Nafferton.

Wringe, C. (1988) *Understanding Educational Aims*, London: Allen and Unwin.

Yahya, D. (1980) 'Secularism: Its Challenges to Islamic Education and Muslim Society', *Journal of General Studies*, Kano: Bayero University, Vol. 1, No. 1: 115–20.

Young, M. F. D. (ed.) (1971) *Knowledge and Control*, London: Collier-Macmillan.

Young, R. (1980) 'Autonomy and Socialisation', *Mind* LXXXIX, 356: 565–76.

Part IV

EDUCATION FOR AUTONOMY AND DEMOCRATIC CITIZENSHIP

EDUCATION FOR DEMOCRATIC CITIZENSHIP IN SCHOOLS

Ken Fogelman

THE INCREASING ATTENTION TO CITIZENSHIP EDUCATION

Attention to and concern about education for citizenship appears to have increased in recent years throughout the world, at least in terms of the extent of discussion and the number of proposals put forward. Of course, some of the reasons for this vary from country to country, but it is possible to identify several common themes (see, for example, contributions in Timmer and Veldhuis 1996). These include concerns about:

- low levels of participation in local and national elections;
- a perceived rise in intolerance, xenophobia and racism;
- the apparent alienation and marginalisation of some young people from the mainstream of society.

In Europe there are two additional elements which give a particular flavour to the debate, namely the desire to promote understanding of and an informed debate on the development of the European Union; and the challenge to education of preparing young people for participation in the newly democratic countries of Eastern and Central Europe. Hammer (1995), though writing specifically about Hungary, offers a list of issues which can certainly be taken as more generally applicable to the former communist countries:

- the public's lack of experience with public discourse;
- traditional reliance on state paternalism;
- the conflict between the notions of public and private;
- the lack of a sense of social-communal responsibility;
- the traditional role of the intelligentsia and political elites;
- the reluctance to embrace a pluralism of ideas;
- the weakening growth of public involvement in politics.

It would be wrong to suggest that all such issues are unique to the newly democratic countries in Europe or in other parts of the world. Conover *et al.* (forthcoming), for example, have written of the relative lack of public political discourse in Britain as compared with the United States.

Virtually all writers on citizenship education acknowledge that there are many influences and that the role of schools must be limited. However, they are equally unanimous in arguing that schools have a vital part to play in preparing young people for democratic participation (see, for example, Edwards *et al.* 1994).

SOME INTERNATIONAL EXAMPLES AND COMPARISONS

There are two severe difficulties in attempting any comparative analysis of approaches to citizenship education. First, there is no systematic information available, obtained on any comparable basis. Second, as a consequence, information has to be taken from official documents or partial accounts of particular examples of practice. It is therefore frequently difficult to judge the extent to which such accounts truly reflect actual practice in the majority of classrooms in any country. Nevertheless there are a number of sources which do provide interesting insights into the variety of interpretations of citizenship education.

Before turning to some specific examples it is helpful to summarise a model of such variation, provided by Osler and Starkey (1996). They write of two dimensions to citizenship education. The first is structural/political as against cultural/personal; the second is described as minimal as against maximal versions. Thus, the minimal, structural/political version of citizenship education emphasises knowledge – of rights and democratic processes – whereas the minimal, cultural/personal approach is more about identities and emphasises personal feelings and choices. The maximal, structural/political version goes beyond knowledge, emphasises inclusion and promotes a model of the good society; the maximal cultural/personal version emphasises competence and participation and aims to develop skills to effect change. Although more complex, such ideas are not dissimilar to the distinction drawn by Cogan (reported in Fogelman, forthcoming) between 'mechanistic' citizenship education (essentially old-fashioned civics education) and an 'associationist' approach.

Discussions of the importance of participation and the development of skills extend beyond the content of the formal curriculum and how it is organised and lead to more general questions about the nature of a young person's experience in school. A concept which is frequently mentioned in this context is that of participation. Stradling (1987) has elaborated on this, writing of citizenship education as being *about* participation, *for* participation and *in* participation. Education about participation entails content and knowledge. Education for participation provides skills such as powers of analysis and criticism, but also attitudes and values such as commitment to the community and integrity. Education in participation is based in action and experience. A central concept is that of empowerment (cf. Fielding's discussion in this volume).

Many would argue that citizenship education also has implications for teaching methods and styles. This is not a matter of stark alternatives in teaching methods, but many of the objectives of citizenship education do seem to imply, for example, a greater emphasis on group teaching as against whole class teaching, more collaborative and co-operative approaches, greater use of student projects and other student-led activities, and more use of resources outside the classroom (see, for example, Kitson 1993, Newspapers in Education, 1995).

Examples from a number of countries illustrate how this broader concept of citizenship education is increasingly favoured. Clough, Menter and Tarr (1995) describe a TEMPUS project in Latvia which is based on 'reflection in action' and on 'interdisciplinary enquiry which is rooted in the everyday experience of society'. Although their project is mainly concerned with teacher training, they also describe activities in schools, which entail the modification or development of materials to encourage more active learning and to take account of the plural nature of the community, and also the introduction of schools councils. Similarly, Ahmetova and Rachmanova (1995), writing about recent developments in Russia, highlight increased democracy in choosing curricula, greater involvement of public and non-governmental organisations and the creation of new textbooks in order to teach 'democratic motivation'.

In Slovakia, what Mistrik (1996) terms 'cultural education' is said to have as its main aims:

- education towards the realisation of cultural identity;
- education towards a multicultural view and perception;
- education towards an ecologically oriented culture;

and, in the classroom, this translates into greater use of discussion, games, excursions and other community links.

Three striking examples of active learning and participation come from Hungary, England and Norway. Hammer (1995) provides guidelines for the teacher and a students' booklet to support a series of 'forums' based on discussion of three alternative solutions to, and theories about, six issues: unemployment, poverty, crime, youth at risk, grading in schools, and Hungary's national security. In a similar way, Talbot's (1995) pack provides materials which can be used either in separate lessons or to mount a conference on equal opportunities issues, covering background knowledge, assertiveness, public speaking, committee skills, media skills and debate.

The Norwegian example is rather different, consisting of a booklet which is distributed to upper secondary students and which provides guidance on, for example, how students should take responsibility for their own learning and on the role of student councils and class representatives. Interestingly, the language in which it is written takes for granted that such ideas will be acceptable to the school and its teachers in ways that could not be assumed in many other countries. For example, it discusses 'ways in which work in the class can be conducted so as to give you an opportunity to play an active part', and asserts, 'The student council should maintain an ongoing discussion throughout the school year concerning how to give pupils greater influence at school' (The National Council for Educational Resources 1994).

Jones (1996) has reviewed a number of national texts for their references to education for European citizenship. Drawing upon examples from France, Denmark, Germany and the Netherlands, she too identifies a general trend for descriptions of citizenship education to emphasise the extension of skills, attitudes and values, as well as knowledge, and the need for learning to be active, participatory and relevant. However, she also draws attention to one problematic area – ambiguities in underlying definitions of citizenship and a lack of distinction among local, national, European and global citizenship. This is a common tension in citizenship education curricula, particularly, though not exclusively, in countries which see citizenship education as one means of introducing young people to their pre-communist history and traditions. However, most writers would sympathise with Dekker and Portengo (1996: 176) that 'Citizenship includes the whole of knowledge, together with insights, beliefs, opinions, attitudes, emotions, values, behavioural intentions, and behaviours of an individual in relation to the political system of which he/she is a member on a local, regional, national and/or international level.'

THE RECENT HISTORY OF CITIZENSHIP EDUCATION IN ENGLAND

In this context, England is a prime example of a country where it is important to distinguish between what appears in official documents and the reality of the classroom. Citizenship education has never had a formal place in the school curriculum in England. Of course, this reflects the fact that, prior to the 1988 Education Reform Act, there was no national curriculum and, therefore no school subject that was compulsory (with the exception of religious education which was specified in the 1944 Education Act). That there was some uniformity in what schools taught was the result partly of tradition and partly of the influence of public examinations taken at the age of 16.

Citizenship education was not a traditional subject. Therefore, whether it was taught at all depended on the interest and enthusiasm of individual teachers or schools. Such enthusiasm did exist. Batho (1990) has identified and reviewed the teaching of civics and citizenship in English schools since the Victorian era. The late 1920s and the 1930s were a period when discussion of the topic, and some activity in schools, was particularly intense, largely in response to fears about the spread of totalitarianism (Association for Education in Citizenship 1935).

More recently, but before the introduction of the National Curriculum, there were several initiatives with regard to specific topics or activities, which might now be seen as coming under the general heading of citizenship education, although that term might not have been used at the time. These included community service and involvement (e.g. Preecy and Marsh 1989), political awareness (e.g. Stradling 1975) and education for democracy and human rights (e.g. Starkey 1991, Stradling 1987).

However, education for citizenship has received more attention since the beginning of this decade when, towards the end of the process of implementing the first version of the National Curriculum, the then National Curriculum Council produced a series of documents on the 'whole curriculum' (e.g. NCC 1989 and 1990a). (These documents relate to England only. There have been similar developments, but with different emphases and detail, in the other countries of the United Kingdom.) The first of these documents introduced the idea of three cross-curricular elements: dimensions, skills and themes. These were subsequently elaborated in Curriculum Guidance 3 (NCC 1990a), which identified:

- dimensions
    a commitment to providing equal opportunities for all pupils
    preparation for life in a multicultural society
- skills
    communication
    numeracy
    study
    problem solving
    personal and social
    information technology
- themes
    economic and industrial understanding
    careers education and guidance
    health education
    environmental education
    education for citizenship.

It is important to emphasise from the outset that the themes were not part of the National Curriculum. Although Guidance 3 does contain the statement 'It is reasonable to assume at this stage that [the themes] are essential parts of the whole curriculum', elsewhere it is stated that they are 'by no means a conclusive list'. In several places it is emphasised that it is for schools to decide how the themes might be tackled. Above all, the themes, unlike the subjects of the National Curriculum, were not, and never became, part of what schools were required to teach by statute and regulation.

Guidance 3 was followed by five further guidance documents, one on each of the themes, the final one of which (NCC 1990b) was on education for citizenship. Although once again there was much emphasis on the content being a 'framework for debate' and not a 'blueprint or set of lesson plans', the guidance offered was quite detailed and consisted of three elements: objectives, content and activities.

Objectives were further subdivided into:

- knowledge (of the nature of community, roles and relationships in a democratic society, the nature and basis of duties, and responsibilities and rights);
- cross-curricular skills (essentially as listed above from Guidance 3);
- attitudes;
- moral codes and values.

For the content, eight 'essential components' were outlined, each accompanied by areas of study and some suggested activities:

- the nature of community;
- roles and relationships in a pluralist society;
- the duties, rights and responsibilities of being a citizen;
- the family;
- democracy in action;
- the citizen and the law;
- work, employment and leisure;
- public services.

There is much which can be debated about this framework – its completeness, the clarity of some of the terms, the lack of an international perspective, and the underlying concept of citizenship which it appears to assume (see, for example, Bottery 1992). Nevertheless, it remains the clearest and fullest description of a possible curriculum for citizenship education which has been offered in England to date.

Although the National Curriculum Council documents are the ones with which teachers are most likely to be familiar, there are references to citizenship education in two other important publications. During the same period as the guidance documents were in preparation within the NCC, the Speaker's Commission on Citizenship (1990) was deliberating. Although it did not have the formal status of the NCC, the political origins of the Commission and the patronage of the Speaker of the House of Commons ensured publicity for its report and recommendations. It is also possible that its influence was more direct, as it did submit evidence to the NCC at the time when its guidance was in preparation.

The Commission was concerned with what it termed 'active citizenship' throughout the community, but a substantial proportion of its recommendations addressed educational issues and implications. In some respects its approach was distinctive from that of the NCC. For example, it accepted the challenge of attempting a definition of citizenship, drawing mainly upon the approach of Marshall (1950) and his distinction among the civil, political and social elements of citizenship. Second, the Commission did adopt a more international perspective, specifically by recommending that the study of citizenship should take account of the main international charters and conventions to which the UK is a signatory.

In other respects the Commission's approach was not dissimilar to that of the NCC. It recommended that citizenship should be part of every young person's education, and it offered a description of citizenship education as including: understanding the rules; the acquisition of a body of knowledge; the development and exercise of skills; and learning democratic behaviour through experiences of the school as a community.

A further important document which has appeared since the publication of the NCC guidance is the report of the National Commission on Education (1993). Despite its title, this was an independent body which undertook a comprehensive review of education in England and Wales. Among its recommendations was that citizenship education should be part of the compulsory core curriculum from the age of 7. The report states that:

> We consider the teaching of citizenship of great importance. We define the subject in a broad way to concern the relationship between individuals and the world they live in. It relates not only to this country but to the European Community and the world as a whole. It concerns the institutions of democracy and the rights and responsibilities of individuals in a democratic society; the creation of wealth; the role of public and private employers and voluntary organisations; and the opportunities which people have to shape or play a creative part in the life of the community.
>
> (1993: 56)

The essential point about all these documents, including those from the NCC, is that, unlike the regulations relating to the National Curriculum, they have no statutory force. They can be seen as a stimulus to schools, and as providing suggested frameworks for content and approaches to citizenship education and the other cross-curricular themes, but it has been open to schools to decide whether to adopt them in their entirety or in part, to adapt them to their own purposes, or to ignore them completely.

The probability that they would be ignored was increased by the many changes and pressures on schools which have been compulsory, in particular the problems associated with the implementation of the National Curriculum. As it worked its way through the school system in the early years of this decade, it quickly became apparent to teachers, and eventually to politicians, that it was unmanageable. Its detail had been laid down by committees, whose members were experts in, and enthusiasts for, their particular subject. It was perhaps predictable that the result was a curriculum which was over-specified, and which did not fit into the time available. In addition there were problems with the associated system of regular assessment, which had come to be seen as overly bureaucratic and demanding of teachers' time.

For these reasons, in 1993 the government established a review of the National Curriculum and its assessment, with a remit to reduce and simplify (Dearing 1994). During the period of consultation, many of those committed to citizenship education (and the other cross-curricular themes) made representations that the opportunity should be taken to reinforce their importance. However, given the context and atmosphere within which the review was taking place, it was not surprising that this did not happen. Apart from the transporting of some aspects of environmental and health education into the science curriculum, there was no mention of the themes, either of their content or of the cross-curricular concept. For the time being at least, these had become unmentionable as they were seen as a complication and an additional burden.

Of course, Dearing was aware of wider issues. As he wrote in his report:

> Education is not concerned only with equipping students with the knowledge and skills they need to earn a living. It must help our young people to: use leisure time creatively; have respect for other people, other cultures and other beliefs; become good citizens; think things out for themselves; pursue a healthy lifestyle; and, not least, value themselves and their achievements.
>
> (Dearing 1994: 2)

It was no doubt the compelling need to tackle and reduce the existing compulsory curriculum that prevented further elaboration of these ideas.

Through its detailed recommendations for the reduction of the content of the National Curriculum subjects, a major outcome of the Dearing review was the recommendation that the total National Curriculum should be more flexible and reduced to account for only 80 per cent of the time available, the use of the remaining 20 per cent to be decided by individual schools. As these, and all other recommendations of the review, were accepted and are being implemented by the government, it might be hoped that citizenship education would be one option considered favourably by schools for their discretionary part of the curriculum. However, many teachers have still to be convinced that the new curriculum will fill only the amount of time intended. Furthermore there continue to be other pressures on schools, not least from the continuing, even though reduced, national assessment. Results are published for individual schools, often in the form of league tables, and can have a major impact on the reputation and popularity of a school. They are also an important factor in the judgements of school inspections. Schools may well therefore feel that it is in their best interests to devote any discretionary time to further teaching of basic skills and other assessed subjects.

THE SCHOOLS' RESPONSE

During the past seven years there have been a number of surveys conducted in order to assess what has actually been happening in schools that might be described as citizenship education. Whilst it is important to identify the varying timing of these studies in relation to the curriculum developments and documents described above, findings have in fact been generally consistent and, in terms of teachers' attitudes at least, surprisingly positive.

Questionnaires for a survey of secondary schools throughout England and Wales, conducted for the Speaker's Commission, were distributed in 1989, just prior to the publication of NCC guidance but at a time when teachers would have known that citizenship education was under discussion (Fogelman 1990 and 1991). A high level of activity was reported, though with substantial variation both among schools and across different age ranges within schools – activity levels becoming greater for older children. For example, about half of secondary schools reported that their 12–13 year olds were engaged in community-related activities, rising to 85 per cent for 15–16 year olds. The most commonly reported activities were: visiting or helping the elderly in their homes, or in hostels or hospitals; working with children in nursery or primary schools; working with people with disabilities; and environmental projects.

Although relatively few schools reported that they gave no classroom time to citizenship education, for those that did so it was irregular and infrequent. Just 1 per cent indicated that they taught citizenship mainly as a separate subject. Much more frequently it was included in more familiar subject areas, such as humanities, home economics or English. Most commonly, for 95 per cent of schools, it was tackled within personal and social education.

Fieldwork for another study of secondary schools, by Whitty *et al.* (1994), was carried out in 1991–2. They found widespread support for the cross-curricular themes from teachers, but again actual practice was much more variable, and their representation in school policy documents relatively rare.

More recent evidence comes from a survey carried out, after the Dearing Review, in the spring of 1995 (Saunders *et al.* 1995). This study, which included both primary and secondary schools, again found relatively positive attitudes to citizenship education: 43 per cent of primary schools and 62 per cent of secondaries said that it is an essential or very important part of the curriculum, and few schools reported that they were not addressing it at all. On the other hand, it was still the case for almost all schools that there was no mention, or only a very brief one, of citizenship education in the school development plan. About two-thirds of schools (both phases) stated that pressures on the timetable had been a major constraint on their ability to provide citizenship education; lack of funding for resources and lack of staff expertise were also mentioned by significant numbers. This was also reflected in the very small numbers of staff who had experienced any in-service education in this area.

Schools were also asked about their intended use of the discretionary time made available by the Dearing Review. This elicited several rather pointed comments on whether the discretionary time really existed; but the majority of both primary and secondary schools anticipated using it for either basic skills or National Curriculum subjects. Nineteen per cent of primary schools and 25 per cent of secondary schools said that they intended to use the time for developing skills for adult life.

Edwards and Trott (1995) describe a more qualitative study of ten primary schools. Systematic and specific teaching of citizenship education was rare. The major emphasis was on activities with a community focus and on school ethos, with planned opportunities for the development of skills and attitudes, but with less attention to developing knowledge and understanding.

The most recent and detailed study, but of primary schools only, is reported by Kerr (1996). Again, the main findings are consistent with those of earlier studies. About three-quarters of schools claimed to be addressing citizenship, but approaches were very varied. Attitudes to the subject were positive, but schools continued to feel constrained by lack of time, lack of resources (there being little awareness of those resources which are available) and lack of guidance.

THE CURRENT SITUATION

A further difficulty in writing about the situation in England is that it is rapidly changing. As already indicated, we have experienced a period during which citizenship education has been virtually unmentionable at political and official levels. Literally in the last few months, this has changed dramatically, to where it appears to be discussed almost daily by politicians and in the media.

There appear to be three influences now at work. First, the framework for the regular inspection of schools carried out by the Office for Standards in Education (OFSTED 1995) includes a section on spiritual, moral, social and cultural development. Interpreting this has been problematic for both inspectors and schools, but there is clear and substantial overlap with the objectives and activities of citizenship education. More than half the primary schools in Kerr's study reported that aspects of education for citizenship were included in the evidence presented to inspection teams.

Second, there has been something of a moral panic, engendered by media representation of behaviour and discipline problems in a small number of schools. Political and media debates about this frequently refer to the desirability of citizenship education.

Third, and more encouragingly, the government promised teachers that the implementation of the Dearing Review would be followed by a five-year moratorium on further changes to the curriculum. A side effect of this has been to create space for more fundamental consideration of the curriculum and its purposes – a debate of the kind which many felt should have taken place before the introduction of the National Curriculum. The Schools Curriculum and Assessment Authority (successor to the NCC) has mounted a series of conferences and seminars on, for example, the values which schools should be promoting. At the time of writing, a report is about to be published and consulted upon and is likely to lead to published guidelines.

It is encouraging for those who have tried to sustain the debate that citizenship education is again high on the agenda, but it has to be hoped that those responsible for the implementation of any new version of it do not overlook the fundamental point made by Carr and Hartnett (1996: 187):

> A distinctive feature of a democratic society is that it accepts that no single image of the good society can be theoretically justified to an extent that would allow it to be put beyond rational dispute, and that the arguments and disagreements to which such disputes give rise ought not to be concealed or repressed.

REFERENCES

Ahmetova, I. and Rachmanova, E. (1995) 'Civic Education in Russia' in A. Osler, H. Rathenow and H. Starkey (eds) *Teaching for Citizenship in Europe*, Stoke-on-Trent: Trentham Books.

Association for Education in Citizenship (1935) *Education for Citizenship in Secondary Schools*, Oxford: Oxford University Press.

Batho, G. (1990) 'The History of the Teaching of Civics and Citizenship in English Schools', *The Curriculum Journal* 1, 1: 91–107.

Bottery, M. (1992) 'Education for Citizenship in the 21st Century', *Curriculum* 13, 3: 196–201.

Carr, W. and Hartnett, A. (1996) *Education and the Struggle for Democracy*, Buckingham: Open University Press.

Clough, N., Menter, I. and Tarr, J. (1995) 'Developing Citizenship Education Programmes in Latvia' in A. Osler, H. Rathenow and H. Starkey (eds) *Teaching for Citizenship in Europe*, Stoke-on-Trent: Trentham Books.

Conover, P. J., Crewe, I. M. and Searing, D. D. (forthcoming) 'The Nature of Citizenship in the United States and Great Britain: Empirical Comments on Theoretical Themes', *Journal of Politics*.

Dearing, R. (1994) *The National Curriculum and its Assessment*, London: Schools Curriculum and Assessment Authority.

Dekker, H. and Portengo, R. (1996) 'European Citizenship: Policies and Effects' in W. Friebel (ed.) *Education for European Citizenship*, Freiburg: Filibach Verlag.

Edwards, J. and Fogelman, K. (1993) *Developing Citizenship in the Curriculum*, London: David Fulton Publishers.

Edwards, J. and Trott, C. (1995) 'Education for Citizenship in Key Stages 1 and 2', *The Curriculum Journal* 6, 3: 395–408.

Edwards, L., Munn, P. and Fogelman, K. (eds) (1994) *Education for Democratic Citizenship in Europe – New Challenges for Secondary Education*, Lisse: Swets and Zeitlinger.

Fogelman, K. (1990) 'Citizenship in Secondary Schools: A National Survey', Appendix E in Speaker's Commission on Citizenship, *Encouraging Citizenship*, London: HMSO.

Fogelman, K. (1991) 'Citizenship in Secondary schools: The National Picture' in K. Fogelman (ed.) *Citizenship in Schools*, London: David Fulton Publishers.

Fogelman, K. (forthcoming) *Uppsala University and Council of Europe In Service Training Programme for Teachers: Report of the Rapporteur General*, Strasbourg: Council of Europe.

Friebel, W. (ed.) (1996) *Education for European Citizenship*, Freiburg: Filibach Verlag.

Hammer, F. (1995) *Critical Choices for Hungary*, Budapest: The Joint Eastern Europe Centre for Democratic Education and Governance.

Jones, M.G. (1996) 'National Texts on European Citizenship' W. Friebel (ed.) *Education for European Citizenship*, Freiburg: Filibach Verlag.

Kerr, D. (1996) *Citizenship Education in Primary Schools*, London: Institute for Citizenship Studies.

Kitson, N. (1993) 'Drama' in J. Edwards and K. Fogelman (eds) *Developing Citizenship in the Curriculum*, London: David Fulton Publishers.

Marshall, T. H. (1950) *Citizenship and Social Class*, Cambridge: Cambridge University Press.

Mistrik, E. (1996) *Aesthetics and Civics (Cultural Dimensions of Civic Education)*, Bratislava: HEVI Publishing House.

National Commission on Education (1993) *Learning to Succeed*, London: Heinemann.

National Council for Educational Resources (1994) *The Guide*, Oslo: NCER.

NCC (1989) *Circular Number 6. The National Curriculum and Whole Curriculum Planning: Preliminary Guidance*, York: National Curriculum Council.

NCC (1990a) *Curriculum Guidance Number 3: The Whole Curriculum*, York: National Curriculum Council.

NCC (1990b) *Curriculum Guidance Number 8: Education for Citizenship*, York: National Curriculum Council.

Newspapers in Education (1995) *Citizenship Through Newspapers: National Edition*, London: The Newspaper Society.

OFSTED (1995) *Guidance on the Inspection of Schools*, London: HMSO.

Osler, A. and Starkey, H. (1996) *Teacher Education and Human Rights*, London: David Fulton Publishers.

Osler, A., Rathenow, H. and Starkey, H. (1995) *Teaching for Citizenship in Europe*, Stoke-on-Trent: Trentham Books.

Preecy, R. and Marsh, J. (1989) *Community Links with GCSE*, London: Community Service Volunteers.

Saunders, L., MacDonald, A., Hewitt, D. and Schagen, J. (1995) *Education for Life*, Slough: National Foundation for Educational Research.

Speaker's Commission on Citizenship (1990) *Encouraging Citizenship*, London: HMSO.

Starkey, H. (ed.) (1991) *Socialisation of School Children and their Education for Democratic Values and Human Rights*, Lisse: Swets and Zeitlinger.

Stradling, R. (1975) *The Political Awareness of the School Leaver*, London: Hansard Society/Politics Association.

Stradling, R. (1987) *Education for Democratic Citizenship*, Strasbourg: Council of Europe.

Talbot, M. (1995) *Active Citizenship: Training for Equal Opportunity to Participate*, Stafford: Network Educational Press.

Timmer, J. and Veldhuis, R. (eds) (1996) *Political Education: Towards a European Democracy*, Amsterdam: Instituut voor Publiek en Politiek and Bundeszentrale fur Politische Bildung.

Whitty, G., Rowe, G. and Aggleton, P. (1994) 'Subjects and Themes in the Secondary School Curriculum', *Research Papers in Education* 9, 2: 159–81.

18

EDUCATION AND CITIZENSHIP IN POST-SOVIET RUSSIA

Nikolai D. Nikandrov

INTRODUCTION

After about seventy years of very stable society which had the proclaimed aim of building communism Russia has been undergoing a period of transformation since 1985 – the year when Gorbachev came to power as Secretary General of the Communist Party. This is not to say that there had been no previous changes in the economy and the social sphere. But at no time before had there been an attempt to encroach upon the *sancta sanctorum* – Marxist-Leninist teaching. This proclaimed in short that the future of all peoples of the world was to be communism and that capitalism was to die either by its natural death of internal contradictions in any given country or by the world socialist revolution helped by the socialist camp – i.e. by the countries where socialist regimes had already been established. The stable political system meant a uniform education system in which political education was a very important part. The term *education for citizenship* was hardly ever used then, but political indoctrination along Marxist lines was never put in doubt.

Gorbachev was prepared to go some way towards democratisation, but still for him the two guiding principles 'more democracy, more socialism' went hand in hand. So for all the change that took place in Russia under Gorbachev it was only modest compared with the drastic reforms under Yeltsin. These amounted to a revolution, a *coup d'état* when all economic and social values of the past (equal rights for all; planned economy; building communism as the ultimate aim of the society) were proclaimed null and void.

But after the destruction of the past, there came a time when some positive values had to be put in place of the old ones. Not long before the presidential elections of June/July 1996, President Yeltsin mentioned the necessity of formulating the national goals of Russia – which meant, in fact, the admission that for about five years we had been drifting along towards nobody knows what. It meant, too, that Russia, which had been united for a long time, must now find its national identity being torn aside by conflicting interests of various groups of population and various republics – some of them part of Russia (God knows for how long still) and some newly independent. Now

215

more often than ever before many people recall how the disintegration began with Yeltsin's famous appeal to heads of administrations 'Take as much sovereignty as you can swallow', though it should be admitted that some centrifugal tendencies appeared earlier.

This is the background against which civil education, education for citizenship and political education have to be analysed in present-day Russia. Very few people would now agree on a single model of an ideal citizen which can now be construed and pursued as the educational goal. However, no educational system of any size (a particular school or a country) can afford to function without an overt or implicit educational ideal for a long time; I would suggest that the past five years of independent Russia are just about the end of that time in our case. What next? An attempt to answer the question will require a retrospective as well as a prospective view.

HOMO SOVIETICUS (1917–1991)

The title of this section is given without any irony though it was invented by violent critics of the Soviet system and meant (disparagingly) a new breed of people engendered by the Soviet regime. In fact the seventy years of Soviet power did educate the citizen of the Soviet state with several important features – certainly not all of them bad. It should here be noted *en passant* that philosophers and statespeople at all times in history have sought to educate 'a new man' (sic) for a better society and have tried to develop a vision of that new man; so the idea itself deserves perhaps no derogatory evaluation. Of course, the years 1917–1991 make one think of too much precision in so delicate a matter as educating a new man. Still the years do mean cornerstones in Russian history and education. The first date is the year of the Great October socialist revolution – for this was the official name of the event; the second is the year of the dissolution of the Soviet Union. Very often other words such as 'downfall', 'disintegration', 'collapse' are used. The important thing is not to choose the best term but to understand that it was not a natural process like disintegration of a chemical substance or a mountain. It was done by people, some of whom fought for power, others saw possible gains and followed the lead. As always, the ostensible aim was the public good.

The model of man to be educated in the Soviet period was alluded to in successive party and government documents. Perhaps the most important one was the 1961 programme of the Communist Party in which the so-called moral code of builder of communism was stipulated (*Programma* 1961). It contained several commandments which (not unlike the ten commandments of the Old Testament) contained the 'dos' and 'don'ts' of the Soviet man and that man's desirable qualities. Since the concluding words of the document were 'The Party solemnly proclaims: the present generation of the Soviet people shall live in communism!' no doubt the moral code was meant to stay for a considerable period of time. It did (at least on paper) but both at the time it was proclaimed and (especially) as time went on there were considerable discrepancies between the norms on paper and the patterns of behaviour life really encouraged, between word and deed.

Such discrepancies exist in any system. For example, no school – at least in an ordinary sense of the word – teaches its pupils to steal, kill or violate; but these and many other 'immoral' practices still exist, for life frequently encourages or at least does not punish them and the school of life always takes the upper hand. But in the Soviet state it was true with a vengeance. Many did follow the maxims of the moral code – they did work hard for the public good, they did love communism and the socialist countries, they did take care of socialist property (i.e. that which belonged to the people as a whole), they did behave in a humane way to each other in the understanding that man to man is brother (no sexism is meant – it is a quotation from 1961 when the word did not exist, at least in the USSR), they did feel solidarity with all the peoples of the USSR and the working people of the world, etc. But most people tried to evade the many limitations imposed on them by the system. I do not mean the generally condemned crimes against people, property or state security, but such ordinary things as having more than one job, extra-marital sex, or trying to make money by petty trading. Suffice it to say that (to put it mildly) the average Soviet person hardly measured up to the ideal of the moral code.

Strange as it may seem, some of the moral code maxims were taken from much earlier times. It was explicitly stated in the party programme itself:

> Communist morality includes the main moral norms that have been worked out by the people over thousands of years in the fight against social oppression and moral vices.
>
> (*Programma* 1961: 119)

An interesting example of this drawing of historical values into Marxist-Leninist morality is the case of collectivism, or collective responsibility of all people for individuals. H. Daniels and others take the transition between state determinism and individualism as a very important vector of Russian education's development. In fact the opposite of individualism is perhaps collectivism (Daniels 1995). A collectivist – I use the word which I have never seen in written English – is a person who gives priority to the interests of his or her collective, of the group to which he/she belongs (be that a small work team, a large factory or the socialist state as a whole) as compared to his/her personal interests. Some people took that seriously and were 'convinced collectivists', some had to conform for fear of reprisals or in the hope of benefits; very few overtly rebelled. It was of course a difficult thing to distinguish between these groups. However, before the word *collectivist* was coined by the ideologists of the Communist Party, a very strong idea of community belonging (*sobornost*) had been a distinctive feature of Russian life for centuries. The very word '*sobornost*' is derived from '*sobor*' which has a double meaning: first, a gathering of people for worship or discussion; second, a church as a gathering of people and/or a large church (a cathedral). So in fact the *Programma* authors' assertion about some age-old maxims of the moral code is true. But the cementing feature of the code was still the wholehearted dedication to the building of communism. Taking that out would infallibly have meant important corrections in the other maxims and the whole code would have than become a set of loosely connected 'general human values'.

This would all suggest that nothing like personal autonomy could have existed in Soviet times. Ostensibly it still did. In fact, many party and state documents emphasised the importance of personal initiative and independence as important feature of the Soviet man. But implicit in all this was the understanding that certain boundaries should not be trespassed. You could of course take independent steps in your working and/or personal life but, say, criticising the teaching of Marx or Lenin or the 'collective wisdom' of the Politburo (the top leadership of the Communist Party of about twenty members), emphasising some drawbacks of the countries of the socialist camp or, conversely, some advantages of the countries of the capitalist camp were all taboo.

Essentially it was the same all over the Soviet period; there were, however, important variations in degree. Criticising 'Comrade Stalin' when he was alive (he died in 1953) certainly endangered the critic's life or could mean deportation to a labour camp. Criticising the Politburo or its particular steps in later times could mean (although not necessarily) a prison sentence or a forced treatment in a mental hospital. The short-lived 'thaw' (1956–1964) of Khrushchev meant a lot in that political prisoners still alive were let free and the good name was returned to those who had perished. But essentially the taboo-system persisted.

Gorbachev's *perestroyka* (literally 'reconstruction') first softened the climate a good deal and then brought about a radical change. Not only were the taboos eliminated but the critique of the darker side of the Soviet history and social practice was encouraged. The evolution of the criticism and the critics was interesting. First, it was asserted that returning to the early ideas of Lenin would solve most problems (in education, too, 'Lenin's conception of the school' was the solution). When, however, Lenin's ideas and repressive practices were devalued, the same critics (who knew the facts of history quite well and nothing new was added to them) said the ideas themselves were at fault and should be done away with. Gorbachev's reforms slowed down and stalled; before he lost power he had lost the trust and hope people had in him. That notwithstanding I am sure he deserves praise, for the democracy we have now was not fought for and won; it was given to the people by Gorbachev while all later reformers (including Yeltsin) only followed suit.

The *perestroyka* events had a profound influence on education. The year before it began, in 1984, the education reform was proclaimed. But it was soon overshadowed by the much more far-reaching slogans of *perestroyka*:

218

democratisation, humanisation, *glasnost* (openness), market economy, decentralisation, assertion of human rights, etc; school and personal autonomy were among them. But as the reforms slowed down and the disappointment of those who hoped for immediate material benefits grew, most people lost faith in yet another reformer and found themselves in a state of moral disarray with little hope for a life of acceptable quality. So by the time the Soviet Union was disbanded (end of 1991) the former moral values were severely shaken, no new ones were apparent, a new generation of young people had grown up with no value education at all as far as school was concerned and there was a strong bias towards material well-being rather than spiritual, cultural or intellectual values. That was the sum total of the Soviet times and the start of independent Russia.

EDUCATION IN RUSSIA 1991–1996: A SEARCH FOR NEW VALUES

In the hectic time of the late 1980s few people really thought about moral values or the ideal of yet another 'new man'. The standard of life was falling, at times fear of hunger loomed large, the central authorities were challenged by the power-seeking people representing the Soviet republics. At the same time certain groups of people had already felt the pleasure of having legitimate money in quantities not heard of before while others were getting poorer and poorer. A joke of about 1980 had it that under capitalism, wealth is unevenly distributed; under socialism, poverty is evenly distributed. By about 1990 the joke had already little sense, for differentiation of income had gained pace though not yet at the speed of later times. This is not to say that people did not think at all about cultural values, honesty, humane relationships with each other; but the disappearance of habitual feeling of security made them act competitively rather than co-operatively.

There was another reason for the change. During the whole Soviet period there functioned the pioneer and the Komsomol organisations. They were strongly politicised, but politics was not their sole purpose. Essentially they were organisations which united most children (10–14 year olds) and young people (14–28 year olds). These were very large education, recreation and (of course) political indoctrination systems. Their disappearance left a vacuum in the education of collective-minded people while life itself encouraged individualism more and more. Again, this is well noted in the article by Daniels *et al.* (1995). Perhaps the two great slogans of the time were 'a worthy life' (whatever that might mean) as far as the standard of living was concerned and 'general/universal human values'. The drama of the situation in Russia is that of late there have been two value changes. One was that of the *perestroyka* period when Gorbachev initiated very significant liberalisation of all spheres of life in the former USSR. The change itself was (seemingly) very easy to accept by the vast majority of the people. In fact, what was it all about?

Human rights, technically proclaimed in the Brezhnev Constitution and even in the earlier Stalin one (freedom of speech, freedom of the press, freedom of meetings, inviolability of the domicile, etc.), were really to be granted. The power of the party in administering the economic and cultural activity at the centre and in the cities was to be severely curtailed. Key importance was attached to the initiative of the working person. Private property was gradually introduced. All that and much more was gladly accepted by the vast majority of the people. The picture, however, was not that rosy. Some thought the changes had to be still greater initially (e.g. private property should have been allowed without any limitations), others were not prepared for the initiative, still others abhorred to do some things allowed under the new regulations, still others abused the new possibilities to make quick money. Examples are easy to find. Many people just did not want to become owners of factories or shops – others, on the contrary, made full use of the possibilities to organise enterprises of any kind, the choice being only that of the fastest way to make money. Many people thought it immoral to buy a thing in a state shop and sell it for five times the price at the door of the shop – others made it their business. True, Gorbachev wanted to have it all under some sort of control, but he declined authoritarian practices and that was very well (ab)used by some people. It was all a great change in values which was being gradually accepted by most people. The situation became much more acute after Yeltsin came to power in Russia (April 1991) and especially after the coup attempt (August 1991) and the liquidation of the USSR (December 1991). Rapid economic decline followed the dissolution of economic and cultural links that had been built in the course of centuries, not just in the decades of Soviet power. For most people (estimates vary between 40 and 85 per cent) that meant rapid impoverishment. For very few (3 to 5 per cent) that meant making big money in no time. The rest did not feel the change either for the better or for the worse in real terms, while practically all felt the general uncertainty and anxiety.

And, of course, that was another and much more serious change in values. It became virtually impossible to earn decent money by decent means, and whoever wanted to stay afloat had to accept the means that had been abhorred by most. Rackets, robbery, prostitution, drug trafficking, murder bought for money, corruption in government and the police are now so widespread that the situation in the country (especially in large cities) has become, to say the least, generally unfriendly to the people. As far as values are concerned this means a very hard choice for almost everyone. Some people are prepared to stay in 'honest poverty' while rejecting over-commercialisation in all spheres of life. Others have no liking for dubious means to make money but feel economically pressed to accept them. A tiny minority wish nothing better.

But, of course, economic values are not the only values that matter, though they are closely linked with almost everything else. It is of interest to have a look at other values and the role education – more particularly, the school of

220

general education – can play in transmitting them. That education has such a mission is hardly open to question, though terminology matters very much here. Transmission and especially inculcation of values presupposes, in the eyes of many, a sort of pressure, even violence; words like brainwashing and indoctrination also come to mind. Then, seemingly, personal autonomy and democracy have little sense. Nevertheless it is hardly imaginable that education can be limited to transmitting factual, 'positive' knowledge and no values. It is not only a problem of educational philosophy; it is also an understanding of democracy. A very important question is posed: does there or could there exist a peculiarly Russian type of democracy or, since democracy is founded on general human values, can there be only one 'general' type of democracy? I will not try to answer the question in political terms, for example by discussing the pros and cons of a presidential or a parliamentary republic. But there is also a social and human dimension here and, what is still more important, there is a certain perception of democracy prevalent in the Russian society nowadays – i.e. shared by the people, not by politicians. I will agree with Apresyan and Guseynov (1996: 8, 10) that

> democratisation both of the Soviet society in the period of Gorbachev's *perestroyka* and of the post-Soviet Russian society under Yeltsin has proved unfulfilled in its most important expectations. . . . Non-acceptance of democracy as a form of social and state construction is combined with the general understanding by the post-Soviet Russian public opinion of Western democracy as not corresponding to the Russian traditions. . . . It is a fact of life that after the three or four years of reforms which were called 'democratic' the very idea of democracy does not find support in any of the population group.

This is the crux of the matter. Of course a population group is not a tiny number of people who are (or feel themselves as) politicians or professionals in political research. But support for democracy in the population has certainly dwindled – even if it is 'democracy in Russian colours' as people sometimes say without further elaboration. I would say that there exists no special 'Russian colour' in democracy. It is true, though, that considering the peculiarities of the period there are certain limitations in the social realities of democracy in this country. While cherishing the hope that the limitations will be gradually lifted as time passes we should still have them in view – in providing education, too. One thing here is that for the people who have been born and lived in the Soviet society with its lack of individual freedom and with its repressive practices democracy has very often a general meaning which suggests that all limitations in human choice and action may be lifted. Democracy is all freedom with no responsibilities. This understanding had very practical consequences – there was a cry of repression being returned whenever a law, a decree or a practice was introduced to limit appropriation of property, non-payment of taxes, etc. In this sense real democracy can exist only when there is a rule of law and the people are accustomed to it. This is not the case in Russia, where both the people and the state are accustomed to breaking the constitution and other laws. This practice existed long before 1917 and it was well reflected in a saying of those times: in Russia there has always been a good means against bad laws – poor implementation of laws. Witty as the saying is, the practice itself is certainly contrary to what should be. *Dura lex sed lex*, as the Romans said (law is severe but it is law). If the citizens of a state are not law-abiding this is anarchy; though of course it is not such obedience which defines democracy: fear can make people obey in a totalitarian state as well or better.

What happens however is mass violation of law. For example, in the autumn of 1993 parliament was dissolved by the presidential decree – which was against the constitution then in force. After it the building was blocked by armed forces and then burned out by tank and artillery fire with people still in there. Even if the parliamentarians were 'reactionaries' who blocked necessary reforms (though this is not my understanding), the lesson of breaking the law was all the more clear: there never had been a case in world history when a parliament was dealt with in this way. Parliaments have been dissolved in law and against the law but not destroyed by artillery. Another example is of course the case of the Chechen Republic. In 1991 when Yeltsin stood as a presidential candidate he travelled all along the country with his famous phrase: 'Take as much sovereignty (independence) as you can swallow.' The Chechens did try – and the result was the death of about 90,000 people and the destruction of almost the whole republic. Again – even admitting the Chechens were wrong (again, I am not so sure they were) – such a mass violation of human rights, which are now proclaimed in 'the Yeltsin Constitution', is abhorrent.

People took the lessons (and there have been many others such as not paying salaries for months) very seriously: if the state treats us in this way anything is permitted. This is not the only reason, but mass tax-evasion, wide-spread criminal practices of extorting money (the racket) are sometimes – and certainly wrongly – considered forms of social protest against the state that treats people cruelly. It is true that a strong social policy with balancing regulations to protect the poor and the weak is a long way off in Russia and this retards the pace of developing democracy. Many people see it as a sort of moral obligation of the state to treat people in a humane way. If they do not see it in real life they say they do not need 'such' democracy.

All this and the general climate of uncertainty do not help to educate citizens of the new Russia, which I hope is at least on the way to democracy. The discrepancy between the school as an institution and the school of life persists. In a way, people are stimulated by life itself to be autonomous. First, they have lost faith in the government and the state. Second, mass-media, political leaders and the new financial elite make it a point to emphasise in all possible ways that in Soviet times people relied on the state whereas now it is the time of personal initiative and autonomy. However, the initiative and autonomy often lead people to break laws, to behave violently, etc. Suffice it to say that security officers in the street, in the subway, near (and inside) shops and offices are quite a new – and, unfortunately, a necessary phenomenon in Russia.

The education system follows suit. In higher education academic freedom and institutional autonomy really exist. Now higher education establishments have (and use) the right to work out and implement their own content of education. The State Committee for Higher Education encourages this and has published materials to help university professors to work out the contents of education for many fields – with a specific note that they are not a decree but a sample, that the State Educational Standard is only a framework to be supplemented and/or changed by the universities themselves (State 1995; *Programmi* 1996).

For schools of general (pre-university) education the notion of autonomy is not officially used, though they are also very independent in their work. They are also, like higher education, very poorly financed. They are supposed to use as a guideline the experimental standard of general education which (unlike that for higher education) has not yet been approved by the government. But, again, this is a very general framework which is changed by the schools depending on their educational philosophy and other circumstances.

This suggests that the education system educates an autonomous citizen; and it does. However, competition now stands in place of mutual help, individualism in place of collectivism. Many traditional values any school cannot afford to forget (humaneness, compassion, tolerance to other people, patriotism as love of one's own country, etc.) are not forgotten in schools but they are hardly encouraged by everyday life. Needless to repeat that the values taught by life experiences usually prevail over the precepts taught in school. The scope of this chapter makes it impossible to elaborate on the theme, though, in fact, it is a fruitful approach to look at these values in order to understand what kind of person, what kind of citizen is educated (see Nikandrov 1995, 1996).

Although much of what is written above sounds pessimistic, I do hope that 'we shall overcome'. This will take time, but by-and-by the autonomous citizen of Russia with a reasonable understanding and respect for democracy and with a personal appreciation of national and general human values will be a fact of life.

REFERENCES

Apresyan, R. G. and Guseynov, A. A. (1996) 'Demokratia i grazhdanstvo' (Democracy and citizenship) *Voprosi filosofii* (Problems of philosophy) 7: 3–17.
Daniels, H., Lucas, N., Totterdell, M. and Fomina, O. (1995) 'Humanisation in Russian education: a transition between state determinism and individualism', *Educational Studies* 21 (1): 29–39.

Kaufman, C. (1994) 'De-Sovietizing educational systems, learning from past policies and practice', *International review of education* 40 (2): 149–58.

Nikandrov, N. D. (1995) 'Russian education after perestroyka: the search for new values' *International review of education* 41 (1–2): 47–57.

Nikandrov, N. D. (1996) *Vospitanye tsennostey: rossiyskiy variant* (Values education: the case of Russia), Moscow: Magister Publishing House.

Programma Kommunisticheskoy Partii Sovetskogo Soyuza (The Programme of the Communist Party of the Soviet Union) (1961), Moscow: Politizdat.

Programmi avtorskikh kursov po gumanitarnym i sotsial- no-ekonomicheskim distsiplinam dlya vysshey shkoly (Programmes of personal courses in the humanities and socio-economic disciplines for higher education) (1996), Moscow: State Committee of the Russian Federation for Higher Education).

State Educational Standard of Higher Professional Education: Official Publication (1995), Moscow: State Committee of the Russian Federation for Higher Education.

19

THE FAMILY AND THE PRIVATE IN EDUCATION FOR DEMOCRATIC CITIZENSHIP[1]

Penny Enslin

INTRODUCTION: SCHOOLS AND FAMILIES

It is commonly assumed that families and schools are, or should be, complementary partners in education. But are they, given feminist concerns about the family and its influence? This chapter argues, first, that families tend to exercise an influence that is in some respects antithetical to the development of democratic citizenship. Second, arguments against critical scrutiny of gendered practices on the grounds of the family's status as a private sphere need re-assessment. While the discussion engages with international debates, its starting point is South Africa and its project of reconstructing schooling and consolidating the democracy achieved in 1994.

FROM APARTHEID TO DEMOCRACY

South Africa's remarkable transition to democracy, marked by the election of 1994 and confirmed in the constitution adopted in 1996, is regarded in the public philosophy as much more than merely a formal achievement. The new constitution of May 1996 belongs to a citizenry which is trying to overcome traditions of oppression, segregation, exploitation and authoritarianism, and to establish a non-sexist as well as a non-racial democracy. Yet while much has been said and written to celebrate the achievement of liberation, this democracy is still new – stronger in the habits of resistance and still formulating the detailed implications of the moral vision produced by victory over apartheid.

This vision is reflected in a widely shared public understanding of what democracy means in this context: there will be citizenship for all, the views of all will be heard, participation in decision-making will be promoted, there will be wide consultation as seen in the process of encouraging public comment on drafts of the new constitution, and there will be open and transparent government and freedom of information. These characteristics of the new democracy suggest both publicness of procedure in government and a public of active citizens. Popular organisations, like unions, civic organisations and other community-based organisations, have self-consciously created models of debate, consultation, mandates carefully negotiated by leadership with its members, report-back and criticism. All of this implies, in the words of the *Reconstruction and Development Programme* (RDP), the policy framework of the African National Congress (ANC), 'thorough-going democracy' (ANC 1994: 7), the establishment of a *culture* of democracy which will pervade the life of the society, not only a formal system of election and representation. Hence the popular assumption that all institutions ought to be 'transformed' if the transition to democracy is to be complete. I argue in this chapter, as a contribution to the exploration of the educational implications of this vision of democracy, that the family is one such institution.

Schooling is one area in which South Africans have developed a popular understanding of democracy. Schools were an important site of resistance to apartheid, and they are now also one of the central challenges in the reconstruction of South Africa. Black students played a crucial role, from the historical turning point of the Soweto uprising in 1976, through a series of boycotts in the 1980s, and as partners with teachers and parents in the formulation of People's Education, as an alternative to apartheid education (Hyslop 1988). But this contribution was made at a heavy cost. The democratic government elected in 1994 inherited an educational system which was not only divided, unequal and dysfunctional. The student politics of protest had been accompanied also by the virtual collapse of the authority of both teachers and parents.

The reconstruction of the educational system comprises several formidable tasks. These include restructuring nineteen segregated departments of education into nine non-racial provincial departments and one national ministry, and of reallocating resources which discriminated against black and especially rural schools, as well as creating structures that will enable schools to function effectively. An assumption in this latter regard has been that parents must be given an effective role in school governance (Ministry of Education 1996; Province of Gauteng 1995), that their influence and interest will play a role in both democratic management of schools and in reasserting the authority over the youth which was lost during the years of school-based resistance. This presents some problems which need to be understood in the context of the history of apartheid.

Under apartheid white and black parents were allowed to play markedly different roles in the schooling of their children, a reflection of the very different treatment given to black families compared with white families. Colonialism and subsequently apartheid itself exercised a devastating effect on black families. Migrant labourers were compelled to seek work on the mines and in the cities, leaving women and children behind in increasingly overcrowded and impoverished reserves. Those women who followed male family members to the towns and cities were subject to various restrictions. Influx control laws prevented large numbers of women and children and the aged from leaving the reserves, while in the cities migrant workers tended to be accommodated in single-sex hostels. As the family structure of traditional tribal society was eroded, a growing number of families, rural and urban, came to be headed by women. Yet their situation was often contradictory; while their position as heads of households increased their independence and authority, it was contradicted by their minor status in the eyes of the law and the deeply entrenched patriarchal attitudes of the African community (Walker 1991: 149).

Apartheid laws reached right into the family, constituting it racially and determining who was allowed to be family to whom; some families were destroyed by statutory race classification, which classified their members as belonging to different racial groups and therefore not entitled to reside in the same group area. Yet by contrast, Afrikaner nationalism fostered a sentimental though also patriarchal ideology of the (preferably large) white family as the cornerstone of society. While white parents were able to exercise sometimes considerable influence in their children's schools, through parent-teacher associations and governing bodies, the influence of black parents was considerably less. The Christian National Education (CNE) Policy of 1948, an expression of Afrikaner nationalist ideology, awarded considerable authority to white parents over the schooling of their children. The Policy declared that the home should complement the church and the state in the control of schools, which derive their authority from parents in whose hands the control of the school should primarily reside (Institution for Christian National Education 1948: Article 8).

This principle was not to apply to black parents, whose children's education would be conducted under the trusteeship of whites. The Policy invoked the parent–child distinction in infantilising blacks, justifying white domination by depicting them as being in a state of cultural infancy and requiring the parental guidance of whites. The Bantu Education Act of 1953 provided for the establishment of a school committee at each school, some of whose members were to be elected by parents, and for local school boards each to control several school committees. These structures were intended to carry the burden of administering and also financing segregated and unequal schools for black children, providing 'an illusion of self-government' (Hyslop 1987: 1). But they lacked legitimacy and, especially from the 1970s, in some urban areas there was opposition to state policy from school committees and school boards (Hyslop 1987: 16–17). The influence of black parents on schools was thus considerably less than in white schools. Their children's schools were subject to heavy bureaucratic controls and, from the late 1970s, to state repression and in some instances to the intervention of the security forces.

It is therefore understandable that current proposals are for a strong role for parents in the governance of schools (ANC 1994: 131; Ministry of Education 1996; Province of Gauteng 1995). New regulations recognise the need for training of members of governing bodies, that parents need to learn skills in order to participate effectively in school governance (Ministry of Education 1996:

Chapter 3 Section 18; Province of Gauteng 1995: Chapter 4 Section 27). But the relationship between parents, as authority figures in families, and the project of democratising education which these proposals assume raises a problem.

The Reconstruction and Development Programme (RDP) implicitly identifies the problem, in the meticulous attention which it pays throughout to the situation of women in South Africa, especially black and rural women, to the inequalities and exclusions they have suffered in the past, and to their needs in areas such as education, employment, access to land, housing and health care. The RDP calls for gender equity and for women to be represented in all institutions; people must be educated in the principle of non-sexism (ANC 1994: 65). Yet the programme acknowledges that 'girls and women are educated and trained to fulfil traditional roles that perpetuate their oppression' (p. 62).

And here lies the central problem in turning to parents as an element in the democratisation of education. For the family, in the various forms it has taken, as an expression of different ethnic and religious traditions as well as an institution damaged by apartheid, is the central institution in the reproduction of traditional roles which oppress women, discouraging them from exercising autonomy in both the public and the private. Patriarchal or familial authority is not traditionally exercised in a democratic manner; girls and women are not traditionally party to it. The family as presently constituted is not a place to turn to if we are trying to develop autonomy and democratic habits.

To raise these issues is to challenge another tradition common to many cultures internationally (O'Neill 1993: 320) which holds that the family is a private sphere which should be protected from public (or state) intervention. In turning now to examine the feminist critique of the family, and noting how its oppressive tendencies undermine the aims of both education and democracy, I will argue against the assumed association of the family with privacy.

THE FAMILY AND THE PRIVATE

The distinction between the public and the private has been one of the distinguishing features of mainstream liberalism, which has been characterised by its proponents as defending the personal freedom of the individual against public or state interference. This defence crucially urges that a line be drawn – and vigorously held – between public and private, or political and personal (Shklar 1989: 23–4). In a recent development John Rawls (1993) has reformulated this distinction as one between public and non-public. For Rawls, defending liberalism as a political doctrine whose principles do not depend on any one comprehensive moral or political doctrine for their justification, public reason does not apply to the domestic sphere, which operates in terms of the comprehensive doctrines.

228

The feminist challenge to mainstream liberalism has focused on the role of the distinction between the public and the private in maintaining as well as explaining and challenging the oppression of women. The public sphere, it argues, is largely the preserve of male participants. By contrast and relatedly, women are still widely considered to be suited to and hence responsible for the private sphere, to which they tend to be confined for part and sometimes all of their lives, but in which they still tend to be dominated by men.

Feminist analyses of women in the private sphere have focused critical attention on the family. The work of Susan Okin (1989, 1994) is the most important single contribution to this critique, also offering a sustained engagement with Rawls's work. Her argument in *Justice, Gender and the Family* (1989) highlights the unequal power exercised by men and women in families, which is largely derived from the unequal wages usually brought to the household. Housework and care of children are not equally shared. Women's dependence on their husbands' income usually results in men taking major decisions and in some cases in women's remaining with men who batter them. The injustices of the family, which go beyond those mentioned above, have profound consequences for many of their members – including educational ones. Claudia Card (1993) discusses the significance of what she calls the 'moral damage' which results from sex oppression. In primary relationships with men, women suffer 'institutionalised dependence', including dependence on them for approval. But they often find themselves attached to men who 'define and value themselves by what they take to be their own achievements while they define and value us in terms of our relationships to them' (1993: 204). Our self-esteem, she observes, is affected by our primary personal relationships, starting with our parents, who can leave their children disadvantaged all their lives if they handle their relationships with them badly. While feminist writers have drawn to our attention the disadvantages for women which result from harmful primary personal relationships, their observations should also alert us to dependent and other destructive relationships which are morally damaging to male members of families, and regarded as a private matter.

For societies committed to the development of democracy, the feminist critique of the family poses a serious problem, by showing that some of its traditional practices are not themselves democratic. Hierarchical exercise of authority and allocation of roles and duties, the exercise of private power in such a way that the views of all adults and older children are not equally heard and participation in decision-making is not equally shared, contradicts what are regarded as appropriate features of democracy, such as those cited in the previous section of this chapter. This means that in democracies, as well as other types of polity, we have an institution in which citizens spend a large part of their lives, but which is democratic in neither its practices nor, because of their impact on their members' education, in its wider effects. This has important consequences both for education and for the project of democratisation of the society. The selves which girls acquire in the family may deter them from aspiring to educational and other goals which contradict the assumption that their primary role is to meet the needs of others. The development of democracy in the public sphere depends on the development of individual citizens who are accustomed to expressing their needs and listening to the needs of others. 'Someone who is accustomed either to dominate or to be subordinated in personal life is unlikely to be able to treat others as equals in the context of democratic decision-making' (Gould 1983: 8). For educational purposes, I shall show, the public good is dependent on the private, and requires intervention in it.

To be critical of the family as a private sphere is not necessarily to reject privacy as of no value. Why is privacy, including those forms usually sought in the context of the family, valuable?

The first of three reasons for valuing privacy explored by Okin is that it is a necessary prerequisite for intimacy and for developing personal relations (1991: 87). While it is often assumed that this intimacy is to be found in the domestic sphere, Okin points out that various theorists have observed that real intimacy is often not available to women and children in the domestic sphere, which is not always free of the threat of force. Many families do not provide opportunities for privacy and relationships within them are often not intimate.

For Okin, a second argument often offered for the importance of privacy is that it provides an escape from public roles. But while the domestic sphere might provide such respite from public roles for men and the opportunity to 'be oneself', for most women it offers no such escape. For they may have limited public, non-domestic roles and their domestic roles may be so demanding as to allow no such escape. The opportunity to 'unmask' may only be possible outside the 'private', domestic situation.

A third, related, argument is for privacy as a 'space for mental self-development' (Okin 1991: 89), the opportunity to enjoy solitude and to become engrossed in an activity of one's choice. But, under the present gender structure, this feature of privacy is available to men more than to women, who are expected to be available to see to the needs of others.

Privacy might be more feasibly enjoyed outside of the family. Marilyn Friedman explores friendship as a site of intimate relationships less prone to abuse and 'privatised power imbalances' (1993: 74–5). As Friedman shows, friendship offers moral growth derived from a friend's different experiences and perspectives. We can note, reading Friedman against Okin's description of the domestic, that in a relationship of friendship, which is not a socially ascribed one (Friedman 1993: 208), privacy provides the opportunity to escape one's usual, domestic roles and to seek self-development.

While cultural differences may mean that conceptions of privacy vary between societies and cultures, the arguments above show that families cannot be assumed to be places of privacy. They do not always operate in the equal interests of all their members, some of whom may have to seek privacy outside the family. We can also deduce from them a significant feature of the public–private distinction: that the family or domestic sphere should be treated neither as the equivalent of the private nor as its exemplar.

Feminist writers have proposed various interventions in the family, requiring that it become a public issue and challenging the mainstream liberal distinction between public and private. Among the policy and legal reforms which Okin proposes are: equal entitlement to a household's earnings, that after divorce both households should have an equal standard of living, and provision by employers for day care for employees' children and for parental leave and flexible working hours (1989: 176–83). Iris Young argues that public policy should support 'the ends and purposes of families' (1995: 553) while encouraging not only the traditional form of family. She proposes measures aimed at providing such support: reproductive freedom, father obligations, welfare reform, full employment and guaranteed income, and mothers' houses. John Exdell lists a further set of feminist policies which the goals of equalisation of power and opportunities warrant, including pay equity, abortion rights, government-funded child care and the regulation of family relationships by state policy (Exdell 1994: 449).

These are all examples of public intervention, mostly in the form of state intervention, although the two are not equivalent. I contend that none of them is obviously likely to undermine privacy by abusing it. While the provisions regarding reproductive freedom in particular touch on the personal and are the focus of controversy, it can be argued that they would be more likely to enhance opportunities for women and men to enjoy intimate relationships, and to escape from the public in ways that allow for self development.

EDUCATION, THE FAMILY AND PRIVACY

The practices of many families undermine the aims of education and present a problem for both the project of democratising a society and for programmes to democratise school governance by increasing the involvement of parents. Yet the mainstream liberal view is one that continues to oppose the intervention of schools in the traditions of families.

In a recent paper, Terry McLaughlin (1995) applies Rawls's distinction between public and non-public in considering approaches to diversity in the common school. Sympathising with Rawls's attempt to set the aims of education within a political rather than a comprehensive notion of liberalism (1995: 243), McLaughlin considers the question of what influence the public can legitimately have over the non-public. Distinguishing between 'public evaluation' in the context of a liberal democracy, and the values of the non-public, he argues that schools ought to pay attention to both promoting 'basic social morality' and the civic virtues of a democracy as public values, while illuminating rather than criticising non-public values (McLaughlin 1995: 241).

From a feminist perspective, McLaughlin's proposal is likely on application to endorse by default features of the domestic which are components of the comprehensive doctrines which it will seek to illuminate – including those which oppose or undermine autonomy for girls and women. If girls as well as boys are to be sufficiently prepared in the course of their education to exercise the qualities of democratic citizenship, such as those cited by Rawls – knowledge of their rights, to be self-supporting, to understand and participate in their political culture and its institutions, and to be co-operative members of society who respect fair terms of co-operation – then it seems that schools have no option but to counteract those aspects of the domestic or familial context from which pupils come to school that undermine these goals. Where the beliefs and personal qualities of pupils undermine their potential to participate in the public and the non-public, they require intervention.

What kinds of educational intervention in relation to families and to the private does this suggest? While not rejecting McLaughlin's recommendation that schools illuminate a range of non-public values including those about the family, there are three aspects of such intervention. First, the school curriculum should include a critical focus on families and 'family values'. In this regard Colin Wringe (1994) recommends that the ideological and moral support accorded the traditional family should be made clear, along with the encouragement of recognition of the flexible forms that modern families take. In the South African context, this requires acknowledgement of a range of different family units, from extended and nuclear families, to polygamous and matrifocal and other single parent families, as well as those in which adult siblings create households and those comprising grandparents living with grandchildren. It cannot be assumed that either parents or families presuppose the presence of the other. And, in a recommendation which connects with Friedman's examination of friendship and its significance:

> We should cease to accord family life and family affection the privileged place they have in the projected ideal future that is supposed to lie ahead of young people; instead we should recognise the value and richness which the individual life of diverse and transient commitments may hold for some.
>
> (Wringe 1994: 88)

Second, defending the position that the state ought to provide resources – 'material and educational' – which will change the domestic balance of power, Exdell makes some specific educational recommendations, emphasising the importance of developing the faculty of autonomy. He argues the need for sex education and 'gender consciousness-raising' in the public school curriculum (Exdell 1994: 449), that girls should be taught both the skills and the independence to be self-supporting, and that boys and girls should learn egalitarian relationships within the family (1994: 453).

This last recommendation implies a third, quite direct intervention, given the power of the family and the argument that families often fail to provide opportunities for their members to pursue what is valuable in privacy. Schools ought also to provide opportunities for children to learn to develop and sustain fulfilling personal relationships, both including and outside of those ascribed by kinship. The opportunities they provide for the pursuit of interests of one's own choosing should be seen as valuable in finding opportunities for unmasking and for self-development, developing a sense of privacy. To do this, schools ought to recognise and respect children's privacy, as well as teaching them to recognise the 'public criteria for educational achievements' (Macmillan 1995: 110, 115). If our selves are a mixture of the given and the chosen, the education of the self is a matter of learning to understand the given, including our primary family ties and all that comes with them, and choosing new relationships and selves free of what Friedman calls the 'a priori morally decisive authority' of the family. It also poses the possibility of 'unconventional values, deviant life-styles, and other forms of disruption of social traditions' (Friedman 1993: 218–19).

In arguing that schools should address the family and privacy in these three ways, I make two claims. The first is a procedural principle, that we should not try to separate radically the private and the public and reject public scrutiny of the private. The second is a substantive principle: that there are oppressive family contexts which undermine the development of the autonomy appropriate to full development of democracy and they require public scrutiny and educational intervention.

CONCLUSION

In the public sphere, particularly in politics and government, progress has been made in South Africa towards gender equality since the transition to democracy. More women now sit in parliament – 24 per cent of the members compared with the world average of 10 per cent (*The Star* 1996b: 15). Although at four out of twenty-five the number of women cabinet ministers is less impressive, it is an improvement on the record of the previous regime. In local government, elections in most parts of the country in late 1995 returned women as 18.75 per cent of the councillors and to 14.4 per cent of executive positions in local government (*Sunday Independent* 1996: 13).

But in other respects progress has been slower. For example, the constitution of May 1996 recognises both traditional leaders and customary law, stating that when applicable it must be applied by the courts, but subject to the constitution. The future of customary law awaits detailed determination by legislation. This leaves large numbers of women – including not only black women with strong traditional ties but also Muslim and Jewish women – subject to customary law. This implies that they will continue to be subject to certain forms of discrimination and restrictions on their autonomy, including for African women being treated as minors and having a diminished right to ownership of property. The position of the ANC Women's League is that 'customary laws and the institution of traditional leaders are oppressive to women' (*The Star* 1996a: 5) and that they negate the rights of women.

In spite of such calls, the ANC as a whole has not treated this issue as a priority. It is presumed that the issue will be fought partly in the courts, as aspects of customary law are challenged on the basis of the constitution and the Bill of Rights, which states (Section 9) that neither the state nor any person 'may unfairly discriminate directly or indirectly against anyone' on grounds which include gender, sex or marital status. This presumption assumes that a constituency traditionally discouraged from participation in politics and from challenging traditional authority will have the resources to take these issues, some of which may be regarded as a private matter, to the courts.

One of the necessary conditions for this process to gain momentum is public debate, involving the media and community organisations, as well as exploration of these issues in schools. This does not necessarily imply, as might be objected, unrestrained attack on all customs and traditions. Such debate, democratically conducted, would invite participants to consider the implications for gender equity of relevant traditional practices. By encouraging parents as members of a democratic public – indeed as members of different democratic publics debating their own traditions as well as bearers of authority in families to consider such issues – those traditions which prejudice the educational and other interests of girls could be reconsidered. Viewed as contributing to the proposed training to be offered to parents involved in school governance, such debate offers the possibility for those aspects of family traditions to be modified without the destruction of privacy, indeed opening opportunities for the development of privacy, rather than its destruction. Similarly, neither should the public be equated with the state, for the public may include non-state bodies in civil society as well as members of the public.

Does my argument indicate abandonment of the distinction between private and public? I think not. It is important to make the distinction, to assert that there are some matters which are of general concern and require publicity, public consideration and sometimes intervention, and others not. But the public and the private are not completely separable. The challenge of the distinction is not to make it, but to decide how the two are interrelated and how they ought to influence one another.

NOTE

1 This chapter draws from papers presented at the annual meeting of the Cambridge Branch of the Philosophy of Education Society of Great Britain, September 1995, and the annual meeting of the Society, Oxford, March 1996.

REFERENCES

African National Congress (1994) *The Reconstruction and Development Programme*, Johannesburg: Umanyano Publications.

Card, C. (1993) 'Gender and Moral Luck' in O. Flanagan and A. Rorty (eds) *Identity, Character and Morality: Essays in Moral Psychology*, Cambridge, Mass.: MIT Press.

Exdell, J. (1994) 'Feminism, Fundamentalism and Liberal Legitimacy', *Canadian Journal of Philosophy* 24, 3: 441–63.

Friedman, M. (1993) 'What are Friends for?', *Feminist Perspectives on Personal Relationships and Moral Theory*, Ithaca: Cornell University Press.

Gould, C. (1983) 'Private Rights and Public Virtues: Women, the Family and Democracy' in *Beyond Domination: New Perspectives on Women and Philosophy*, Totowa, New Jersey: Rowman & Allanheld.

Hyslop, J. (1987) 'Aspects of the Failure of Bantu Education as a Hegemonic Strategy: School Boards, School Committees and Educational Politics 1955–1976', University of the Witwatersrand, History Workshop.

Hyslop, J. (1988) 'School Student Movements and State Education, Policy: 1972–87', in W. Cobbett and R. Cohen (eds) *Popular Struggles in South Africa*, Sheffield and London: Africa World Press.

Institute for Christian National Education (1948) 'Christian National Education Policy' reprinted in B. Rose and R. Tunmer (eds) (1975) *Documents in South African Education*, Johannesburg: Ad. Donker.

Macmillan, J. (1995) 'Some Thoughts on Privacy in Classrooms' in J. Garrison and A. Rud Jr. (eds) *The Educational Conversation: Closing the Gap*, Albany: State University of New York Press.

McLaughlin, T. (1995) 'Liberalism, Education and the Common School' *Journal of Philosophy of Education* 29, 2: 239–55.

Ministry of Education (1996) 'Draft South African Schools Bill' reprinted in *The Sunday Times*, Sunday 9 June: 7–10.

Okin, S. (1989) *Justice, Gender and the Family*, New York: Basic Books.

Okin, S. (1991) 'Gender, the Public and the Private' in D. Held (ed.) *Political Theory Today*, Cambridge: Polity Press.

Okin, S. (1994) 'Political Liberalism, Justice, and Gender', *Ethics* 105, 1: 23–43.

O'Neill, O. (1993) 'Justice, Gender and International Boundaries' in M. Nussbaum and A. Sen (eds) *The Quality of Life*, Oxford: Clarendon Press.

Province of Gauteng (1995) *School Education Act*, Pretoria: Provincial Gazette Extraordinary, 8 December.

Rawls, J. (1993) *Political Liberalism*, New York: Columbia University Press.

Shklar, J. (1989) 'The Liberalism of Fear' in N. Rosenblum (ed.) *Liberalism and the Moral Life*, Cambridge, Mass.: Harvard University Press.

The Star (1996a) 'ANC women demand female oppression's end', 18 April.

The Star (1996b) 'Women must walk together to put their stamp on government', 23 May.

Sunday Independent (1996) 'Under-representation of women in local government skews decisions', 31 March.

Walker, C. (1991) *Women and Resistance in South Africa*, 2nd edn, Cape Town: David Philip.

Wringe, C. (1994) 'Family Values and the Value of the Family', *Journal of Philosophy of Education* 28, 1: 77–88.

Young, I. (1995) 'Mothers, Citizenship, and Independence: A Critique of Pure Family Values', *Ethics* 105: 525–56.

20

PROFESSIONAL EDUCATION AND THE FORMATION OF DEMOCRATIC RELATIONSHIPS BETWEEN 'EXPERTS' AND 'ORDINARY' CITIZENS

Terry Phillips

INTRODUCTION

If all citizens are to share in the autonomy implied in the notion of democratic citizenship, the society's 'experts' – among them its professionals – must enact democratic processes in their practices. Experts, by definition, 'possess' specialised bodies of knowledge and have expertise in a range of specialised skills. Knowledge increases the possibility of informed professional decision-making while skill enables the successful accomplishment of practical professional tasks. Professional education *aims* to create experts but in the process it may well reinforce hierarchically structured institutional frameworks and inhibit lay citizens' autonomous potential. Modern democratic societies are founded on the concept of citizen involvement and partnership. 'Experts' have an important role to play in modelling and enabling the processes of mutual critical reflection which make genuine democratic partnership possible (see Heathcote, in this volume).

In democratic societies professional education must encourage the putative professional to challenge and work toward the reconstruction of institutionalised dependency behaviours and values. The empowerment of young people to participate proactively in autonomous citizenship is dependent upon the provision of a professional education in which *all* professionals, not just teachers, learn to perceive themselves as partners in the dialogic deconstruction and reconstruction of expert–non expert inequality.

KNOWLEDGE, SOCIAL PRACTICE AND CULTURE

The social practices and theories of our culture are shaped and reshaped in the course of human interaction (Mead 1934; Goffman 1959; Bhaskar 1991;

237

Shotter 1993; Gergen 1989, 1994). There is an interplay of discourses as one set of theories is tried out against another, one set of practices tested against another, or theories and practices brought into contention with each other (Kress 1985; Lotman 1981/1990; Bakhtin 1981; Gardiner 1992). Any significant cultural shift is part of this interplay.

Bourdieau argues that an individual's social practices are so embedded in the common culture that eventually he or she sees them as 'natural'. The individual develops a *habitus,* a way of doing things, which responds to context from within an ideological framework whose values and rules of engagement are no longer evident to him or her (Bourdieu 1977, 1990). Knowledge is embedded in action, which is in turn embedded in the culture. Vico suggests we develop a common feeling *(sensus communis)* about the world that makes it possible for us to practise and understand without recourse to explication (Vico 1709/1965, 1988). Like Bourdieu, he proposes that knowledge is developed through common ways of doing and understanding. We learn who we are, how to do things, what counts as relevant knowledge, through being immersed in our culture.

I would argue that ways of thinking (cognitive practices) are also developed out of a *habitus*. An individual's attitude of mind, their cognitive disposition, is shaped by the cognitive *habitus* of their society, embedded in which is the *habitus* of its elite members, the professionals. If this is so, then the layperson–expert interaction is a key arena for the construction of many of the understandings and dispositions which develop and sustain the habitus that in turn shapes the 'ordinary' citizen's autonomy.

UNDOING CERTAINTY

Professionals have access to 'authorised' knowledge and are well versed in the 'approved' practices of a given field. They have privileged knowledge and experience that makes it possible for them to assume the role of official arbiter of both theory and practice in that field. While they cannot completely escape the cultural 'entrapment' described by Stolzenberg (1978), they do have power to shape the detailed ground-rules of interaction in *particular* contexts. As a consequence, they may develop a perception of themselves as able to *determine* ways of behaving in the society as a whole. The lay-person or 'ordinary' citizen, on the other hand, is likely to see themself as having to follow patterns already established elsewhere by more powerful others.

People whose institutionalised status and field expertise give them positions of authority are often hesitant about making themselves vulnerable by giving away some of their expertise. If they acknowledge there may be a number of alternative ways of looking at an issue they reveal that their expertise is based on judgement and choice rather than certainty. They make transparent the fact that their decisions depend on values and not *a priori* 'truth'.

In a situation where decisions are made on the basis of claims to expert knowledge, autonomy remains unachievable in practice for anyone whose expertise is not authorised. And yet most democratic societies would wish their citizens to be autonomous in their decision-making about their own education, health and welfare. To change the habitus to promote such autonomy it is necessary to institutionalise dialogic interaction in the professional–layperson interaction. This requires the fostering of confidence about uncertainty and the creation of conditions for mutual exploration of what each party is uncertain about. In dialogue, uncertainty is agentive because it compels participants to examine what they have until now treated as axiomatic. This creates a climate in which the interrogation of what has previously been taken-for-granted becomes commonplace. The interests of a democratic society are furthered where professionals, recognising the tentative nature of their expertise, listen more often and lay people, seeing the professional at ease with uncertainty, make their own voices heard despite a felt *lack* of expertise.

If the society is evolving from an autocratic one, professionals must work with clients to reconstruct current layperson–expert relationships to include the possibility of dialogue for mutual understanding. In the new context all participants in the conversation will be free to play with the 'imaginary' (Shotter 1993), envisage a range of alternative solutions to the educational, health or welfare 'problems' that are their particular concern, and negotiate a plan of action to which they contribute equally.

There is a complication. To deconstruct an idea or a practice that is currently taken-for-granted you first have to be aware that it is one of a number of possibilities. By definition something is taken-for-granted when we have forgotten that there are alternatives. It is so deeply embedded in a historically constructed culture that it is no longer available under normal circumstances for analysis and critical reflection. To quote David Carr:

> What distinguishes [the] reflective components of action and experience from the pre-reflective 'immersion' . . . is that here the temporal object, experience, or action is taken apart, broken down into its elements, so that each can be attended to separately. This means of course that it no longer occupies the position of 'background' . . . and requires a function or a value in a larger structure.
>
> (Carr 1986: 56)

It follows that reflection must itself become institutionalised and the orientation towards analysis must become a central part of what is taken-for-granted in a culture. Which raises two related questions. How does any community develop a habitus in which questioning, analysis and critique are central? In what antecedents are the models for interrogative behaviour to be found?

CONSTRUCTING THE DIFFERENCE BETWEEN AUTONOMY AND DEPENDENCE: AN EXAMPLE FROM THE CLASSROOM

Before looking more closely at the role of professional education in developing and maintaining *habitus* for citizen autonomy, it is worth considering the role of school-based education in constructing early dispositions to dependence/independence.

It is evident from studying children in classrooms that they do not become autonomous simply because they are given more opportunity to work independently. Children, like the rest of us, interpret current experience in the light of previous experience. If, for instance, discussion 'tasks' in a particular class are normally a form of exercise, then the children in that class will treat every 'discussion' as an occasion for 'doing' the teacher's agenda. Autonomy is not achieved by means of one-off events that run counter to a well-established classroom culture.

Striking examples of the persistence of learner dependence in circumstances where autonomy is potentially possible come from classroom research into the behaviour and conversation of 7 to 12 years olds working collaboratively at the computer. SLANT Project researchers expected to find that computer-mediated activities would increase student autonomy by encouraging a greater focus on decision-making (Mercer, Phillips and Somekh 1989).[1] What they found instead was that children in one classroom would often respond quite differently from others using the same or similar programmes in a different classroom (Mercer *et al.* 1992).

While some groups of children working at a problem-solving activity hardly discussed their proposed solutions at all before pressing a key to continue, groups in other classes discussed their thinking at some length before taking action (Fisher, Dawes and Moyes 1992). Similarly, while some groups engaged in computer games and simulations by arguing a case for making one move rather than another, others moved through the steps of the activity with minimum delay for discussion (Phillips and Scrimshaw 1992). While the groups studied were influenced to some extent by the nature of the software they were using, responses to the same or comparable software varied sufficiently from classroom to classroom to raise the question; what other factor(s) is at work?

The answer to this question seemed to lie in differences of culture in the various classes studied. Where 'getting on with the job in hand' was habituated into the culture, discussion at the computer was typically about what had to be done to complete the next step in a programme. Where 'standing back to reflect' had become part of the habitus, children turned away from the computer screen more often to solve a problem through discussion. Open-ended computer software created the potential for children in all the classes to become involved in planning and debate about possible outcomes, but this potential failed to become an actuality in the classes where the normal *modus operandi* was for teachers to take the decisions and children to follow.

The research showed that in some classrooms instrumental communication was valued above communication for understanding. In these classrooms children expected to deal in information exchange where the transfer was from teacher as 'expert' to pupil as 'dependent non-knower'. When the computer was introduced into the classroom, it stood as a surrogate for the teacher as 'expert'. But the research also showed there are classrooms where discussion and decision-making continue when computer-mediated activities are introduced, with the children treating the computer as a voice in the conversation rather than a source of authority. In these classes, knowledge was commonly the subject of analysis, critique or speculation and teachers adopted the role of 'co-learner' wherever possible. They were places, in fact, where students learned to value their own 'expertise', their own 'voice', because of the model presented by their teacher.

THE ROLE OF PROFESSIONAL EDUCATION AND TRAINING: AN EXAMPLE FROM NURSING

Children in school learn many of the limits and possibilities of belonging to the society through interaction with teachers. As they become adult citizens and enter the wider world what they have learned is reinforced or modified in interactions with a wider range of professionals. Professionals themselves learn through interactions with more experienced professionals. If teachers, nurses, doctors and others are to actively facilitate democratic citizenship by modelling the kinds of behaviour that enable it, they must have experienced it for themselves. Because the education and training of nurses in England has undergone a massive cultural change in the past decade, it offers us insights into the problems of creating a new habitus even where there is a declared intention to do so. It also indicates some of the principles by which change is accomplished.

The regulatory body for nursing education in England (the ENB) aims to promote the preparation of independent practitioners with the knowledge and skill to be autonomous decision-makers. In pursuance of this aim, course providers are required to prepare students to reflect on practice and evaluate it (ENB 1990, 1993). We might have expected this to have led to a universal increase in student challenges to established practice, revealing independent thought as well as autonomous practice, but it has not happened universally. In many institutions where nurses learn their profession, students *do* behave in significantly different ways than in the past. In particular they ask questions more often and take action to find out, through reading research, when they are confronted with complex situations. They no longer accept everything without question just because it represents 'what has always been done'. Nor do they wait to be told what to do when they encounter a novel situation.

241

In as many other institutions, however, students persist in behaviour which reinforces the status quo and keeps them dependent. They continue to follow established practice without subjecting it to critical scrutiny, preferring to adopt the prevailing professional habitus. They perceive the act of challenging practice as 'making a fuss' (Bedford *et al.* 1992; Phillips *et al.* 1994; Bedford *et al.* 1995).

Why is it, then, that what is taught during courses of professional preparation for nurses often fails to transfer into practice? Is it that, on the whole, the theory part of professional preparation takes insufficient account of the practical, as suggested by Elliott (1991), Carr and Kemmis (1986) and Schon (1987)? Or is it, as recent research evidence seems to suggest, that while theory and practice are often pretty well integrated in course design, reflective practice and autonomous action are rarely modelled in the practice of the higher education teachers who provide students with their role-models?

ACE and TYDE Project data[2] indicates that many nurse educators do two things which contradict the avowed aim to promote the kind of autonomy-promoting reflective practice noticed by, among others, Benner (1984), Schon (1987) and Cox, Hickson and Taylor (1991). First, they signal in their teaching that they value taxonomised and 'authorised' knowledge for its own sake; second, they refer to so-called 'good' clinical practice without making explicit or evaluating the criteria by which it has been judged to be good (Phillips *et al.* 1994). Both actions construct the student role as a largely dependent one by asking students to accept uncritically the 'expert' judgement of their teachers. Nurse educators who simplify the complexity of the issues on which decision-making centres reinforce their own authority and discourage students from engaging dialogically with them or with knowledge itself. By presenting the world in ways that suggest it is amenable to division into discrete categories by people like themselves with 'sufficient' authorised knowledge, they discourage students from bringing their own relevant but unauthorised expertise to bear. In effect, these educators determine relevance by maintaining the categorical boundaries of field knowledge. Students are positioned as 'listeners' or silent interlocutors in a monologue. They are obliged to remain silent until the day they have learned enough to be 'trusted' to go it alone. Autonomy is depicted as something for the future, something that *follows* education rather than an integral part of it.

Students who encounter educators who make explicit the relationship between knowledge, practice and values seem to be motivated to discuss both theoretical and ethical principles for practice, drawing on their personal experience and understanding. Encouraged by lecturers who present information and ideas for exploration rather than non-critical acceptance, they begin to perceive the examination of alternatives and the discussion of values as a key part of student–lecturer interaction (Bedford *et al.* 1992). Educators interact with students in ways which suggest that participation in democratic dialogue is 'natural'.

MODELLING CRITICAL REFLECTIVE PRACTICE: A STRATEGY FOR CHANGING THE HABITUS

Novices often learn a role by interacting with experienced role holders. If teachers model professional nursing as primarily a matter of expertise, then they provide students with a theory in action that foregrounds dependence on the knower, and in that sense devalues autonomy. Such a model places professional knowledge above everyday knowledge and discourages interplay between them. It also discourages novices from *evaluating* the trustworthiness of the professional knowledge, by failing to consider frameworks for critique. The novice practitioner is simply invited to apply 'given' knowledge without first evaluating it. On the other hand, nurse educators who demonstrate a perception of nursing knowledge and practice as 'texts' produced by multiple authors, or 'conversations', created by many 'voices', model learning as a dialogic process. They show what it means to explore the ideal in relation to the actual, and theory in relation to practice. They provide evidence of what it means to live with ambiguity and avoid over-simplification. They demonstrate, in interaction, that genuine autonomy comes from being able to take responsibility for making choices in situations where there may be a number of appropriate alternatives.

A competent and truly autonomous practitioner must be able to operate across contexts and apply principles in a context-sensitive way (Dreyfus and Dreyfus 1980; Dreyfus 1982; Benner 1984). It is generally believed therefore that reflection on practice, where practical thinking in one situation is made explicit, built on and used in another, should be developed through discussion (Carr and Kemmis 1986; Schon 1987; Phillips *et al.* 1994). The move from novice, who assesses each clinical situation as if it were a one-off, to competent practitioner, who perceives nursing or midwifery holistically, demands dialogue before, during and after action. In this way, action and reflection impinge upon each other and over time result in changes both in the practice ('what' is done and 'how' it is done) and in the theoretical framework for that practice ('why' it is done) (Phillips *et al.* 1994).

PRINCIPLES FOR ENABLING AUTONOMY IN PROFESSIONAL EDUCATION

Observation of nurse education in classrooms and clinical placement environments, together with interviews with lecturers, clinical practitioners and students across an extended period of time, lead Phillips *et al.* (1994) to propose a range of principles and strategies for facilitating reflection and critique. They proposed, for example, that there should be a principle in nurse education that the assessment of clinical practice be based upon student/assessor discussion of a range of forms of evidence. They then suggested that the strategies to ensure this would include the provision of designated time for discussion, the use of documented evidence about a student's practice as the basis of discussion, and the provision of a record – in writing – of the evidence discussed, the advice given, the issues raised and debated, and the principles that were agreed for making an action plan. A second principle proposed was that the assessment of nurse education should encourage the development of a critique of both theory and practice. The strategies for development of a critique were to include the provision of a dossier (or portfolio) of various items that brought together theory and practice, and provided evidence of students' knowledge, understanding and attitudes. Amongst these were to be: issues-based papers presented by the student to the class, reports on post-placement discussions of dilemmas experienced in practice, significant extracts from student diaries or journals constructed during practice, reports of case studies or projects undertaken. This evidence, taken together, was to be used to determine the student's ability to examine critically the particular and situation-specific in relation to the general context of nursing.

These principles are founded on the fieldwork evidence that clearly defined structures and strategies are necessary to ensure student autonomy in practice as well as rhetoric. They make explicit the need for an enabling framework of dialogue and critique. The research showed unequivocally that, without such a structure, the activities of analysis, reflection and discussion were inclined either to be squeezed out of the curriculum altogether or to be pushed into the margins.

EDUCATIVE DIALOGUE TO SUSTAIN THE CULTURE FOR DEMOCRATIC CITIZENSHIP

When taught by experts who rarely test their knowledge and skills against other theories and practices, novice professionals commonly become non-interrogative themselves. There is a high probability that once qualified their meetings with the 'ordinary' citizens who become their clients will reiterate inequality by constructing the clients as dependent laypersons. Dialogic conversations, however, in which the expert accepts the problematical nature of their own knowledge and skill and is ready to facilitate the interaction as a mutually educative event, brings about new understandings on the part of both interlocutors. They recognise the fact that the autonomous professional has to organise apparently contradictory information, analyse that information critically, make judgements on the basis of the analysis, and take appropriate action bearing the contradictions in mind. It is essential, therefore, that a curriculum for autonomy has structures and strategies in place which will facilitate all of these processes. The more concrete these are, the more probability that dialogue will occur at a 'local' level, that is, in teacher/student interactions. The more often dialogue happens at the local level, the more the 'global' culture will become an established dialogic one in which democratic citizenship is able to flourish. The one cannot be maintained without the other.

STRUCTURES AND STRATEGIES FOR CHANGE:
A SUMMARY

Optimal conditions for the development of democratic autonomy across a society are found where its macro-structure and its micro-structures are in harmony. At the macro-structural level the development of autonomy requires frameworks that ensure the devolution of decision-making and judgement, while at the micro-structural one it needs interaction strategies that facilitate critique. Structures and strategies are worked out *in practice* and are always open to reiteration or modification *in practice*, at the point of praxis where the macro and micro meet. The institutionalisation of dialogic processes which enable democratic autonomy occurs where not only its micro-level mechanisms and strategies but also its macro-structures encourage it. Ways of thinking and doing are constructed in actual interactions, but are affected by codes set up by the society as a whole; while at the same time a society's codes are constructed by what happens in actual interactions.

In a democratic society, what it is that counts as appropriate knowledge and acceptable practice is constructed dialogically. Because of this fact, the definition of what counts as appropriate is itself subject to change; dialogicality encourages reflexivity and permits the re-construction of 'what has been mutually acceptable until now' into 'what is mutually acceptable at the present time'. In a healthy democratic society which is sufficiently secure in its democracy, the structures and strategies by which democracy is accomplished are themselves open to scrutiny, critique and change through the self-same dialogic process.

Autonomy is not a 'thing' or an 'outcome' but a multi-faceted process. It includes the whole complex of processes through which individuals learn, judge, make decisions and act to manipulate and transform the world for human purposes. It requires that it is part of the way of life of all citizens, but especially of the professionals who are significant role models, to expect – having critically reflected on their theories, practices and their structures and strategies for examining them – to begin the process over again.

NOTES

1 The SLANT – or Spoken Language And New Technology – Project (1991–1993) was funded by the Economic and Social Research Council. The research was carried out jointly by a research team from the University of East Anglia (UEA), Norwich and the Open University, Milton Keynes. The writer was a member of the UEA team.
2 The Assessment of Competence in Nursing and Midwifery Education (ACE) Project (1991–1993) and the Evaluation of Pre-Registration Nursing and Midwifery Degrees (TYDE) Project (1992–1995) were funded by the English National Board for Nursing,

Midwifery and Health Visiting. Both national evaluations were carried out by a team from the Centre for Applied Research in Education (CARE) at the University of East Anglia, Norwich. The writer was Co-Director of both evaluations.

REFERENCES

Bakhtin, M. (1981) *The Dialogic Imagination: Four Essays by M. M. Bakhtin*, edited by M. Holquist (translated by C. Emerson and M. Holquist), Austin: Texas University Press.

Bedford, H., Phillips, T., Robinson, J. and Schostak, J. (1992) *The Assessment of Competence in Nursing and Midwifery Education (The ACE Project). Final Report*, London: ENB.

Bedford, H., Leamon, J., Phillips, T. and Schostak, J. (1995) *The Evaluation of Three and Four Year Degrees in Nursing and Midwifery (The TYDE Project): Interim Report*, London: ENB.

Benner, P. (1984) *From Novice to Expert: Excellence and Power in Clinical Nursing Practice*, California: Addison-Wesley.

Bhaskar, R. (1991) *Philosophy and the Idea of Freedom*, Oxford: Basil Blackwell.

Bourdieu, P. (1977) *Outline of a Theory of Practice*, London: Cambridge University Press.

Bourdieu, P. (1990) *In Other Words: Essays Towards a Reflexive Sociology*. Cambridge: Polity Press.

Carr, D. (1986) *Time, Narrative, and History*, Bloomington: Indiana University Press.

Carr, W. and Kemmis, S. (1986) *Becoming Critical: Knowing Through Action Research*, Geelong, Victoria: Deakin University Press.

Cox, H., Hickson, P. and Taylor, B. (1991) 'Exploring Reflection: Knowing and Constructing Practice' in G. Gray and R. Pratt. (eds) *Towards a Discipline of Nursing*, London: Churchill Livingstone.

Dreyfus, S. (1981) *Formal Models v Human Situational Understanding: Inherent Limitations on the Modelling of Business Expertise. Office, Technology, and People*, USAF Contract No: F49620-79-C-0063 Mimeo paper.

Dreyfus, S. and Dreyfus, H. (1980) *A Five Stage Model of the Mental Activities Involved in Directed Skill Acquisition*, mimeo paper, USAF Contract F 49620-79-C-0063, Berkeley: University of California.

Elliott, J. (1991) *Action Research for Educational Change*, Milton Keynes: Open University Press.

English National Board for Nursing, Midwifery and Health Visiting (ENB) (1990) *Regulations and Guidelines for the Approval of Institutions and Courses*, London: ENB.

English National Board for Nursing, Midwifery and Health Visiting (ENB) (1993) *Regulations and Guidelines for the Approval of Institutions and Courses*, London: ENB.

Fisher, E., Dawes, L. and Moyes, L. (1992) *Discussion in the Primary School: Teachers Developing Their Strategies for Encouraging Investigative Talk Amongst Children Using Computers*, paper presented to the Conference of the British Educational Research Association, Stirling University, November 1992.

Gardiner, M. (1992) *The Dialogics of Critique: M. M. Bakhtin and the Theory of Ideology*, London: Routledge.

Gergen, K. J. (1989) 'Warranting Voice and the Elaboration of Self' in J. Shotter and K. J. Gergen (eds) *Texts of Identity*, London: Sage.

Gergen, K. J. (1994) 'The Social Construction of Personal Histories: Gendered Lives in Popular Autobiographies' in T. Sarbin and J. Kitsuse (eds) *Constructing the Social*, London: Sage.

Goffman, E. (1959) *The Presentation of Self in Everyday Life*, New York: Doubleday.

Kress, G. (1985) *Linguistic Processes in Sociocultural Practice*, Victoria, Australia: Deakin University Press.

Lotman, Y. (1981/1990) *Universe of the Mind: A Semiotic Theory of Culture* (translated by A. Shukman), London: I. B. Taurus.

Mead, G. H. (1934) *Mind, Self, and Society*, Chicago: University of Chicago Press.

Mercer, N., Fisher, E., Phillips T. and Scrimshaw, P. (1992) *Spoken Language and New Technology in the Primary Classroom. Final Report of the SLANT Project*, London: ESRC.

Mercer, N., Phillips, T. and Somekh, B. (1989). 'Research Note: Spoken Language and New Technology', *Journal of Computer Assisted Learning* 7: 195–202.

Phillips, T. and Scrimshaw, P. (1992) *Playing By the Rules: Adventure Games and the Development of Expectations About Working With Computers in Primary Classrooms*, paper presented to the Conference of the British Educational Research Association, Stirling University, November 1992.

Phillips, T., Bedford, H., Robinson, J. and Schostak, J. (1994) *Education, Dialogue, and Assessment: Creating Partnership for Improving Practice*, London: ENB.

Schon, D. (1987) *Educating the Reflective Practitioner*, San Francisco: Jossey-Bass.

Shotter, J. (1993) *Conversational Realities: Constructing Life Through Language*, London: Sage.

Stolzenberg, G. (1978) 'Can an Enquiry into the Foundations of Mathematics Tell us Anything Interesting About Mind?' in G. Miller and E. Lenneberg (eds) *Psychology and Biology of Language and Thought: Essays in Honour of Eric Lenneberg*, New York: Academic Press.

Todorov, T. (1984) *Mikhail Bakhtin: The Dialogical Principle* (translated by Wlad Godzich), Manchester: Manchester University Press.

Vico, G. (1709/1965) *On the Study Methods of Our Time* (translated by E. Gianturco), New York: Bobs-Merrill.

Vico, G. (1988) *On the Most Ancient Wisdom of the Italians* (translated by L. Palmer), Ithaca: Cornell University Press.

21

AUTONOMY AND EDUCATION

An integrated approach to knowledge, curriculum and learning in the democratic school

David Aspin

INTRODUCTION

Amongst the prime prerequisites for the effective functioning of modern democratic states, four are crucially related to education. These are: (1) that citizens should be able to sustain their own existence and that of the state; (2) that citizens should be able to participate in its institutions and contribute to the direction of its affairs; (3) that citizens should ensure that the social goods of life in the democratic state are extended to all its citizens; and (4) that citizens should be free to use those social goods to choose and construct a satisfying quality of life. To be prepared for all of these endeavours citizens will need to be given access to a high quality and empowering education that will equip them for the obligations, choices and decisions they will be called upon to make. The notions of the personal *autonomy* and democratic *involvement* of citizens in a democracy are crucial here: without either of them democracy could not be sustained or flourish and individuals could not work out patterns of preferred life-options for themselves in it. Both presuppose a high quality *education for democracy*, attained through an integrated approach to knowledge, curriculum and learning, in a democratically structured and managed school and school system.

EDUCATION, KNOWLEDGE AND THE CURRICULUM: A CRITIQUE OF SOME CURRENT CURRICULUM PHILOSOPHIES

Significant differences subsist between countries and educational systems in their approach to the design and implementation of curriculum as part of their educational reform efforts.

Recent reform efforts in some countries suggest that education is seen primarily in instrumental terms – valuable only insofar as it leads to ends of economic efficiency and effectiveness. For many governments education has a promotive or service function; the metaphors employed by them represent education as an hydraulic instrument for increasing national economic development, or as an engine or vehicle to be driven along the road to national economic recovery. Yet others see education as a *commodity*, the obtaining of which enables people to use its 'added value' outcomes as goods to exchange for some larger advantage.

Another group sees a prime function of schooling as inducting coming generations into the traditions, knowledge and culture that are central to developing as a human being in that society. On this view students are 'entitled' to access to all the great and good things 'that have been thought, said and done' (cf. Matthew Arnold 1969) in the advancement of humankind, and that form the starting-points for future cultural understanding and endeavour. These 'entitlements' can be concentrated into a number of areas of cognitive achievement, culture and value. Learning in these provides the building blocks for a life in society that will enable people to understand, enjoy and become bearers of civilisation and culture in all their forms. This kind of 'educatedness' furnishes young people with the cultural identity and cognitive basis on which they can found their attempts to develop strategies for coping with the demands of the modern world.

Others still seek to define educational goals transcending immediate economic, political or social concerns. Education properly conceived, on this analysis, gives people entry into and competence in the various forms of intelligence and rational thinking, without which any approach to other questions is impossible (cf. Hirst 1973 and Gardner 1983). In and through such modes of experience and understanding people are able to make sense of their experience and communicate about it intelligibly with others of their kind. The different modes of understanding constitute the totality of the rational apparatus by means of which human beings can understand and appraise the reality they share, face the dilemmas of existence and tackle the exigencies with which it faces them.

Such approaches to curriculum, although they continue to underpin the reform efforts of many countries, have been under considerable challenge for many years. It has been argued that their theses are functions of a particular set of meta-theoretical preconceptions about the nature of philosophy, science and society, exhibiting adherence to empiricist epistemologies, against which Dewey inveighed so trenchantly (Dewey 1907; cf. Aspin 1997). The status of such theses is claimed to be in all essentials no more than that of a dogma (cf. Langford 1973), to the refutation of which Quine and many others have devoted considerable logical power (Quine 1951, 1953, 1969; Quine and Ullian 1978).

Modern curriculum thinkers (Phillips 1971; Hindess 1972; Kleinig 1973; Langford 1973; Watt 1975; Evers and Walker 1983) contend that proposals emanating from such curriculum theories carry no particular epistemic warrant or authority and have no more uncontested rightness, self-evidence or plausibility about them than any other set of proposals for the curriculum of educating institutions. An education for democracy requires an alternative approach.

A PRAGMATIC CONCEPT OF KNOWLEDGE

In seeking to frame an alternative account of knowledge in the curriculum of educating institutions, we might begin by averring that knowledge claims of any kind belong in the public realm; they have to show what Dewey called 'warranted assertability' (Dewey 1938a). In making a knowledge claim to others, we confer upon them the right to believe and behave as if what we tell them we know is 'true' and may be acted upon. Knowledge, on this premise, is public, objective and testable: what matters here is the kind of evidence that we accept and against which we are willing to test our future thinking and acting. It is from such evidence and claims that we make our selection of activities for educational curricula.

The presumption in favour of our acceptance of claims made upon a common framework of knowledge and understanding is our membership of a society that is 'open' to the checking of such claims to know. It is only on the assumption of the possibility of error that we assert claims to know something (cf. Wittgenstein 1953). We have to substantiate our knowledge claims: the requirements of intelligibility and public communication dictate this. But we also accept that our claims are liable to error or correction: paradoxically, when we claim 'to know' something, we are also thereby tacitly inviting our interlocutors to share *but yet to scrutinise critically and check what we say for possible error.* Knowledge is public but, in 'open' societies, it is always open to checking, criticism and falsification.

Knowledge is thus uncertain, unstable and liable to refutation. It exposes the various grounds from which knowledge claims are articulated, and subjects them to critical scrutiny, the elimination of errors, and every possible attempt at disconfirmation (so Popper 1949, 1969, 1972). It is only when such claims have successfully resisted all attempts at overthrow that they may be *provisionally* accepted as having 'warranted assertability', and the theories from which they emanate as constituting the temporary 'most progressive' research programmes (Lakatos 1976).

The theories that have greatest cognitive value are those that operate to the best functional advantage. As Quine remarked: 'Creatures that are inveterately mistaken in their inductions have the pathetic but praiseworthy tendency to die before reproducing their kind' (Quine 1969: 126). So, embarking on our intellectual journey, we adapt our best theory for the best informed attack upon the problems that face us, doing it in an *ad hoc* fashion, appraising its theoretic strength, adjusting, correcting and adding to it in pragmatic fashion as we go along (cf. Neurath 1932).

This is the concept of knowledge which we may be better off bringing to the elucidation of its educational purposes within today's schools aiming at quality in the most important part of their mission: to develop and disseminate what presently counts as 'best current provisional theory' and to apply it to the tentative solution of the problems with which our communities in the modern democratic state are faced.

A PROBLEM-BASED APPROACH TO CURRICULUM PLANNING

Curriculum philosophy, seen in this light, is an activity of theory construction, correction, comparison and contention, engaged in for the purpose of providing temporary best solutions to problems, the lack of answers for which is otherwise threatening to human well-being and social harmony. Selecting knowledge for educational curricula is an activity of facing problems, planning, criticising and tentatively adopting as yet unfalsified hypotheses proffered as solutions to the problems onto which they are directed (cf. Bridges and Hallinger 1992; Robinson 1993).

Such *problems* provide a set of agenda for educational address and curriculum action that replace concentration on defining larger-scale 'aims of education'. To go by Popper's account (Popper 1960), a total and comprehensive solution, in which such large-scale and overarching 'aims of education' might have their place, will never come. Rather, we should tackle the problems, topics and issues that beset an 'open society' and its educating institutions. The only realistic educational undertaking is to adopt pragmatic approaches to problems that press in on us today.

These days one could quickly construct a pragmatic curriculum to enable learners to make a start on understanding and attempting to provide solutions for a range of such problems in democratic societies. These might include the following:

1 the concern of all countries to extend and augment the literacy of their citizens;
2 the need for people to acquire the knowledge, skills and competences required to operate in modern economies;
3 the problem of relationships in the workplace, in the home, with other people, and with other countries;
4 the problem of healthy lifestyles and avoiding risk-taking behaviours;
5 the problem of the *humanisation* of educational curricula.

Our attack on such problems will require schools and other educating institutions to provide access to learning and study in those areas and forms of cognitive operation by means of which the question of understanding, dealing with and solving those problems, and a myriad others like them, can be most appropriately tackled. In this way students may be enabled to develop their autonomy by learning how to *make up their minds for themselves* in such matters.

THE NEED FOR AN INTEGRATIVE PERSPECTIVE

In arguing for a problem-based approach to matters of curriculum choice and construction, I do not imply that schools should abandon those areas of cognitive concentration and learning activity, from which their curricula have been hitherto constructed. Rather, I suggest an evolutionary way forward, which builds on and extends what we have done in the past. This is achieved in three ways. *First*, we may gather together and direct the knowledge we gain in those fields of interest and intellectual enquiry on to problems of overriding human preoccupation and vital social concern – examples of which have been delineated by Bruck (1993) as including: health and the human body; housing and living space; transport and mobility; energy and resources; money and wealth; love and human relations; technology and the environment; information and the media; culture and leisure, and so on.

Second, and following Bruck, I want to argue that schools need to encourage in the curriculum a stress on, and the development of, an *integrative perspective*. This proposal does not entail the abolition of traditional knowledge and curriculum structures; rather it seeks to fuse them and focus their several contributions on to a range of problems, in the solution of which all have a common interest. The stress on, development and adoption of such an integrative perspective will do much to take our students beyond the confines of separate and distinct subjects and disciplines which their school curriculum and educational environments have hitherto embodied.

Third, as Bruck points out, there is still one more barrier to overcome before schools can develop the integrative curriculum. The new kind of intersubjective and integrative enquiry, for which I am arguing, does not rely exclusively on the printed text and the purely literary mode of communication: *it involves the use of all available media of communication*, including computers, multimedia, television, video and telematics, and audio-visual and electronic technologies. For giving students access to and the right to employ all the new methods of communication and cognitive growth lets them govern their own learning in ways with which they are increasingly most familiar. New learning technology transcends the territorial demarcations of traditional subjects and encourages the development of novel and iconoclastic forms of conception, imagination and intellectual creativity. Such new modes of conceptualisation and cognitive advance will encourage the development and deliberate fusion of the kind of integrative perspective for which I argue here.

As one way of making one step forward on the road to evolutionary curriculum change here advocated, we might make the following tentative suggestion: that *integrative studies might for the present be focused at the post-compulsory level*. They might be best placed in separate 'centres' staffed by specially skilled teachers, skilled in integrating diverse areas of knowledge from different domains and in directing them on to the problems, topics and issues of abiding interest and personal and social concern. For it is only through the study of and attack on problems that schools and centres of learning will be able to work out schemes of curriculum action. In so doing they can broaden students' understanding and help them develop and increase their sense of personal autonomy, community involvement, and social and political responsibility.

Increases in personal autonomy and civic responsibility are called for and brought into play in the contributions citizens make to understanding, criticising, implementing and evaluating the decisions of policy-makers working out solutions to the problems that have bearing upon them. Education for life in a participative democracy is therefore the culmination of a series of curriculum experiences that have as much as anything else to do with the idea of education, not merely as induction but, more pointedly, as an active preparation for the future. And that will clearly require a degree of cognitive maturity, powers of wide-ranging and dispassionate appraisal, and the capacity for rational judgement and choice in those students who are to function as citizens in such a state. It is they who will benefit most from such an approach, as regards the development and exercise of their autonomy and sense of community involvement.

KNOWLEDGE, COMMUNICATION, AUTONOMY AND DEMOCRACY

There is good reason for seeing education for autonomy as a necessary part of preparation for participation in the affairs of the modern democratic state. For me the prime focus for democratic values in education comes from one of the central concepts in education – the concept of *knowledge*.

Entering the world of knowledge and pursuing truth in all their various forms involves the learner in a number of quests. These include the search for evidence by which existing knowledge is objectified, communicated and assessed; the generation, growth, dissemination, communication about and criticism of new knowledge; the impartial and careful scrutiny and assessment of various cognitive claims we encounter; and the need to establish and internalise stable and agreed criteria of meaning and intelligibility in all interpersonal discourse. All these activities involve ethical imperatives; all of them are democratic. The ethical/socio-political values that characterise democratic education are a function of *educating* institutions' epistemological preoccupations.

I also want to argue for the inherence of certain democratic principles in speech and discourse generally. I contend that the presumption of equality, toleration and shared interest is implicit in every occasion of human communication. Just as human discourse is an activity that is the very stuff of morality (cf. Hare 1952), so I claim that the activity of learning, speaking and understanding a language is also in some sense a democratic enterprise. It presupposes the same commitment to telling the truth, to treating interlocutors as equals, to allowing freedom of expression, to tolerating what people say, and respecting their rights to parity of esteem. This point is made by Ackerman (1980) in his account of 'conversation' and its presuppositions as being an exemplification of the moral/democratic form of life and of liberal education at work. Such an education not only teaches people to communicate and to converse; it teaches them *eo ipso* to be autonomous moral agents, sensitive, benevolent and considerate human beings – and good democrats.

THE NEED FOR TRAINING IN DEMOCRATIC ACTIVITIES

Ackerman (1980) and Powell (1970) point to a key presumption of democracy: that democracy, of all types of informal social relationship and formal institutional arrangement, requires a well-informed and liberally educated citizen body to exercise its powers and to participate in debate relating to decision making, the outcomes of which will prove binding on all citizens. This presumption, and the requirements following from it, places enormous emphasis on education and the production of a curriculum for democracy. It implies that the future citizen will not only be exposed to all the various forms of knowledge and understanding on which their exercise of their franchise requires them to draw; future democrats will need to be immersed in and committed to keeping abreast of intellectual advances and cognitive developments. The dynamic and pragmatic character of understanding, appraising and judging involved in participating in the democratic form of life in a rapidly changing environment necessarily requires this of them and brings it on.

More than that, however: understanding, appraising and judging will not be enough by themselves to ensure democratic participation in the processes of policy formation, implementation and assessment that the modern citizen is called upon to make. Not only must future citizens be given exposure to and provided in their schools with the opportunity for the acquisition of knowledge appropriate for the democratic form of life: there must also, as Powell argues, be opportunity for engagement and practice in *activities* appropriate to a democratic form of life and in that set of organisational and administrative arrangements in which democracy is embodied. Adoption of these procedures and practices both formally in lessons at school and participation in the formal and informal activities that characterise a school's organisation and administration are vital functions in preparing the young for their contribution to the life and institutions of democracy.

Thus the study of problems in any lessons or curriculum activity at school, seen as an educating institution, is usually part of an effort on the part of a teacher to (a) bring their students to recognise and solve problems of similar structure with different values for the variables, and then (b) to enable them to *select as problematic* certain questions which interest or puzzle them, to frame them as clear problems, to recognise what would count as evidence for their solution, to frame an hypothesis and, as Dewey says (1938a), to 'undergo' its consequences. The aim of all truly educational processes seems, on this analysis, to be the reaching of a kind of autonomy (even if limited) *in whatever field is studied*. For, as I see it, education typically involves acts like *judging, questioning, considering, criticising, doubting and making up one's mind for oneself*.

We might say that an essential and ineliminable part of agency in any kind of enterprise is *the power of autonomy* – of having independence in judgements or conduct, especially in moral or political matters. If one cannot decide moral or political issues *for oneself* then one cannot be held to have made a free choice, and, for that reason, one cannot be held responsible for the consequences. That would put one on a par with those suffering mental illness, animals and babies.

MANAGING THE DEMOCRATIC SCHOOL

It follows that one cannot achieve a good democracy without a good education. Its achievement is not a question of force, nor of power, although it can be reasonably argued that it is necessary sometimes to force people to be free, as for instance in the case of compulsory voting in Australia. However paradoxical we might think that situation to be, the following may be confidently asserted: if a school is run by autocrats, it will not be likely to produce democrats. A school will hardly produce democrats if it is *not* run by people committed to and living the principles of the democratic form of life and government. If we can encourage our students to strive to achieve some understanding of, competence in and commitment to the instruments of democracy, and if they can see and have some practice in democracy actually at work in our schools, then we might be reasonably confident that they will become democrats (cf. Chapman, Froumin and Aspin 1995).

This is where schools can perform a great service to the democratic ideal. Knowledge and acceptance of democracy is not enough; it requires active engagement in it. This in turn presupposes training and education. It will be important that, in creating and managing a school committed to democracy, there be constant application and utilisation of the principles of accountability and of criticism in the development and implementation of policy, particularly when certain substantive questions arise, such as 'How can we improve our language teaching?' or 'How can you introduce humane values to the curriculum?'

On this basis, the democrat needs to be prepared to come with proposals for developing democratic values in schools and centres of learning, and to be prepared to criticise them. If that is true, it follows that a major key to the democratisation of schools is the democratisation of principals. For they are the prime agents of the changes necessary to create and manage effectively the change from the autocracy, hierarchy and patriarchy of the present to the democratic schools we might all hope to see in the future.

AUTONOMY AND MUTUALITY IN SCHOOLS AND SCHOOL SYSTEMS

Although I have stressed the importance to be attached to the development of personal autonomy as a key feature of life as a citizen in a modern democracy, I should also enter a note of caution against the almost aggressive pursuit of individualism and individual choice which some modern liberal states have recently displayed. What must also be noted, as against that emphasis, is that our world is a complex conjunction of communities and groups of individual human beings; we do not live, indeed we could not start our existence or survive, if we lived on desert islands. The personal freedom and individual choice that is so much prized by exponents of the market philosophy is only possible as an outgrowth of the knowledge and values that other members of society have opened up to us, and given us as an intimation of what choices are available and what choosing, and the calculation of its consequences, might mean. For most of us this has first been made available through our schooling experience.

It is a paradox of our existence that our autonomy requires the work of other persons. It is given to us and increased by our education; and that requires the learning of language and the transmission of knowledge. Both of these are social activities and public enterprises in which at least two people must engage in an interaction predicated upon the assumption of the mutual tolerance and regard that is only embodied in the institutions of society. Without the one, there cannot be the other; and without that key institution called education, there can be neither. The educational paradox is that autonomy is the flower that grows out of seeds planted and tended by heteronomous hands (Chapman 1993).

Personal autonomy is the fruit of our upbringing and education – whether carried out informally or formally in institutions established, staffed and resourced for the purpose. Some institutions of this kind are privately funded; many more are provided out of the public exchequer. Those of us with resources contribute to the exchequer on that basis. It is that contribution which grants us licence to access those good things that society wishes to be available for enjoyment by its members and to subsidise such access by others not so well off as we might be.

Reference to such contributions brings out the mutuality and interdependence of our economic arrangements for funding and running our society and providing appropriate levels and kinds of service for the benefit of all its constituents. This includes those who, because of history, handicap, weakness or sheer misfortune may not be able to contribute much to it at the moment but still need its support. This makes society and its various institutions, especially the school and other centres of community learning, the forum in which individuals can develop their pattern of preferred life options (cf. White 1982). In this way they increase their personal autonomy; in this all sections of the community co-operate mutually for social justice and the benefit of the societal whole. Individual freedom becomes a precondition for social equity; and equity a precondition for individual freedom.

At the present time across the international arena there is a great deal of talk about devolution, local management of schools, or self-managing schools; and there is much concentration in such discourse on independence, individuality, autonomy. To an extent this is good: autonomy is perhaps the key feature in any developed and self-conscious awareness of an individual's or institution's sense of identity and their own worth. But it would be a great mistake to allow this debate on changed administrative structures and relationships in education to be suborned to the discourse of 'the market' and of economic rationalism, with its emphasis on aggressive individualism and the complete freedom of choice, as if to imply that schools, and the individuals within them, were in some way self-contained and hermetically-sealed units, absolutely separate and free from all other-regarding considerations or obligations.

I want to argue instead that the concept of education as a public good provides a decisive refutation of that concept of educational partition. We should argue instead that, in a public system of education, there can be no such thing as a completely autonomous or independent self-governing school. To be sure, a certain amount of school autonomy may be readily countenanced and extended in certain areas of decision-making. It is a paradox, however, that autonomy can only be rendered intelligible and made to work within the confines of a relationship with the system and the community based on a mutuality of benefit and regard.

Schools conceived thus enjoy a mutual relationship with the system and the community of which they are a part. The system ensures the basic protection of rights for all students; at the same time schools enjoy a mutual relationship with the community in which parents and other significant groups are able to have their voices heard in regard to matters of fundamental value and goals. There is also a mutual relationship within the school among school-based personnel, as decision making is shared, owned and supported. In return the school enjoys a greater degree of autonomy in selection of community related goals and the fitting of resources to meet those goals; it also enjoys a greater sense of its own standing and importance in providing community leadership, in promoting the value of education among all its stakeholders, and in this way promoting the idea of the learning community and the values of life-long education. In sum, the model of relationships between school, system and community should mirror those of the strong, robust autonomous individual in mutual relationship with the society of which he/she is a part – the model and goal in the provision of quality education in a democracy (Chapman 1993).

A CONCLUDING NOTE

We should, though, be wise to take note of one final, and vitally important, point: 'education', 'autonomy' and 'democracy', as well as being targets for our endeavour and goals for our striving, are also very often 'hurrah' terms (as Ayer 1971 would call them). For this reason one is uncomfortably aware that definitions of them will inevitably be functions of the definer's most profound metaphysical, ideological and moral preconceptions and commitments. To that extent definitions of these terms, and their translation into various forms of practical realisation, are, as well as being highly prescriptive, also highly contentious – and completely open to appraisal, critique and the most strenuous efforts at correction and falsification. Indeed in any 'democracy' that is perhaps the one feature that we most commonly seek to identify – its constant concern for and preoccupation with *self-examination, self-criticism, self-review and self-assessment*.

What is special about and saves the democrat in my view – and this, I believe, is finally the prime justification for preferring democracy over every other form of government – is that she follows the Popperian path in accepting and embracing that very attempt at refutation. The democrat places a premium upon exposing even the most cherished of her beliefs, definitions, policies and plans to public scrutiny, review and possible refutation. The very activity of democratic debate is itself a deduction of its being and value.

REFERENCES

Ackerman, B. (1980) *Social Principles and the Liberal State*, New Haven, Conn.: Yale University Press.

Arnold, Matthew (1969) *Matthew Arnold and the Education of the New Order: A Selection of Arnold's Writings on Education*, edited with an introduction and notes by P. Smith and G. Summerfield, London: Cambridge University Press.

Aspin, D. N. (1997) *Logical Empiricism and Post-Empiricism in Educational Discourse*, London and Durban: Heinemann. See Chapter 1.

Aspin, D. N. and Chapman, J. D. with Wilkinson, V. R. (1994) *Quality Schooling: A Pragmatic Approach to Some Current Problems, Topics and Issues*, London: Cassell.

Austin, J. L. (1975) *How to Do Things with Words* (The William James Lectures at Harvard University) 2nd edn, edited by J. O. Urmson and M. Sbisa, Oxford: Clarendon Press.

Ayer, A. J. (1971) *Language, Truth and Logic*, Harmondsworth: Penguin.

Bloom, B. S. *et al.* (1956) *Taxonomy of Educational Objectives: The Classification of Educational Goals Handbook I: The Cognitive Domain*, New York: Longmans.

Bond, E. (1976) 'An Introduction to "The Fool"', *Theatre Quarterly* 6 (21): 33–8.

Bridges, E. M. with Hallinger, P. (1992) *Problem Based Learning for Administrators*, Oregon: ERIC Clearing House for Educational Administration, University of Oregon.

Bronowski, J. (1973) *The Ascent of Man*, London: BBC Publishing.

Bruck, J. (1993) 'Break the Disciplinary Barriers', *The Australian Higher Education Supplement*, 10 November.

Chapman, J. D. (1993) *Autonomy and Mutuality*, Inaugural Address given at The University of Western Australia, 13 October.

Chapman, J. D. and Aspin, D. N. (1994) 'Effective Schools and the Curriculum Redefined: Implications of the OECD Activity on the Effectiveness of Schooling and of Educational Resource Management' in M. Skilbeck and P. Hughes (eds) *Education for the Twenty-First Century*, Paris: OECD.

Chapman, J. D., Froumin, I. and Aspin, D. N. (eds) (1995) *Creating and Managing the Democratic School*, London: Falmer.

Davidson, D. and Hintikka, J. (1969) *Words and Objections: Essays on the Work of W. V. Quine*, Dordrecht: D. Reidel.

Davidson, D. (1980) *Essays on Actions and Events*, Oxford: Clarendon Press.

Davidson, D. (1984) *Inquiries into Truth and Interpretation*, Oxford: Clarendon Press.

Dawkins, J. S. (1988) *Strengthening Australia's Schools*, Canberra: Australian Government Publishing Service.

Dewey, J. (1907) 'The control of ideas by facts', *Journal of Philosophy* 4 (12): 111.

Dewey, J. (1938a) *Logic: The Theory of Enquiry*, New York: Holt, Rinehart and Winston.

Dewey, J. (1938b) *Experience and Education*, New York: Macmillan.

Dewey, J. (1966) *Democracy and Education*, New York: Free Press.

Edel, A. (1973) 'Analytic Philosophy of Education at the Crossroads' in J. F. Doyle (ed.) *Educational Judgements*, London: Routledge & Kegan Paul.

Evers, C. W. and Lakomski, G. (1991) *Knowing Educational Administration*, Oxford: Pergamon.

Evers, C. W. and Walker, J. C. (1983) 'Knowledge, Partitioned Sets and Extensionality: A Refutation of the Forms of Knowledge thesis', *Journal of Philosophy of Education* 17 (2): 55–70.

Fromm, E. (1960) *Fear of Freedom*, London: Routledge & Kegan Paul (first published as *Escape from Freedom* 1941).

Gardner, H. (1983) *Frames of Mind: The Theory of Multiple Intelligences*, New York: Basic Books.

Habermas, J. (1972) *Knowledge and Human Interests*, London: Heinemann Educational Books.

Hamlyn, D. W. (1971) *The Theory of Knowledge*, London: Macmillan.

Hare, R. M. (1952) *The Language of Morals*, Oxford: Clarendon Press.

Hindess, E. F. (1972) 'Forms of Knowledge', *Proceedings of the Philosophy of Education Society of Great Britain* 6 (2) July: 164–75.

Hirst, P. H. (1973) *Knowledge and the Curriculum*, London: Routledge & Kegan Paul.

Illich, I. (1971) *De-Schooling Society*, New York: Harper and Row.

Kleinig, J. (1973) 'R. S. Peters' Use of Transcendental Arguments', *Proceedings of the Philosophy of Education Society of Great Britain* 7 (2) July, 149–66.

Kuhn, T. S. (1973) *The Structure of Scientific Revolutions*, Chicago: Chicago University Press.

Lakatos, I. (1976) 'Falsification and the Methodology of Scientific Research Programs' in I. Lakatos and A. W. Musgrave (eds) *Criticism and the Growth of Knowledge*, Cambridge: Cambridge University Press.

Langford, Glenn. (1973) 'The Concept of Education' in G. Langford and D. J. O'Connor (eds) *New Essays in Philosophy of Education*, London: Routledge & Kegan Paul, Ch. 1.

MacIntyre, A. (1972) *Against the Self-Images of the Age*, London: Duckworth. (Part 2, Chapters 13, 15 and 16 'Hume on "is" and "ought"'; '"Ought"'; "Some More about "Ought"' ').

Neurath, O. (1932) 'Protokollsätze', *Erkenntnis* 3: 204–14.

Passmore, J. P. (1967) 'On Teaching to be Critical' in R. S. Peters (ed.) *The Concept of Education*, London: Routledge & Kegan Paul.

Peters, R. S. (1965) 'Education as Initiation', Inaugural Lecture at the University of London 1963, repr. in Archambault, R.D. (ed.) (1965) *Philosophical Analysis and Education*, London: Routledge & Kegan Paul.

Peters, R. S. (1966) *Ethics and Education*, London: Allen & Unwin.

Phillips, D. C. (1971) 'The Distinguishing Features of Forms of Knowledge', *Educational Philosophy and Theory* 3 (2): 27–35.

Popper, K. R. (1949) *The Logic of Scientific Discovery*, London: Hutchinson.

Popper, K. R. (1960) *The Poverty of Historicism*, 2nd edn, London: Routledge & Kegan Paul.

Popper, K. R. (1969) *Conjectures and Refutations*, 3rd revised edn, London: Routledge & Kegan Paul.

Popper, K .R. (1972) *Objective Knowledge*, Oxford: Clarendon Press.

Powell, J. P. (1970) 'On Justifying a Broad Educational Curriculum', *Educational Philosophy and Theory* 2 (1), 53–61.

Quine, W. V. (1951) 'Two Dogmas of Empiricism', *Philosophical Review* 60: 20–43.

Quine, W. V. (1953) *From a Logical Point of View*, Cambridge, Mass.: Harvard University Press.

Quine, W. V. (1969) *Ontological Relativity and Other Essays*, New York: Columbia University Press.

Quine, W. V. (1974) *The Roots of Reference*, LaSalle, Ill.: Open Court.

Quine, W. V. and Ullian, J. S. (1978) *The Web of Belief*, 2nd edn, New York: Random House.

Robinson, V. (1993) *Problem-Based Methodology*, Oxford: Pergamon.

Ryle, G. (1949) *The Concept of Mind*, London: Hutchinson.

Watt, A. J. (1975) 'Transcendental Arguments and Moral Principles', *The Philosophical Quarterly* 25: 40–57.

White, J. P. (1982) *The Aims of Education Re-stated*, London: Routledge & Kegan Paul.

Wittgenstein, L. (1953) *Philosophical Investigations* (trans. G. E. M. Anscombe), Oxford: Blackwell.

22

REDESIGNING INSTRUCTION TO CREATE AUTONOMOUS LEARNERS AND THINKERS

John Arul Phillips

This chapter starts from observations about the changing character of society around the Pacific Rim and in particular in south and east Asia. It observes the shift from an essentially agrarian to a manufacturing and information-oriented society in which the workplace, the marketplace and the home have become increasingly complex organisations and the parallel shift from essentially autocratic to increasingly democratic governments requiring a higher level of participation of their citizens.

Schools have however failed to keep up with the implications of these changes. They have not yet taken seriously the obligation on educational institutions in a democratic society to cultivate both the attitudes and skills required of a self-determining and questioning citizenry which can choose those who will govern, hold government to account and itself participate in the process of government. Schools continue to be preoccupied with teaching curriculum content rather than the critical processes which enable children to think for themselves in a society which is less predictable, rapidly changing and increasingly complex. This chapter will:

- discuss the importance of teaching the process of learning and its goal in creating autonomous learners and critical thinkers;
- propose ideas for the incorporation of those skills associated with critical, and creative thinking in the curriculum, while taking into consideration the examination orientated system of education in the Pacific Rim; and
- discuss possible strategies for the implementation of these ideas in the classroom and the role of teachers, textbook writers, evaluators, curriculum developers and administrators in their application.

The chapter is written from a perspective in the Asia Pacific region, but the issues are global. Indeed some of the oldest democracies as well as some of the newer ones might benefit from more vigilant attention to the foundations of critical and creative thinking in the school curriculum.

THE CHANGING CHARACTER OF SOCIETY

As nations in the Asia-Pacific region are ushered into the next century, concern has been expressed with regards to the rapidly changing character of society. Employers have been quite critical of the decision-making and problem-solving abilities of workers they employ. Social leaders view with concern the evaluative abilities of the younger generation in making judgements on issues affecting them. Politicians are uncertain whether the younger generation can think rationally as responsible citizens. Parents are equally concerned about their child-rearing practices and ask whether they are doing the right thing amidst the accelerating changes taking place in their immediate environment. Each nation in the region is aiming towards achieving the status of a modern state focusing on industrialisation, urbanisation, automation and interestingly, decentralisation of power. On the road to modernisation, four areas of development are beginning to make an impact on nations in the region which have important implications for the way in which the next generation of citizens are educated.

The first area of development relates to the information age wherein accessibility to large stockpiles of knowledge in many different fields has been made possible by advancements in digital technology. As aptly suggested by Wurman (1988), 'information anxiety' will be the new disease of the future; that is, the feeling of helplessness at being unable to cope with abundance of information. There is an ever-widening gap between what one understands and what one thinks one should understand. Anxiety expresses itself in feelings of frustration at not being able to keep up with the wealth of information and knowledge that accumulates each day and the speed at which such information is made available. Too much information is coming to the individual and there is little time to deal with it.

The second area of development is taking place in the workplace. Some of the Asian-Pacific nations have progressed in a very short time from a solely agrarian economy to economies that depend largely on an expanding industrial and manufacturing sector. A few of these economies are already moving to a second level of industrialisation, namely in the area of high-technology where automation and computerisation is rapidly changing the workplace. With the new wave of modernisation, the demand is for new technologies, new products and new procedures and for customisation, with individuals requiring products and services which suit and meet their needs. The shift is towards knowledge-based jobs in which people are required to acquire and master a broad spectrum of skills effectively within a short period of time. Business and industrial organisations are beginning to realise that more and more careers are requiring brain power rather than mere muscle power. Hence, it is important to encourage lifelong learning and improve the thinking skills of the workforce to keep pace with changing needs. As proposed by Senge (1990), businesses should invest in the creation of 'learning organisations' in which the quality of thinking and the reflective capacity of the workforce contributes to enhancing productivity and adaptation to the rapidly changing demands of the workplace.

The third area of development is in the sudden expansion of the mass media. People in the Asia-Pacific region are increasingly having access to a plethora of television and radio channels from all over the world, made possible by advances in satellite technology. The globalisation of the air waves is seeing the increasing penetration of American, European and modern Asian influences, which has both its positive and negative side. As it becomes increasingly difficult to sieve and censor information transmitted through the airwaves, reliance on self-censorship by the individual may be the only alternative. However, this presupposes that the individual is able to make choices based on reasoned judgements; is able to detect prejudices, evaluate and determine the credibility of the source of the information. The question is whether young Asians can think critically and extract what is desirable and discard the undesirable from the perspective of their own cultural and religious values. To what extent would these external influences impact on Asian tradition and social mores? There is already a growing fear that more and more young Asians are setting aside their traditional cultural practices and values and opting for a kind of internationalised 'modern' culture which is evolving on its own.

The fourth area of development is the trend towards increasing democracy in some of the governments in the region. The fall of communism, rising affluence and a more educated citizenry are some of the reasons for greater involvement in the decision-making process of governing. Democracy rests on an informed and intellectually able populace that is able to think independently.

THINKING AND DEMOCRACY

Nations in the Asia-Pacific region which have traditionally pursued a system of government with minimal citizen participation are increasingly experiencing a clamour for more participation in public life and freedom to think and express ideas. Even authoritarian systems, seeing the fruits of a market economy, have relented to liberalising aspects of government. There is a growing desire for more participation in the political life of nations, stemming from the realisation that determination of a nation's destiny need not necessarily be left to the monopoly of a few. However, nations that have not had a tradition of democracy realise that their citizens need certain skills and attributes to deal with the intricacies of a relatively more open form of government. Good citizenship is not just merely abiding with the laws of the land but more importantly is 'the ability to think critically about issues concerning which there may be an honest difference of opinion' (Glaser 1941: 5). With more democracy, effective thinking becomes increasingly important as local, national and global issues become more complex and complicated.

Good thinking is a prerequisite for good citizenship because it helps the citizen form more intelligent judgements on issues and to the democratic solution of social problems. There can be no liberty for a society that lacks the critical skills to distinguish lies from the truth. Citizens in a democracy have an obligation to think deeply about issues that affect themselves and society at large, while at the same acknowledging that differences of opinion do occur but they are what constitutes good citizenship. However, effective thinking among citizens is a skill that may not be as highly valued by some societies as is sometimes believed. This is evident in some of the nations in the region where authoritarian systems of government continue to dominate. One needs only to be reminded of how some governments in the region have treated dissidents in their respective situations to appreciate that authoritarian habits die hard.

While acknowledging that young people ought to be encouraged to think, to question, to form their own opinions and even arrive at their own values, the need to respect tradition, cultural values and legitimate authority is also of concern, especially so in the Asia-Pacific region where preservation of tradition is highly valued. The dilemma lies in wanting simultaneously to inculcate critical inquiry and reflectiveness and to transmit a traditional culture and its standards, even though transmission of such values cannot be fully justified on rational grounds. The challenge before educators is finding ways to promote critical inquiry and independent thinking while at the same time respecting traditional values and beliefs. Can the critical thinking abilities of the next generation be developed while maintaining the cherished beliefs of society which may be in conflict?

THINKING AND SCHOOLS

Few would deny that it is the role of school to develop the critical thinking abilities of learners. In fact, teaching has a dual agenda, which unfortunately is sometimes overlooked. First is teaching for the *product* of learning which focuses on the transmission of a body of knowledge through the concepts, principles and theories of the discipline. Second is teaching for the *process* of learning which is primarily concerned with the thinking or cognitive processes involved in the understanding of that body of knowledge. Unfortunately, in practice teaching tends to emphasise the product of learning or content with the assumption that the mental processes involved are equally efficient for all learners. This assumption may not be valid for all learners because students do not naturally acquire the skills of logical reasoning and critical enquiry merely by studying the content of a particular subject.

It is not surprising that some learners who perform exceptionally well in public or national examinations are not necessarily proficient thinkers. This discrepancy is of concern to nations in the region, especially when comparisons are drawn with their counterparts in the United States and Europe. High schools students in western countries have consistently outperformed Asian students on tests measuring critical and creative thinking. It is increasingly evident that schools in the region have been too preoccupied with the mastery and acquisition of facts and concepts while paying scant attention to the application of these facts and concepts in a wide variety of situations. In other words, thinking has been ignored or assumed to be equal for all learners. The need for integrating the teaching of thinking and content is ever more pressing today when learners have to contend with massive amounts of information, both relevant and irrelevant. Content is best studied in a 'thinking' way so that new thoughts, understandings and beliefs may be generated. For example, studying history is a stimulus to historical thinking while mathematical content is transformed into mathematical thinking.

The case for teaching thinking skills is more urgent when one considers the sizeable proportion of learners who, despite having been in the school system, have not sufficiently acquired the knowledge, skills and attitudes to perform in the rapidly changing economies of the region. These are learners who lack intrinsic motivation to perform in school tasks. Various efforts have been directed at identifying factors contributing to low academic performance but efforts to reduce the problem has not been forthcoming. Krouse and Krouse (1982) identified two main factors contributing to low academic performance, namely poor socio-economic background and inefficient mental models of learners. Poor performers are more likely to come from economically disadvantaged families with low parental involvement. In addition, academically weak learners are more likely to possess inefficient cognitive or thinking strategies, which is partly responsible for their low self-esteem and negative attitude towards learning.

Though improvement of the socio-economic status of learners is beyond the ambit of the school system, the improvement of their mental models is within the realm of instruction. Intervention by teachers in improving the cognitive performance of learners may have far reaching consequences in improving learner self-concept, self-control, motivation and attitude towards learning. Unfortunately, schools seem to be organised more along the lines of the 'Matthew effect' (Stanovich 1986), in that those that need the most and best instruction are more likely to get the least and worst. This phenomenon is worsened with the dominance of public examinations in the education systems of the Asia-Pacific region. Learners who are academically weak and are unable to perform at a satisfactory level as demanded by national examinations are given less attention. It partly reflects the assumption of society that success is not for all and one should expect that it is the destiny of some learners to end at the bottom of society (Coles 1978). Fortunately, there is growing realisation that nations in the region can ill-afford to have a segment of the potential workforce deficient in relevant thinking and cognitive skills which would impair efforts to create the kind of knowledgeable, autonomous and independent thinkers which both the economy and a democratic society demand.

TEACHING THINKING

A phenomenon which has swept across education world-wide since the 1980s is the resurgence of interest in the teaching of thinking or cognitive skills in schools. Nor is it surprising that, in an era in which the development of high technology has coincided with a movement in the direction of more democratic government in the Asia-Pacific region, this region too is sharing in that interest. The teaching of thinking skills is not new. Renewed interest in the psychology of thinking has largely been spurred by the advent of the cognitive revolution. Intensive research in cognitive science has provided a deeper insight into how humans think, solve problems and make decisions. Interest in teaching for thinking stems from the realisation that such skills are poorly performed by students in schools, and not surprisingly even in institutions of higher learning. Even business organisations are realising the importance of effective thinking among its workforce. For example, workers on the factory floor are encouraged to share their thoughts and provide feedback to management to improve productivity.

The teaching of thinking in schools has, however, been relegated to the background due to the belief that thinking cannot be taught and that they need not be taught, but it would be wrong to assume that thinking will emerge automatically as a matter of development or maturation. There is increasing evidence to suggest that higher-order thinking can be improved through instruction. Even though learners are capable of a multitude of mental processes such as the capacity to compare, to contrast, to classify, to induce and deduce, to infer, to generalise, to find patterns and predict, not all are able to perform these skills spontaneously and naturally. Furthermore, learners are not inclined to think critically or acquire the enquiry skills of a particular subject area as a result of having studied that subject (Glaser 1985). Being aware of this deficiency, some teachers have taken steps to re-examine current instructional practices and look for ways to bring thinking to the classroom.

One of the crucial issues in developing the thinking abilities of learners is deciding on the approach to be adopted, whether thinking skills or content should be given priority. Some have argued that in order for learners to think, they need to think about something because thinking cannot take place in a vacuum. Others have suggested that learners need not have a vast store of knowledge to think. They can engage in thinking activities based on their experiences and whatever current information they possess. Still others propose that learners can acquire thinking skills while simultaneously learning a body of knowledge, on condition that teachers are able to organise appropriate activities (Phillips 1996). The theoretical position that the practice of different kinds of thinking on the content learned enhances mastery which in turn facilitates recall will be more readily accepted by education systems in the Asia-Pacific region because recall for examination purposes is an important consideration.

A PROGRAMME FOR TEACHING THINKING

This theoretical position suggests that an approach based on the *infusion of thinking skills* would be the more appealing for implementation in the region, since it would require least disruption of existing curricula. The role of examinations is dominant to the extent that any attempt to stray from the national curriculum would be considered a waste of time and effort. The goal of thinking is to arrive at a decision and find solutions to problems and this entails the manipulation of an array of thinking or cognitive skills. The programme proposed is based on the premise that these skills can be taught and that the performance of these skills can be enhanced through systematic instruction. Basically, the programme addresses three components; namely, the subjects or disciplines, the learner and the teacher or instructor.

The *subjects or disciplines* component constitutes the content to be taught. Every field of knowledge (science, social science, language, arts) can be used to teach thinking. Thinking and knowledge are interdependent, and it is inconceivable to think of thinking as not involving knowledge because thinking about nothing is an exceedingly difficult thing to do. However, there is evidence to suggest that people possessing the same knowledge might differ in how skilfully they apply what they know in the solution of problems. Each subject area or discipline has its own set of process skills. For example, in science, there are science process skills which manifest in scientific thinking. Similarly, in economics there are specific process skills that explain how an economist thinks.

The *learner* component refers to the type of thinking skills that are to be acquired by the learner. To create autonomous learners and independent thinkers, two types of thinking need to be emphasised; namely, critical and creative thinking. Critical thinking is defined as 'reasonable reflective thinking that is focused on deciding what to believe or do' (Ennis 1987: 10). In other words, the thinker strives to analyse arguments carefully and examine the evidence upon which a conclusion is arrived at. The critical thinker uses standards in making judgements, employs strategies of reasoning and arguments and uses reliable information in support of judgement made (Swartz and Perkins 1990). Creative thinking is the ability to organise cognitive operations that yield novel, unusual and extraordinary ideas and results. To be creative one has to think divergently which requires originality (generation of unusual ideas), flexibility (generation of different ideas) and sensitivity towards problems (Guilford 1959). To be able to think critically and creatively requires the manipulation of an array of micro-thinking skills. For example the skill of comparison, prediction, evaluation, summarisation, interpolation, application, hypothesis testing, inferencing, generalising and so forth. In other words, at each stage of critical or creative thinking, the individual calls upon one or more of these micro-skills.

Related to these types of thinking, the learner is also supposed to acquire certain dispositions or attitudes that reflect and encourage thinking. A good thinker welcomes problematic situations and is tolerant of ambiguity. A good thinker is also self-critical, looks for alternative possibilities and seeks evidence from many perspectives. A poor thinker is rather impulsive and tends to give up easily but a good thinker is reflective, deliberative and is persistent. While the poor thinker overvalues intuition (which may be useful in some instances), the good thinker believes in the value of rationality. The good thinker is open to multiple suggestions and considers alternatives while the poor thinker prefers to deal with limited possibilities and is more reluctant to seek alternatives (Glatthorn and Baron 1985).

The *teacher or instructor* component holds the key to the successful implementation of the thinking skills programme. The teacher has to be convinced that the primary purpose of instruction is not only to impart knowledge but to develop the thinking skills of learners. The teacher also has to be equipped with a deep understanding of the skills to be developed. Each of the skills need to be operationally defined, the rules and procedures for teaching of the skills have to be identified, why they are important, when learners will need to use them and how to redesign instruction to incorporate the teaching of these skills. As suggested by Beyer (1984), efforts in developing thinking will be hampered if there is no attempt to identify the obstacles to teaching thinking and align instruction accordingly.

In developing the thinking skills of learners, the teacher or instructor is looked upon as a model thinker. As a model, the teacher demonstrates as frequently as possible the processes of thinking and this is accomplished through 'think aloud' protocols. It has been realised of late that merely providing learners with opportunities to think is insufficient. Teachers need to identify the individual thinking skills and systematically teach them through modelling. The teacher is looked upon as the expert while the learner is the novice. It is hypothesised that if novices are allowed to observe how an expert executes a particular skill, they would be more aware of their own metacognitive processes when they later execute the skill on their own (Flavell 1976). The expert says out loud what he or she is doing while executing the thinking skill. It is important to say all of one's thoughts out loud so that the novice will understand how an expert thinks. After having seen how the expert executes a particular skill, it is the turn of the learner to execute the skill. The learner is encouraged to think aloud while executing the particular skill and this is observed by both the teacher and other learners. As learners describe what is going on 'inside their heads', they are more likely to be more aware of their thinking processes which is a prerequisite for autonomous thinking. The teacher observes the think aloud protocols of learners and comments when necessary. Learners are also encouraged to compare the different think aloud sessions of their classmates and identify the strengths and weaknesses of each. Finally, learners are given problems or situations and are left on their own to apply the thinking skills learned.

TOWARDS A CULTURE OF THINKING

Merely having a thinking skill is no assurance that learners will use it. Such skills have to be practised in an environment that encourages thinking. But, the highly centralised and examination driven system in the Asia-Pacific region may not be supportive of an environment that encourages thinking. Traditional values place a high premium on adherence and the questioning attitude may be frowned upon. However, if the thinking of learners is to be developed, a culture of thinking has to be created. A culture of thinking refers to an environment in the school, the home, the workplace and even the streets where language, values, expectations, habits and behaviour reflect the enterprise of good thinking (Tishman, Perkins and Jay 1995).

The role of the school in the creation of a culture of thinking is crucial and the place where such enculturation can occur effectively is the classroom. Teachers are the ones who establish the educational climate, structure learning experiences and who have power over the processes that take place in the classroom. Teachers need to be aware that certain of their behaviours, perceptions and attitudes have a powerful influence in shaping the thinking abilities of their learners. Teachers have at their disposal a variety of ways in organising classroom instruction to stimulate thinking. The underlying principle of such organisation is to encourage learner participation in the teaching-learning process. It would be quite impossible to encourage thinking if the teacher did most of the talking (which teachers generally find difficult to minimise). Among the methods suggested is the Socratic-type discussion and co-operative small group sessions. In each of these sessions, learners participate in debating issues, giving alternative views and evaluating different viewpoints. Learners could be working on a thinking task in small groups, individually or even as a whole class.

Teacher response behaviours also have an important effect on the thinking behaviours of learners. The extent to which these behaviours extend or terminate thinking depends on the way in which teachers react to answers and questions posed by learners. Sometimes it is the tone of voice and the manner in which questions are answered that curtails thinking. Besides that, the manner in which language is used in the classroom also influences the thinking of learners. Using precise terminology of thinking indicates to the learner how to perform the particular skills (Costa and Marzano 1987). For instance, the repeated use of words such as *compare, predict, classify and analyse* increases the likelihood of internalisation of the skills associated with the terminology which eventually becomes part of the learners' repertoire of vocabularies.

CONCLUSION

Besides the direct teaching of thinking skills to create autonomous learners and independent thinkers, writers and publishers of textbooks and curriculum materials also play a role in infusing thinking skills. Many of the existing curriculum materials need to be re-examined and perhaps rewritten in an approach that encourages learners to think. Another area that needs reform is the evaluation and assessment systems widely practised in the region. Examinations exert such a powerful influence on what transpires in the classroom at all level of schooling. Despite adopting the most recent advances in psychometric technology, assessment tends to emphasise evaluating low-order cognitive outcomes of achievement. Changes in the testing methods and the kinds of outcomes measured will have far-reaching consequences in the teaching of thinking. If it can be shown that higher-order thinking is evaluated, teachers may be more inclined to teach for such outcomes. Though this is not the purpose for which the thinking ability of learners is developed, at least it provides the impetus for wide implementation of a thinking skills programme.

The aim of teaching thinking is to better prepare students for today's increasing complex and rapidly changing world; whether it be in the workplace, school or democratic community. The probability of succeeding economically and politically in democratic terms will be greatly enhanced if citizens possess a high level of reasoning proficiency. 'Thinking is at the heart of what it means to be human; to fail to develop one's potential in this regard is to preclude the full expression of one's humanity' (Nickerson 1987: 32). However, a citizenry which is informed and reflective and able democratically to resolve problems for the purpose of improving society is something which has to be worked for and nurtured through a school system which is dedicated to this purpose – and this is dedication which needs to be constantly renewed in any society which aspires to satisfy democratic principles.

REFERENCES

Beyer, B. (1984) 'Improving thinking skills – Defining the problem', *Phi Delta Kappan* 65 (7): 486–90.

Coles, G. (1978) *The Learning Mystique: A Critical Look at Learning Disabilities*, New York: Pantheon.

Costa, L. and Marzano, R. (1987) 'Teaching the language of thinking', *Educational Leadership* 46: 29–33.

Ennis, R. (1987) 'A taxonomy of critical thinking dispositions and abilities' in J. B. Baron and R. J. Sternberg (eds) *Teaching Thinking Skills: Theory and Practice*, New York: W. H. Freeman and Company.

Flavell, J. (1976) 'Metacognitive aspect of problem solving', in L. Resnick (ed.) *The Nature of Intelligence*, Hillsdale, NJ: Lawrence Earlbaum Associates.

Glaser, E. (1941) *An Experiment in the Development of Critical Thinking*, New York: Teachers College, Columbia University.

Glaser, E. (1985) 'Critical thinking: Educating for responsible citizenship in a democracy', *National Forum* 65: 24–7.

Glatthorn, A. and Baron, J. (1985) 'The good thinker' in A. L. Costa (ed.) *Developing Minds – A Resource Book for Teaching*, Roseville, CA: Association for Supervision and Curriculum Development.

Guilford, J. (1959) 'Traits of creativity' in H. H. Anderson (ed.) *Creativity and its Cultivation*, New York: Harper & Row.

Krouse, J. and Krouse, H. (1982) 'Toward a multimodal theory of academic underachievement', *Educational Psychologist* 16 (3): 151–64.

Nickerson, R. (1987) 'Why teach thinking?' in Baron, J. B. and Sternberg, R. J. (eds) *Teaching Thinking Skills: Theory and Practice*, New York: W. H. Freeman and Company, 27–37.

Phillips, J. (1996) *Developing Critical and Creative Thinking in Children*, Petaling Jaya: Lingua Publication Co. Ltd.

Senge, P. (1990) *The Fifth Discipline: The Art and Practice of the Learning Organisation*, New York: Doubleday.

Stanovich, K. (1986) 'Matthew effects in reading; Some consequences of individual differences in acquisition of literacy', *Reading Research Quarterly* 21: 360–7.

Swartz, R. and Perkins, D. (1990) *Teaching Thinking: Issues and Approaches*, Pacific Grove, CA: Midwest Publications.

Tishman, S., Perkins, D. and Jay, E. (1995) *The Thinking Classroom: Learning and Teaching in a Culture of Thinking*, Boston: Allyn and Bacon.

Wurman, R. (1988) *Information Anxiety*, New York: Doubleday.

INDEX